M000303719

Child and Adolescent Therapy

Related Titles of Interest

Handbook of Prescriptive Treatments for Children and Adolescents
Robert T. Ammerman, Cynthia G. Last, and Michel Hersen (Editors)
ISBN: 0-205-14825-5

Teaching Social Skills to Children and Youth: Innovative
  Approaches, Third Edition
Gwendolyn Cartledge and JoAnne Fellows Milburn
ISBN: 0-205-16507-9   Paper   0-205-16073-5   Cloth

Child Psychotherapy: Developing and Identifying Effective
  Treatments
Alan E. Kazdin
ISBN: 0-205-14387-3

Handbook of Psychotherapy with Children and Adolescents
Thomas R. Kratochwill and Richard J. Morris (Editors)
ISBN: 0-205-14804-2

The Practice of Child Therapy, Second Edition
Thomas R. Kratochwill and Richard J. Morris (Editors)
ISBN: 0-205-14397-0

School Refusal: Assessment and Treatment
Neville J. King, Thomas H. Ollendick, and Bruce J. Tonge
ISBN: 0-205-16071-9

Child and Adolescent Psychotherapy: Process and Integration
Robert M. Leve
ISBN: 0-205-14907-3

Behavior Management in the Schools: Principles and
  Procedures, Second Edition
Richard M. Wielkiewicz
ISBN: 0-205-16459-5   Paper   0-205-16458-7   Cloth

Child and Adolescent Therapy

Margaret Semrud-Clikeman
University of Washington

Allyn and Bacon

Boston • London • Toronto • Sydney • Tokyo • Singapore

Copyright © 1995 by Allyn & Bacon
A Simon & Schuster Company
Needham Heights, Massachusetts 02194

All rights reserved. No part of the material protected by this copyright
notice may be reproduced or utilized in any form or by any means,
electronic or mechanical, including photocopying, recording, or by
any information storage and retrieval system, without written
permission from the copyright owner.

Library of Congress Cataloging-in-Publication Data

Semrud-Clikeman, Margaret.
    Child and adolescent therapy / Margaret Semrud-Clikeman.
        p.   cm.
    Includes bibliographical references and index.
    ISBN 0-205-15026-8
    1. Child psychotherapy.   2. Adolescent psychotherapy.   3. Clinical
child psychology.   4. School psychology.   I. Title.
RJ504.S45   1995   95-2154
618.92´8914--dc20   CIP

Printed in the United States of America

10   9   8   7   6   5   4   3   2   1   99   98   97   96   95

This book is dedicated to the children of Mequon-Thiensville Schools and Massachusetts General Hospital with whom I was fortunate to work. It is also dedicated to the two men in my life—my father, Ray Semrud, who taught me how to trust and love, and my husband, John Clikeman, who taught me how to reach for my goals.

Contents

PART II   *Beginning the Process*

Preface

An extensive review of the relevant published books on child therapy points to a need for a comprehensive book on this subject, a book geared toward the school psychologist and clinical child psychologist for both training and continuing education purposes. The volumes on this subject that now exist generally fall into one of two categories. Most of the books are edited and contain chapters for various childhood psychopathologies without a common treatment or theoretical thread. These books approach child therapy from a psychopathology viewpoint and not from a developmental stance. In this case, the emphasis is on the psychopathology and not on the treatment and may be useful for students with previous training in therapeutic techniques.

Other books on child therapy present therapeutic interventions for one type of disorder (i.e., attention deficit hyperactivity disorder) or for one part of the clinical process (i.e., interviewing). These books are useful for specialized practices but for training purposes selected chapters are utilized rather than the whole book.

The book you have before you presents a conceptual framework that provides for the development of therapeutic interventions with children, adolescents, and their families. This theoretical approach has its roots in developmental object relations theory evidenced by practitioners such as D. W. Winnicott, John Bowlby, and Fred Pine, combined with the social-behavioral theory of Albert Bandura and Jean Piaget, and the cognitive behavioral approaches and family systems theory of Virginia Satir. Chapters include child interviewing techniques, diagnosis and case formulation, family variables, stages of the therapeutic process, therapy with children with exceptional educational needs (learning disabilities, neuropsychological deficits, mental retardation, and behavioral disorders), group therapy, and consultation techniques.

Child and Adolescent Therapy is designed to appeal to faculty members charged with the responsibility for training school psychologists, child clinical psychologists, and school counselors. As such, the book focuses on the development of basic skills of interviewing and therapy which can be further refined later. The book is meant to be read by students as well as by practitioners who want to update their therapy skills. To this end, the book seeks to provide concrete case examples and exercises for skill development. Although research studies are provided to illustrate therapy issues, the major emphasis is on development of skills.

This book is based on my 20 years of clinical experience with children and their families. The case examples are drawn from this experience and are composites of many children I have seen over the years. As I have found from practice, children can teach you a great deal about child development and their resilience when faced with emotional distress. The patience and strength of children who are experiencing emotional difficulties resonate with hope for the adults who love them and work with them.

Acknowledgments

I learned not only from the children and their parents but also from patients and sensitive supervisors and friends. I particularly thank Agie Laev, Jim Gardner, and Dorothy Loeb for their assistance in my development as a school psychologist. I further acknowledge the support and knowledge of my therapy supervisors at Massachusetts General Hospital including Dennis Norman, Robert Reifsnyder, Carol Taylor, and Cynthia Rankin.

I wish for those of you reading this book to have the good fortune that I had in my training, to work with people like these. I would also like to acknowledge the professionals who reviewed my manuscript and helped me immeasurably with their recommendations: Anne Teeter, University of Wisconsin–Milwaukee; Peggy Ollerhead, School Psychologist, Roland Park Country School in Baltimore, and Laura Corkery, Middle Georgia Psychoeducational Center in Macon.

About the Author

Margaret Semrud-Clikeman worked as a school psychologist in Wisconsin for 13 years before pursuing her doctorate at the University of Georgia. During her years as a school psychologist, she worked with numerous children and adolescents and their families, coping with problems ranging from mental retardation, neurological disorders, significant emotional disability, to physical disorders. She provided intensive treatment to individuals and groups and worked in a setting that valued a multidisciplinary approach.

Margaret completed a predoctoral internship in clinical psychology at Massachusetts General Hospital/Harvard Medical School. During that time, she practiced long-term psychotherapy with children and adolescents as well as adults. She has completed a course in family therapy with direct family therapy supervision and was then awarded a two-year Neuroscience Fellowship from Massachusetts General Hospital/McLean Hospital/Harvard Medical School. This fellowship provided support for research in the neuroscience area. Her dissertation was selected for the Outstanding Dissertation National Award by the Orton Dyslexia Society.

Professor Semrud-Clikeman recently completed a study utilizing volumetric MRI measurements to compare attention deficit disorder children with matched controls. These results have now been published in the *Journal of the American Academy of Child and Adolescent Psychiatry*. She has presented her work at numerous national and international forums and recently presented a paper on short-term therapy at the National Association of School Psychologists' national convention in Seattle.

Margaret is currently an assistant professor in educational psychology at the University of Washington in Seattle. She continues to work as a school psychologist one day a week in a Seattle-area school district and maintains a private practice.

Child and
Adolescent Therapy

1

Beginning Thoughts

Imagine that you are anxiously awaiting the arrival of your first client. Although you have completed your beginning courses in therapeutic techniques, this is your first opportunity to practice these skills. You know you will meet with your supervisor later in the day to go over the session, but that gives scant comfort at this time. "Please let me not make a fool of myself," you say to yourself. You are prepared with questions, activities, and games for the child. Questions cross your mind, and you waiver between a hope that the parents will cancel and an equally strong hope that the child will come on time. "What if the child won't talk to me at all? What will I do then? What if the child tells me something that I can't handle?"

The child you are waiting for is Teddy, a 10-year-old who has been referred to you for assistance with his behavioral difficulties. His teacher reports that he has difficulty paying attention in class, is involved in frequent fights on the playground, and has completed few assignments this quarter. In addition, Teddy has been absent more than a third of the class year. When he does come to school, he is often sleepy. Your classroom observation of Teddy was of a thin child who looks apathetic and somewhat sad. He has difficulty paying attention to the teacher, squirms in his chair, frequently drops his materials on the floor, and finishes little of his work. Observations of Teddy on the playground show that he is usually talking with the adult supervisor or walking by himself.

Teddy comes to your office with his teacher. When you talk to him, he answers in one-word sentences or says "nothing's the matter." You send him back to his classroom wondering how you will help him and what feedback you can give to his teacher. His records indicate that he is an only child who lives with his mother. A phone interview with his mother provides information that Teddy has been in several schools over his five years. She also tells you that she is a single parent who works the swing shift at a local factory. Teddy is usually unsupervised after school and often stays up until she comes home from work at 11 P.M. Although she sounds cooperative, Teddy's mother also appears to be overwhelmed with her responsibilities.

This case is representative of many cases that are referred to school psychologists, child clinicians, or counselors in the course of their daily work. As a beginning therapist facing such a case, it would not be surprising for you to feel overwhelmed by the problems Teddy shows. Like other therapists, you have entered this field because you felt you could "help" and had ideas that such "help" would be readily asked for by children and parents. Unfortunately, not much thought may have been given to situations that might not be easily resolved or in which "help" might not be welcomed by the identified client. In addition, little thought may have been given to how you may react to certain situations—particularly those that may make you feel helpless and powerless. It is important for the beginning as well as the seasoned clinician to realize that such situations will occur and to acknowledge the feelings they provoke.

The purpose of this book is to provide beginning clinicians with useful strategies that can assist in working with children and adolescents. The basic premise is that child/adolescent therapy, perhaps more than adult, requires working with systems in the child's life, including the family, school, and at times, the community. Basic differences between adult and child/adolescent therapy involve the role of development on cognitions as well as the need to involve significant others in the treatment. The following sections in this introductory chapter outline the basic issues involved in working with children and adolescents.

Issues in Practice and Training

Generally the child therapist has at least three clients: the identified child; the parent or caretaker; and the school environment including teachers, peers, and administration. In Teddy's case, the child does not openly wish for assistance. He may become amenable to treatment once he has established a relationship with the clinician. His mother, although overtly cooperative, has little time, energy, or resources to assist Teddy. Although Teddy's teacher may be the most logical route for intervention outside of the therapeutic relationship, it is important for the beginning (and the experienced) clinician to remember that the teacher may well be looking to you for a solution. Before beginning treatment, you need to be cognizant of any ethical concerns that may arise during treatment.

Ethical Concerns

The ethical principle of competence is one of the first issues to address. It is important for the clinician to determine her or his own limits of competency in working with certain populations. The beginning clinician may well ask, "How can I be competent in any area when I am just starting?" The assessment of competence must include issues of training and experience. The scope of your practicum and internship experiences lay the foundation for later practice. When you are unsure as to your competence, it is reasonable to ask for supervision from an experienced colleague.

Most clinicians face new types of clients and must ascertain their competence to provide treatment. Where there is concern as to competency, the clinician will seek out consultation or supervision. Supervision is provided during the practicum and internship experiences and should amount to roughly one hour of supervision for every three hours of therapy. In many school districts, school psychologists and counselors meet weekly to discuss cases. This is a ready source of supervision for the beginning clinician. If this supervisory structure is not already in place, then it would be wise to discuss this matter with the senior psychologist on staff. Ready access to a supervisor or consultant may not be as easily obtained by clinicians in private practice. In this case it is necessary to build a support network for yourself in order to allow for consulting about different cases. There are usually organizations that can provide introductions to other professionals in your field.

Who's the Client

Another basic issue in treatment is to determine who the client is that you are treating. One of the most difficult lessons to learn is how to assess the expectations of those who refer clients to you. It is always important to ask yourself "Who's the client?" when interviewing the referring party. This is not to say that the child may not also have a problem, but it is not as common for the child to seek help as it is for the teacher and/or parent to seek help for the child. On the other hand, I have had children seek help to "get the teacher off of my case." In this situation, the child wishes assistance with an adult, and sometimes the clinician must secure cooperation from the adults involved in order to proceed with treatment. In both cases it is important to involve the person referred as well as the referral source in planning treatment goals. Chapter 4 discusses further the development of these goals.

Although the teacher or the parent may initially present the problem, you may find it necessary to work with the child and consult with the adult in order to provide the best possible service. It is rare that the clinician seeing children or adolescents can work in a vacuum by seeing only the client. While this model may work for adult therapy, it rarely works for children. Children are rarely empowered to change their behavior without the cooperation and assistance of important adults in their lives. At the very least, you need to have contact with one major player in the child's life, be it parent or teacher. At times there is resistance by the adults in working on the problems. Ways to resolve these issues will be more fully developed in later chapters.

Unfortunately, adults often have misconceptions about what therapy is and may believe that a few sessions in a psychologist's (or counselor's) office is sufficient for a cure. Thus, at times you may feel you are expected to work magic in your office. During the initial interview it may become apparent that the child and parent or teacher do not necessarily have congruent needs and/or expectations. It is therapeutically important to resolve these differences during the course of treatment. If the intention for psychotherapy is to bring about more adaptability (Koocher & Keith-Spiegel, 1990), then it will be necessary to address these expectation differences at an appropriate time.

On some occasions, it is more appropriate to work with the teacher or parent than with the child on a problematic area of development. This tactic can be most appropriate when the child is resistant to coming for therapy and the parent/teacher is willing to assist in intervention or when change in the parent–child or teacher–child relationship is seen to be the goal of the intervention. In determining who is the client, you need to conduct a thorough interview with all parties involved while simultaneously beginning to develop a case formulation on the underlying issues involved in the case. This process is an important issue not only for practice, but also for training. In order to evaluate your services, therapeutic goals and aims must be developed. The determination of who is the client is contained within these goals.

Institutional Expectations

When working with a student in a school (or sometimes clinical setting), be aware of institutional expectations. Some schools will expect you to provide short-term therapeutic interventions. Children with longer term needs will be seen as appropriate for referral to an outside agency. Figure 1–1 presents a decision tree for deciding whether a child should be seen in the school or a private clinic; it also gives other options that may be tried such as consultation and group counseling.

Deciding whether a referral to an outside agency is appropriate includes determining what's best for the child. If the child's needs can be best served within the school setting and the child's emotional difficulties are negatively

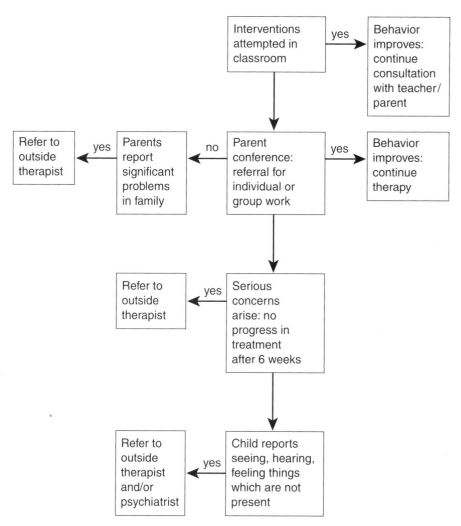

FIGURE 1–1   Points of Decision to Refer to Private Therapist

impacting on learning, then it is within the scope of the school clinician to meet these needs even if they are long term. One way to justify long-term direct service is to utilize group therapy when appropriate, to utilize consultation with teachers (and so provide indirect service), and to keep the administration generally informed as to progress and caseload requirements. In the most difficult cases, it may be prudent to demonstrate that your service delivery is cost-effective when compared to costs the district would bear in paying for private services. When necessary, the law provides for therapy services to "handicapped" children for them to be able to learn. Upon determining the need for special education services, the multidisciplinary team will generally also determine whether the child requires therapy in order to benefit from the proposed educational program. Note, however, that not all children are candidates for individual therapy just because they have emotional difficulties. It is the multidisciplinary team's duty to determine when therapy is justified, and the school clinician is an important member of this decision team.

To judge whether it is appropriate to refer a child to another professional, you need to determine the scope of the problem. If the child shows areas of difficulty in learning due to feelings of inadequacy, low self-esteem, and/or depression and these issues cannot be adequately addressed within the academic program, then individual or group treatment is appropriate. Moreover, if the child's acting-out behaviors are interfering with school performance and additional assistance is judged necessary by the multidisciplinary team, then individual or group treatment is also advised. The following example combines both acting-out behavior and sadness.

A fifteen-year-old boy had been in a resource room for learning disabilities since fifth grade. He had made steady progress until the past six months, when his parents divorced. At that time, he had begun to mouth back to female teachers and experience difficulty with completing his work and coming to school on time. His resource room teacher expressed concern about this change and requested additional assessment of his emotional well-being to be included in the three-year reevaluation. This assessment indicated feelings of sadness and anger at his mother, whom he considered had abandoned him following the divorce (he lived with his father at his mother's request), and his feelings that he was unfairly treated by one of his teachers. These feelings were interrupting his ability to benefit from instruction. The multidisciplinary team determined that he required counseling in order to deal with emotional issues that appeared to be affecting his learning. If he had been experiencing these feelings but his learning was not directly affected, then he would not have been an appropriate subject for counseling through the school system.

Territorial Issues

There may be territorial issues as to who works with the child, who with the parent, and who with the teacher. It is important to determine the unwritten rules about service delivery to prevent turf issues from interfering with therapy. For example, I worked in a private setting that considered that the social worker's role was to work with the parent, but was not seen as particularly relevant for the clinician to work with the school. Part of the reasoning for this belief was that it was difficult to obtain reimbursement for school consultation.

It is always important to determine the institutional rules and to adjust them to fit the client, not to fit the client to the institutional rules. In some cases, I found referral of the parent to a social worker for parenting assistance was appropriate. In others I consulted with the director for social work and discussed my need to work directly with the parent on issues related to the therapy. In this manner I was able to forestall any turf issues that might arise. You should be realistic about these institutional rules and use them to serve your client's "best" interest. As long as it is ethically feasible, experienced clinicians have found it easier to work with the system rather than against it.

There is usually more than enough work to go around, although in a school setting turf issues may still be effect. In some schools the school nurse assumes the duty of interviewing parents about the medical and social history of the child. In other schools it is the school social worker. The school psychologist/counselor may be seen as working with the child and not the parent. This demarcation of duties appears clean and easy, but in reality it is not. While the clinician may need to consult directly with the parent, others on the team may block such interaction. The clinician needs to be cognizant of others' concerns and attempt to understand the dynamics behind them. At the very least, in these cases it is important to use a multidisciplinary team approach in which professionals share information and therapeutic approaches.

If there is resistance to a team approach, then it will pay you dividends to begin developing such an approach with cases that have a better chance for success. If you continue to push against such resistance, the resistance is likely to increase. On the other hand, if you perceive the resistance to change and take steps to answer unspoken questions the other professionals may have, then the chance for success is increased. Once someone resisting a team approach feels no counter-resistance, that person may be more willing to listen to alternative treatment plans. Issues which may be implicated in resistance are feelings of insecurity, lack of skills or knowledge, or lack of professional objectivity (Gutkin, 1981).

If the issues are ones of lack of skill or knowledge, it is important to be perceived as willing to share information and knowledge by utilizing co-therapy strategies, modeling different techniques, and using inservices or discussions. When dealing with feelings of insecurity or low self-esteem, you should not challenge the person directly on the issue of teamwork. Offering consultative support for a particularly difficult case can often begin opening doors for mutual benefit.

In other cases, consulting with a professional who is experiencing difficulty maintaining professional objectivity can be difficult. When this happens, try to understand why the person is reacting to a particular child in an overly involved manner. Expressing more emotion than usual about a particular child or couching statements in terms that lead one to believe there is an inevitable outcome are tip-offs that the referring person may be experiencing difficulty with professional distance. For example, a teacher referred an eight-year-old child who had been recently adopted.

> This child was acting out and having numerous fights on the playground. The teacher stated that this child was going to have many emotional problems in adolescence and would not "amount to much" if long-term intensive therapy was not begun immediately. The teacher was frantic for the clinician to begin as soon as possible. Because the clinician believed that some of the difficulty lay in the teacher's propensity for significantly increasing attention to this child whenever he misbehaved, thus reinforcing such behavior, part of the intervention program involved changes in the teacher's behavior.
>
> This program was met with resistance from the teacher, who felt the child's "deep-seated" emotional problems were not being addressed. Over several sessions discussions with the teacher gradually revealed that she had adopted an older child who had gone on to develop severe emotional problems in adolescence and who, now an adult, was unable to settle on a career path.
>
> The unspoken fear the teacher felt was that she would fail again with this child and she was overcompensating for such concerns. The clinician strove to unlink the inevitability the teacher felt was in the child's future and to focus on the child's behavior in the here and now. Support for the skills the teacher possessed bolstered her feelings of efficacy. Once the teacher's issues of inadequacy and failure were unlinked from the child, the teacher was able to work more effectively with the child and corrective action was forthcoming.

Developing a Conceptual Framework

As important as it is for a beginning therapist to develop therapy skills, it is imperative that a conceptual framework provide an underpinning for the provision of therapy. Research on treatment outcome has found that no one theory has a better "cure" rate than another. In fact, many therapists consider the relationship to be key while the theory provides the backdrop for the relationship. The beginning clinician may believe that establishing a relationship is sufficient for therapy to occur. If this was so, then friendships or other relationships could provide therapeutic assistance. In fact, for problems of lesser severity, these relationships can often serve a therapeutic purpose. For most cases referred for assistance, however, more than a relationship is needed for assistance. Without a relationship, a conceptual framework is insufficient for treatment to be successful. After the first few sessions, you need to use the relationship to move to more critical issues.

Many students who choose to pursue training in the therapeutic process possess intuition, are sensitive to nuances and feelings, and have common sense. These skills are necessary in and of themselves but they are insufficient abilities for an effective therapist. It is equally important to have a theoretical framework on which to base clinical judgment and from which to develop treatment goals that can be applied across clients. This framework should also serve to organize your thoughts about a case as well as provide a structure for case formulation and treatment planning. (Case formulation will be discussed in Chapter 4.) As you practice, you will find it necessary to make adjustments to the conceptual framework you adapt. Your therapeutic approach will become tempered by your clinical experiences and your values. An important exercise for the beginning clinician to complete is to write out his or her current theory of counseling/therapy. This exercise provides an opportunity for the student to think through and try on theoretical approaches to therapy to see how they "fit." When I have my students write out their thoughts on therapy, they find it a difficult but enlightening task. It is then helpful to reread the paper after practicing therapy for a while to see how one's views have evolved. One of the purposes of this book is to provide a conceptual framework for understanding the therapeutic relationship as well as to assist you in your professional development.

The case of Teddy at the beginning of this chapter could be conceptualized differently by various theoretical orientations. A behaviorally inclined therapist may structure interventions that include provision of reinforcement for Teddy when he attends in class, remains in his seat, and completes his work. A cognitive-behaviorist may well decide to intervene with Teddy on his behavior as well as his thoughts as he goes about his work. A social skills program may be instituted to assist Teddy in developing friendships. A systems therapist may begin by working with Teddy through teacher and parent interventions. A psycho-dynamic therapist may well wish to investigate Teddy's relationship with his mother and his resolution of psychosexual/social stages. Amidst all of these theories, Teddy may also be referred for evaluation for a possible attention deficit hyperactivity disorder. Some combination of the above models may also be developed. Throughout this book you will find a conceptual framework which utilizes some practices that are behavioral in nature, some grounded in an understanding of how systems work, and others utilizing active listening skills.

A Developmental Therapeutic Model

Behavior can be conceptualized as a function of environmental experiences, the ability to form and utilize relationships, to establish boundaries between oneself and others, and to construct one's self-image from these experiences. These tasks begin in infancy and continue throughout life. The child lays down experiences that shape the adult he or she will become. A child is able to synthesize experiences into a self when provided with an adequate environment that meets most needs. An appropriate supportive parental response at each stage of development is vital to "the growth of the self experience as a physical and mental unit which has cohesiveness and continuity in time" (Kohut, 1971, p. 10). Thus, children who have the ability to utilize relationships (which may or may not be with their parents) will ultimately fare better emotionally than those children who cannot form emotional ties. Research in temperament indicates that some children are biologically predisposed to respond differentially to stimulation. That is, temperament research indicates that behaviors, such as adaptability, ability to be soothed, and activity level, are biologically determined. For example, some children are placid and relate easily to their caretakers while others respond dramatically to stimulation by resisting any type of affection or interaction (Buss & Plomin, 1984). These children may be presented with the challenge to adapt their temperamental proclivities in order to obtain the formation of relationships needed for adequate social–emotional adjustment.

Because children are children, it is necessary to view their difficulties in terms of their development. Development has been conceptualized as a process where new experiences are added and the child is transformed and transforms the experience into schemas based on previous experience (Sroufe, 1979). Certain behaviors are expected at certain stages. The same behavior manifested at a far-removed stage may be indicative of significant problems. Sroufe (1979) suggests that in order to determine if developmental problems exist, it is important to determine *how* the child is meeting developmental challenges as well as the level of the child's adaptation. This view evaluates the child's adaptation while continuing to view the whole child who has developed a behavioral style to cope with environmental and physiological demands.

Psychopathology can be viewed as development "gone bad" and therapy as a way of remediating inappropriate development. If psychopathology is viewed in this manner, then behavior is changeable and a less-than-optimal background can be overcome. Moreover, if mental health is seen as the integrity of the self and psychopathology is an attempt at self-healing, then a corrective emotional experience may assist in modifying behavior (Teyber, 1990). A corrective emotional experience is one that allows the child to play out fears and/or concerns with a therapist. The therapist then allows the child to experience the feelings or to produce usually punished behavior within the relationship without judgment. This does not mean the child is allowed to continue inappropriate behaviors in other settings. Rather, the child is allowed a "safe" place to reconstruct feelings and to replay past behaviors. While this is occurring in individual work, the child's behavior is also modified within the classroom or home. If therapeutic interventions are not structured to take into account parent, teacher, *and* child needs, then the intervention cannot succeed.

The *developmental model* discussed in this text draws from the theories of Harry Stack Sullivan, W. D. Winnicott, and Erik Erikson. These theorists stress the importance of the child's ability to establish and maintain emotional ties to caretakers. When these ties are disrupted, anxiety occurs, with behavior designed to reestablish the ties. If the relationship continues to be threatened, the child's behavior escalates as an attempt for equilibrium. If the caretakers are available to calm the child's fears and behaviors, then the child is able to continue to develop and will internalize the sense of being emotionally attached and valued. Knowing that he or she is able to return to safety if venturing too far out makes it possible for the child to seek out new experiences. Moreover, the child carries the loving regard of the caretaker, which in turn reinforces the feeling of safety.

For example, a child who has achieved "basic trust" as one of the first of Erikson's stages can then elaborate and develop this "trust" through additional stages of development. A child who has not developed this sense of security will be handicapped in the ability to foster and maintain relationships in the following stages of development. Thus, this child will achieve a different type of relationship with important caretakers and will have a different experience from the child who has mastered these initial stages (Sroufe, 1979). There is continuity in the child's development and organization of experience. This continuity of development is an important aspect to utilize in working with children with emotional and social problems. These problems relate in some manner to how the child has organized experience and give a view into his or her constructed world schema.

This book contends that children learn about themselves through the relationships they establish at home and carry into other relationships. This early laying down of expectations about themselves and the world around them is modified through additional experiences during children's lives. When initial relationships are faulty, later experiences can make it possible to align early experiences into a different mold.

Temperamental Variables

The developing self is also impacted by temperamental attributes such as reactivity (Rothbart, 1986), behavioral inhibition (Kagan, 1984), or activity level (Martin, 1988). These temperamental attributes interact with the child's sense of self and life situations. For example, a child with an "easy" temperament may fit in well with any parenting style. This child will respond differently (or possibly more readily) than a child with a "difficult" temperament placed in the same situation. The easy child will be able to adapt to situations while the difficult child may fight the situation, become irritable, and generally be difficult to live with. It is understandable that these children will take different lessons from their experiences. The easy child may well believe that life can be handled and that she or he is capable of dealing with changes. The difficult child may well believe that life is more problematic and that it involves a struggle. One child may make relationships work, subsequently developing a sense of self-efficacy while the other child may be in constant turmoil. Thus, as the child experiences the world, he or she not only develops an expectation for emotional attachments concurrent with a developing unfolding of self, but also begins to forge attributions and cognitions about the workings of the world and his or her place in it.

Just as the child operates on the environment, the environment also serves to shape the child's experiences. There is an interactional quality between both experiences. A child who experiences an early trauma will have a very different life schema from a child whose development is not impacted by a significant environmental event. Moreover, the child's temperament and attachments may certainly impact on how that child reacts to "bumps" in life. There is a transactional effect between the experiences and the child's ability to cope with these challenges. For example, a young adolescent seen in our clinic was experiencing difficulty with his mother. He fought with her continually and challenged her at every opportunity. A complete interview with the mother indicated that this boy, at approximately two years of age, had experienced a significant medical difficulty that required her to place a catheter three times a day in order for him to urinate. This procedure was painful and impacted their relationship. The mother reported the boy would run from her when she approached him. Their relationship did not change even after surgery corrected his difficulty. Although the boy did not "remember" these incidents, he shared that he was always "angry" at his mother, sometimes for no reason he could pinpoint.

In addition to the child's temperament in the interpersonal process, the caretaker also brings her or his personality and temperament to the situation. In dyads where the temperamental style appears to be complementary (easy with easy or easy with difficult), a "goodness of fit" occurs (Scarr, 1984). In other dyads where there is not such a match (such as difficult with difficult), problems arise not only in the formation of the relationship but also in how the caretaker and child interpret each other. In this case if adjustments are not made by the caretaker, the child may be at risk for the formation of a negative self-concept and understanding of emotional attachments. As such there is an interactional quality between the child and his or her experiences with the world where the child's temperament shapes his or her relationships and in turn, these relationships shape his or her understanding of the world.

It is important to note that the quality of the relationship between the caretaker and the child predicts peer relationships in later years (Bretherton & Waters, 1985). Thus, it may well be that the child's early experiences set the stage for willingness or openness to later attachments. There is evidence that early experiences can be modified by later positive experiences but these modifications do not usually fully overcome the emotional disruption of the early years (Rutter, 1987). These difficulties will be explored further in later chapters.

Psychosocial Experiences

Much has been written about the sequence of steps a child progresses through during development. Although not all of these theories will be reviewed here, some issues have a more pronounced effect on the development of the self and of emotional attachments. Among these are the development of autonomy, self-efficacy, and the development of the "self-system" (Harter, 1986).

Children who make the successful leap from home to school, whether it is to day care or kindergarten, are able to internalize their parents' caring for them and bring it with them to school. This separation–individuation process is considered to be the most important goal for the typically developing child (Mahler et al., 1975). As such, the child is able to make the transition from the parent to the teacher (or other caretakers) and expects certain rewards and reassurances from the environment. The newly forged relationships in the school setting provide for additional experiences that assist in the development of the child's sense of self and sense of capability. Children who are secure in their home relationships are more able to take the risk to form additional relationships with peers and with other adults. Although the best-case scenario is for each child to succeed at these developmental steps, some children may be unprepared for the elaboration of their relationships to people outside the family.

Children who are unable to make the change from home to school often worry about their parents and seem concerned that the parents will disappear. Their adjustment is less than optimal, and their learning and social development often suffers. Likewise, children who have experienced early emotional traumas, such as divorce or death of a parent, will often show an overwhelming need to attach to someone who is consistent in their life. This need will continue into adulthood unless experience teaches the child otherwise. A child who is extremely needy and demanding of constant attention may be acting out unfulfilled needs. Similarly, a child who is angry or rejecting may be protecting himself or herself from earlier emotional hurts. If these conflicts are unresolved, this behavior can continue into adolescence and carry into adulthood.

As a child grows and matures, it is important for her or him to master the ability to comfort and soothe herself or himself when faced with anxiety-laden situations. In addition, the child needs to be able to recognize when support is needed and how to go about finding it. In order to seek out such support, the child must feel worthwhile and worthy of emotional succor. Thus, the child's developing self-identity is forged through relationships and becomes the source of self-esteem. Children who have been labeled "invulnerable" are not immune from their negative experiences. They have been able to seek out alternative sources for support of their emotional development (Masten et al., 1988).

The above section details a model for understanding difficulties children may experience while moving through the developmental process. If emotional disorders can be understood in terms of aberrant development rather than "something" wrong with the child, a clinician can then utilize the developmental misstep to assist in providing corrective emotional experiences. The school setting offers the opportunity for the child to develop relationships that can provide opportunities for the building of self-esteem when parents are unavailable, abusive, or rejecting. In this sense, the school or clinical setting can serve as a "surrogate" parent and assist in developing the child's sense of autonomy and self. Moreover, the school setting can also provide support for the parent or teacher who is bewildered by the child and is unable to provide needed succorrance for the child.

Thus, it is important not only to develop an understanding for the complexity of many child development issues, but also to have the opportunity to develop skills in the practice of child therapy. The chapters that follow should provide the developing clinician with a base for skills. The chapters in Part I discuss interviewing techniques. Part II delineates basic counseling skills. The third part discusses group counseling, play therapy, problem-specific treatments, and Part IV includes chapters on indirect service to children and adolescents and consultation.

2

Parent
Interviewing

The initial contact with a parent often sets the stage for later interactions. In a school setting the initial contact may be facilitated through the teacher or principal. Most schools have a policy directing the referral process. Sometimes the system involves an informal meeting between the teacher and clinician to discuss what intervention alternatives may be appropriate. In this way a team approach is followed from the beginning and children are screened as to who may be appropriate for individual or group therapy. A program can be set up with the classroom teacher to deal with difficulties with children that may be deemed not appropriate for individual work.

Another model is a weekly meeting involving a student study team, usually consisting of a teacher, administrator, special educator, and clinician. In this procedure the team gathers needed information and determines the disposition of the case. Such information includes the particular behaviors that have been problematic (for example, acting out, withdrawal), previously attempted interventions, results from parent contacts, peer relations, and academic progress. Each area is reviewed and a decision made as to who will be responsible for working on specific suggestions made by the team.

These processes allow for the development of prior interventions to a referral for special education. Such processes, which document attempted interventions as well as a team discussion of a particular child's need, are required under the IDEA law and Section 504 of the Americans with Disabilities Act of 1973 (29 U.S.C. 794). These meetings also provide an opportunity for information gathering as well as planning for the needed interventions.

The Contact Process

If it is decided that a child should be referred for possible therapy, then a person who is familiar with the parent should make the first contact and explain, preferably in person, why the referral is being made. It is important that either the individual clinician or the student study team brief the person making the initial contact on areas of possible concern. I have found it helpful to brainstorm with teachers how they will present the referral and how they describe my services. Encourage them to ask the parents if they have questions about why the referral is being made and to invite the parents to discuss the referral and return the call at another time. The process for the referral should be fully discussed with the parents and they need to be informed of their right to refuse services. I encourage teachers to have the parents take time to think about the referral and not to give an answer on the spot. I also request the teacher to ask the parents if I may call them to discuss this matter more fully.

For referrals that come directly from one or both parents the process is somewhat different. The parents contact the clinician and request that their child be seen. Usually there is a precipitating reason which has brought a concern to a head, and I always ask what prompted the parents to call at this particular time. It is important to let parents talk about their concerns in full and to encourage them to set up an appointment for a face-to-face meeting *without* the child. Just as you need to discuss other intervention strategies with the teacher in a teacher-generated referral, it is equally important to link up with the parents to set the stage for future meetings to discuss the child. By stressing the parents' part in the intervention process, the clinician can underscore the idea that changes which may come in the child's behavior are due to changes made by the child and the parent, *not* by the clinician. In this manner, therapy is placed in the perspective that the responsibility for change lies with the participants in treatment and not the clinician.

Nontraditional Families

The so-called traditional family is becoming less common in society. This development leads one to question the use of this term while calling divorced families, stepfamilies, and families with different sexual styles "nontraditional." It is important to be sensitive to different family styles when making contact with a parent.

In many divorced families, custody is shared and both parents wish to be involved in therapy. The clinician needs to respect these wishes and share not only the final reports but also the prereferral meetings, parent contacts, report cards, and notices of school functions. You should be aware of opinions of teachers (and of yours) that may impact on your relationship with divorced parents. In some cases I have worked with, joint custody has meant the child spent two weeks at one home and two weeks at another within the same school district. Teachers and administrators felt this arrangement was problematic for the child and disapproved of how the parents were managing their divorce. These feelings were unconsciously transmitted to the parents, who admitted feeling uncomfortable talking about their home life with the teacher and/or principal. While it is very important to discuss the effects, if any, of such an arrangement on a child, the clinician needs to keep an objective view in order to continue to assist the child and parents. If the child cannot cope with this arrangement and it is in the child's best interest to have more continuity in his or her life, then the clinician needs to discuss the behaviors of concern and seek a solution with both parents. At this point it is likely that the family needs more intervention than a school clinician is able or trained to provide. A referral to an outside facility is then recommended.

In families where there is not joint custody, the custodial parent may seek not to include the other parent. It is important not to get caught in any struggle between parents while at the same time encouraging the involvement of the noncustodial parent. School districts and states differ in rules about sharing information with noncustodial parents, so the clinician should seek out the local regulations. Generally both parents have legal access to their child's school records unless there is a court order restricting the records to only one parent. I encourage the custodial parent to share information with the noncustodial parent and to invite him or her to meetings. When there is resistance to having the noncustodial parent participate at the same time as the custodial parent, I will offer a separate meeting for the noncustodial parent.

When step-parents are involved, it is generally a good idea to follow the custodial parent's wishes about involvement in meetings and decision making. While communications, signatures on formal documents, and invitations for meetings need to be addressed to the custodial parent, I will discuss with the parents who will attend the meeting and advise them that it is their decision if the spouse is to attend the meeting.

A difficult situation can arise when divorced parents attempt to use the clinician as a pawn. If one parent confides in you and asks you not to share the information with the other parent, you should remind the parent that you are unable to keep confidential any information which discusses child abuse and/or neglect or which would be subpoenaed in a court hearing.

First Contact

It is prudent to interview parents either on the phone or in person before seeing the child. When making the first call to the parents, determine if it is permissible to call them at work or if the call needs to be made in the evening to their home. If calling them at work, always ask if this is a good time or if you can call at a more convenient time. It is also important to make sure they have sufficient time to talk. If you need to leave a message that you called, it is advisable to leave only your name and number and not why you called. If asked, it is perfectly permissible to state simply that the person will know why you are calling. To state that you are a school psychologist/ counselor/clinical child psychologist calling about the child is not only a breach of confidentiality but may also set up a roadblock when an angry parent calls you back.

When you have successfully made the first contact, be prepared to discuss the reason for referral and invite the parents to come to the school for a meeting. It is important to discuss why you wish to meet with them as well as who may also be attending the meeting. The following dialogue is a typical example of a first contact I had with a parent (previously contacted by the teacher) regarding a referral of her second-grade daughter, who was often found crying in class.

MSC: Hello, Mrs. S., this is Peg Semrud-Clikeman calling from your daughter's school. I am the school psychologist Mrs. R. spoke to you about. I believe you are expecting my phone call.

Mrs. S.: Yes.

MSC: Is this a good time to talk or would you like me to call back at another time?

Mrs. S.: This is fine. I am very concerned about my daughter and I would like you to see her as soon as possible.

MSC: I will be glad to see your daughter but first I would like to meet with you to discuss your concerns in more detail. I'd also like to get your ideas about the reasons behind Linda's behavior. I know you know a lot about your daughter which will simplify my job and maybe we can work together to find out what is bothering her.

Mrs. S.: Do you want me to bring her with me?

MSC: No, I'd first like to meet with you alone. Is it possible, do you think, for your husband to also attend the meeting?

Mrs. S.: He works until 5:00 most days—do you think it's important for him to be there?

MSC: I find that when both parents can attend at least the first meeting, important information is shared. I also have found that many fathers have questions about what happens during counseling and rather than putting you in the difficult position of repeating everything, they can ask their own questions and find out first-hand.

Mrs. S.: Well, I need to discuss it with him and see what he wants to do. I know he wants to be involved so maybe he can arrange to leave work early one day.

MSC: Do you want to talk it over with him, and I can call you back tomorrow?

Mrs. S.: Why don't we schedule an appointment and if it's not OK with him, I'll call you back. Can you meet at 4:00 on Wednesday?

MSC: That's fine. I will meet you by the front door. I anticipate that we will need about an hour. I would like to mail a behavioral checklist to be filled out by both you and your husband prior to our meeting. Is that OK?

Mrs. S.: Fine, I'll see you next week.

Involving Fathers

As the interview shows, the father was also invited to attend the meeting. You should communicate to the parents that both of them are important to the treatment of their child. Asking for the father's attendance in the above interview made this intent evident. Many times the mother is the person with whom the school or clinic speaks and she often bears the burden of communicating what is happening with the child to the father. This practice places a very heavy burden on the mother; she is put into the position of carrying, as is usually the case, bad news to the father and of having to answer all his questions. Couple this charge with a highly emotional state and one can readily see that the interactions between these two significant players can impact substantially on the treatment plans.

It is therefore important to invite the father to at least the beginning interview. Unfortunately, this arrangement may well mean you will need to meet after school hours. However, it will pay dividends for the therapeutic alliance for you to sacrifice a bit of your time to meet with the father and mother together. Having both parents participate in the initial meeting sends a message to the child that this process is important and that there is an alliance between the therapist and the family.

There are times when the mother will seek to circumvent the father's attendance at these meetings. It is important to determine the underlying reason in this situation. If the father has chosen not to be involved in the process, it is important to support the mother's commitment to the process.

In other cases, the father may openly oppose intervention and may attempt to block the therapeutic process. In this instance, you should talk with the mother at length about her commitment to the therapy as well as her ability to carry through on suggestions made during the process. It is important to attempt gradually to engage the father at some level in the intervention. You may only be able to keep him up-to-date on progress, but at least that is some contact. It has been my experience that fathers generally want to be involved and even when they are resistant to the idea of therapy for the child initially, they have the best interest of the child at heart and with time are willing to give the treatment a chance.

In other cases the mother may not wish her spouse to be involved. The reasons behind such an attitude are numerous, and only the most interesting will be delineated here. At times, a mother may feel that it is her role to work with the school and with any "child" problems. By asking for the father to attend a meeting about the child, the mother may feel her authority is being usurped or that it is unnecessary for the father to be involved—that she can handle the problem alone. In this case it would be meaningful to discuss why the father's involvement is important and to invite the mother to come in initially and discuss her concerns, with a later meeting with the father to be arranged as she is ready. Try to support the mother in such a way that she does not feel threatened by your invitation to the father. You will need to communicate indirectly that the father's presence at an interview in no way diminishes the role she will play in the treatment. If she continues to be resistant to the father's participation, you may wish to schedule additional appointments to find out the reasons behind such opposition.

Sometimes the reasons may lie with fear of abuse of herself or her child. If this is the case, it is not likely that the mother will volunteer such information readily. If you are able to establish an ongoing relationship, however, it is more conceivable that such information will eventually be obtained. When there is great opposition to the father's participation, be sensitive to the possibility of abuse either by the father *or* the mother.

Another helpful tactic when the mother resists the father's participation is to call the father to arrange to speak to him. I would suggest that you inform the mother of your intention to call but do not ask her permission. If you decide that such action is necessary for the treatment of the child, then you run the risk of temporarily alienating the mother. It is usually better to attempt to obtain the mother's acquiescence to such a move; however, the welfare of the child has to be at the forefront of any decision. If the father's input is needed, then the risk is justified. After the phone call to the father, offer to set a time to speak to the mother so that feelings can be vented and some discussion can take place. I have experienced a few occasions when the father had no idea he had been invited to a meeting. In such a case, a parent meeting to work out these issues up front is well worth the time.

Setting the Stage

Once you have set up the initial interview time, it is important to be prepared for the session. In the interim between the phone call and the meeting it is wise to arrange a time to observe the child in a few settings. These observations do not have to be long; usually 20 minutes is sufficient to get a flavor of the child's behavior. You might choose to observe during a structured classroom time, an unstructured class (such as art, physical education), and on the playground during recess. When observing a child you may wish to observe a typically behaving child at the same time in order to develop an idea of how the child compares to his or her peers. If you have not had a chance to discuss any concerns with the teacher, it is opportune to schedule a time to do so.

Observing a child in the school setting is obviously easier for a school-based clinician. However, an outside clinician may find it revealing to observe the child, and it may be wise to request parental permission for this procedure. Most parents are more than willing to comply with such a request, and you will also find that most teachers are willing to consult with you.

When a teacher is unaware of a difficulty a parent has seen, it is important to interview the teacher about any concerns in the classroom. If there are few problems in school, then a referral to an outside agency is an option which should be explored with the parents.

Coming to the school can be difficult for the parents, who may have painful childhood memories of their own school days. They may again feel that they have done something "wrong" and will react accordingly. I have had parents who have been so concerned about this setting that they have come to the meeting with alcohol on their breath. On other occasions, parents have come in belligerent and settled down once they found out that the intent of the meeting was not to blame them for poor parenting. Entering the school may bring up negative feelings on the part of the parents, particularly if their own school experience was not good. Remember what may be routine for you—that is, talking about the therapy—is an unusual and often frightening procedure for parents.

I strongly suggest that you not meet in the principal's office. That location too often carries the connotation of discipline and even though the parent is an adult, vestiges of memories of this office may remain.

In preparing for a meeting, I find it helpful to arrange the chairs around a circular table. It is sometimes intimidating for parents to meet without some type of "protection" to hold onto. Since I often take notes, it is also easier for me to sit at such a table. Sitting around a table is less intimidating than you sitting behind your desk with the parents on the other side. Too often the latter feels to the parents like a separation which may hinder the alliance being formed.

Setting Goals for the Interview

It is important to decide what your goals are for the interview. Usually the interview is conducted to obtain background information about the child's history, to understand parental concerns, and to begin to determine the child's need for therapeutic intervention. Having done your homework before the interview begins, you may well have begun to develop hypotheses about the difficulties presented. From these hypotheses it is possible to conceptualize interview questions in the areas thought to be most problematic. This is not to say that the interviewer has prejudged what will occur during the interview—unexpected surprises often surface as a result of the interviewing process. However, if there are reports of previous interventions or assessments, it is usually a good idea to be prepared to follow up on these areas before the interview. A review of the child's school record, as well as a discussion with previous teachers, is always a good idea.

It is also meaningful to determine what an interview is not. An interview is not therapy and it is not parent training. It is important from the outset of the meeting to state that the interview is to gather information. If there is an attempt to move into parent training or therapy, you will find it beneficial to redirect such discussions for another time.

In addition to gathering information, the interview provides an arena for the development of a therapeutic alliance. In this forum the parents meet the clinician and their concerns can be addressed. It is important to enlist parental cooperation and establish rapport with the parents. If the parents feel cut off from the process, there may well be difficulties in the delivery of services. Sometimes, in a clinical setting, the parents will begin missing appointments or canceling treatment. In a school setting the underinvolved parent may well grill the child about the sessions. By establishing contact in the initial stages of the intervention, you will find that parental anxieties about the process will lessen.

Selecting an Interview Format

Before looking at the interview process, it is important to determine the type of interview format. Beginning clinicians may feel most comfortable utilizing some previously developed format. Interviews can include an informal social and medical history, rating scales, or a semi-structured/structured interview for diagnosis. Some or all of these techniques will be utilized, depending on the underlying reason for the interview. If the emphasis of the interview is to determine the child's history and day-to-day functioning, the social and medical history combined with behavioral rating scales may be the appropriate choice. If the interview is being conducted to ascertain a possible diagnosis or to rule out a disorder, then the semi-structured or structured interview is helpful. All these types are more fully discussed in the following section.

Social and Medical History

This type of interview is developmentally based and functions to provide information about the child's day-to-day life. In this type of interview the parent is asked questions about the medical and developmental history of the child. This type of interview is informal and has no set questions. Although it does not seek to provide a diagnosis, questions can be posed which provide sufficient information to rule in or rule out certain types of disorders. Appendix A contains a sample parent interview format. For example, questions about the child's mood, eating and sleeping behaviors, and self-esteem can provide information as to the existence of sadness or, in more extreme cases, childhood depression.

A listing of areas for questioning is often helpful and will assist you in organizing as well as preventing you from forgetting an area for inquiry. For example, my students have found it helpful to type out their questions in advance, leaving a space between questions to write in answers. A sample interview format is shown in Table 2–1.

It is important to gather information about the early stages of the child's life, including questions about the mother's pregnancy, labor, and status at birth. In addition to information on the parents' age, education, and occupation, questions about each parent's history may assist in understanding important family dynamics. Sometimes parents will volunteer information

TABLE 2–1 Interview Format for Developmental Interview

Reason for Referral: Includes dates seen, age, grade, referral source, why now

Family Composition: Ages and occupation(s) of parents, ages and sexes of siblings, anyone else living with the family, pets, where the family lives, how many moves

Developmental History: Birth history, birth weight, age at which developmental milestones attained, temperament, type of discipline most frequently used

Medical History: Any relevant illnesses, head injuries, seizures, and so on; family history of disorders or illnesses (ADHD, learning disability)

School History: Preschool experience, age at entry, quality of experience, any retentions or special education placements, previous psychological evaluations and counseling experiences, social skills

Adaptive Behaviors: Self-help skills, household chores, fine- and gross-motor skills

about their school years; this material can provide insight into how they perceive their child's experience. It is also a good idea to ask who else has lived with the family and who now lives in the family home. A grandparent may have had an impact on a child's development; this information can be invaluable, particularly if there has been a recent loss. If there is a divorce, it is often helpful to know how often the child sees the noncustodial parent and what the relationship is like between the two parents.

Important information about the child's early development includes approximate ages of walking, talking, births of other siblings, illnesses, hospitalizations, high fevers, and injuries. It is also important to question early school experiences. Has the child been in preschool or day care? If so, when did these experiences begin? How did the child adapt to these experiences? What were the parents' feelings about the child's attending these programs? Where there ever separation difficulties when the child attended the programs? Questions about separation of the child and parents due to parental illness or work responsibilities are likewise important.

It is also helpful to ask the parents how they view the child's personality. Has it been easy to establish a relationship with the child? If yes, why? If no, what has caused these difficulties? It also may be appropriate to ask of whom the child reminds the parent. Sometimes a child will remind parents of a family member who has had difficulties. If this is the case, it may be important later to attempt to unlink such an attribution. It helps to find out who the child confides in the most as well as with whom, if anyone, the child experiences difficulty. A sample interview based on these questions follows:

P S-C: We have been talking about John's behaviors and history. I would like to turn to a discussion of what type of child he is.

Parent: Well, he is a gentle and sensitive child. He seems to sense when I am tired or when I need some quiet. Things easily bother him and it's hard for him to forget when someone does something to hurt his feelings.

P S-C: Can you give me an example of this behavior?

Parent: Well, just last week one of his friends said he would come over and play and then something else came up so he couldn't come. John was upset and became very angry and said he would never play with that child again. He was hurt and angry and didn't understand that something else had come up. The boy has called several times since and John refuses to talk with him or do anything with him at school.

P S-C: Do you find that happens when you disappoint him or discipline him?

Parent: Yes. It's hard to handle his hurt feelings. He can hold onto what he sees as an "injustice" for a long time and frequently I feel more punished than he is in the end. I'm afraid that sometimes it stops me from setting limits I should just to avoid the confrontation.

P S-C: When did you first notice this type of behavior?

Parent: When he was very little. At two if I said "no" he would run away and sulk for a very long time. Eventually I would have to seek him out and push him to discuss the event. It was never easy. If something came up so we couldn't do what we said, John would have a tantrum. One time when he was about three, we were going to have a picnic on Saturday. Friday night my husband came down with the flu and we couldn't go. John didn't speak to him for several days.

P S-C: It must be hard to live this way—having to consider if punishing John is worth the effort. I wonder, does he remind you of anyone?

Parent: Mmm. I've never really thought about that but in a way he reminds me of my father. He didn't "go with the flow" as the kids say. Things upset him and he would hold onto grudges for a very long time. We kids were very careful not to anger him because it was never worth the effort to make up later.

P S-C: How do you think this behavior affects your relationship with John?

Parent: I never really feel close to him. When things go well, I enjoy being with him. When we are at loggerheads, I'd just as soon be away from him.

P S-C: It must be hard on you at times to want to avoid your own son.

Parent: It is. He does the same thing at school and I have nothing to offer the teacher to change the behavior. Nothing really works at home.

P S-C: Let's talk a little about some of the things you have tried.

The interview continued with a discussion of discipline and how the parents agreed on what actions to take when John misbehaved. One goal which came out of this interview was to assist John's parents with applying consistent and logical consequences for his positive and negative behavior. A later goal was to help John's mother understand that her method of working with her father was not going to translate well in her relationship with her son.

This interview is also a good time to ask about the child's ability to form relationships with other peers. How does the parent see the child with other peers? Does the child have the opportunity to socialize with other children? You may also find out the parents' socialization practices. In families where the parents do not have friends, children also may have few friends, possibly due to the lack of modeling or importance placed on outside friendships.

Questions about a child's behavior often yield useful data. It is also important to determine what type of discipline is used in the home, who disciplines the child, which behaviors prompt disciplinary actions, and how effective such discipline is. This section also includes questions about the child's ability to make transitions, usual behavior at home, and how the child soothes himself or herself when disappointed. Questions about the child's moods, fears, sleeping and eating practices, and relationships with siblings are also appropriate.

Another area of inquiry is the child's school history—any difficulties or strengths the child may have, if the child has been retained, if any psychological evaluations have been performed, and if the child has previously been in treatment. It is appropriate at this point to ask for a release of previous records not currently available. In this section it is important to ask the parents what types of strengths the child shows at home. It is diagnostic if no strengths can be delineated. It is also appropriate to inquire as to the parents' hopes and fears for their child's future.

One pitfall frequently experienced by novice clinicians is the tendency to rely heavily on the questions he or she is about to ask rather than the *answers* the parents provide. Too much reliance on the questions will not only make the interview repetitious and overly long, it also will make it difficult for you to pick up on clues and hints from the parents that need to be followed up with additional questions. Such follow up allows the interview to flow more naturally and addresses areas that are likely to be important in your work with the child. After reviewing the answers you have written down, you can ask follow-up questions on any area that is not complete. This approach focuses on the parent rather than on the questions. A sample questionnaire is included in Appendix A.

Semi-Structured and Structured Clinical Interviews

Structured and semi-structured interviews are frequently used to determine a diagnosis. These interviews are generally structured around the *Diagnostic Statistical Manual* (Fourth edition; *DSM-IV*, APA, 1994). Questions help determine the presence or absence of a symptom, which can lead to a diagnosis of a particular syndrome. A thorough review of representative structured and semi-structured interviews appears in Semrud-Clikeman and Hynd (1991b).

A structured interview requires the questioner to follow a specific procedure with no deviation from the questions. This yields reliable and perhaps valid data because the standardized procedures generate specific answers. On the down side, it allows little flexibility for follow-up questions or for adjustment of the procedure depending on the child's presentation. Some structured interviews can be administered by trained paraprofessionals, while others require a professional administration.

An example of a structured clinical interview is the *Diagnostic Interview for Children and Adolescents—Revised* (*DICA-R;* Reich & Welner, 1989). This interview is completed separately for both the child (or adolescent) and the parents, sometimes by different interviewers. The interview consists of 267 items and requires approximately 60 minutes to administer. The parents are asked a number of questions regarding the presence of a symptom and are required to answer yes or no. These responses are then keyed to *DSM III-R* Axis I diagnoses (disruptive behavioral disorders, anxiety disorders of childhood and adolescence, elimination disorders, etc.). This interview also contains an assessment of psychosocial stressors, an observational checklist for the clinician, and a section for recording of clinician impressions.

In contrast to the *DICA-R,* semi-structured interviews allow for flexibility of questioning within a certain format. This type of interview begins with an unstructured portion in which the parents are asked why they are seeking help at this time and what help has been obtained in the past. The second part of the interview contains questions keyed to the *DSM-III-R* format and a list of symptoms are asked, requiring yes or no answers. This interview takes approximately 60 minutes and contains an observational checklist to be completed by the clinician following the interview. The *Schedule for Affective Disorders and Schizophrenia for School-Age Children* (Kiddie-SADS or K-SADS; Orvaschel, 1985) and the *Child Assessment Schedule* (Hodges, McKnew, Burback, & Roebuck, 1987) are representative of semi-structured interviews.

While these interviews may well have their place in diagnosis and assessment of psychiatric disorders, they are of less use in the school setting. Given the amount of time needed for administration as well as the keying to a psychiatric diagnostic manual rather than to educational difficulties, they may not be worth the time required. These interviews would appear to be more useful for diagnostic questions related to the need for referral to a child psychiatrist or psychopharmacologist for assessment of possible depression, anxiety, or attention-deficit disorders.

Behavioral Checklists

I frequently request parents to complete a behavior rating scale, either prior to our initial meeting or following the meeting. Behavioral checklists are helpful as a screening device for assessment of overall functioning. Since many of the checklists are standardized, they can also provide a comparison of the child, through the eyes of the parent, to a same-aged peer on several dimensions. Frequently I also ask the teacher to complete the same behavioral checklist. This method allows for a rough comparison of behaviors across situations.

Several behavioral checklists are useful. Since the purpose here is not to review behavioral checklists, the following should be considered representative and not exhaustive. It is helpful to choose a behavioral checklist on the basis of ease of administration and scoring, reliability and validity of the instrument, and the behavioral question you are seeking to answer (discussed in Martin, 1988).

The *Child Behavioral Checklist* (CBCL; Achenbach, 1980) provides measures of externalizing (acting out) and internalizing (anxiety, withdrawal, depression) for boys and girls from ages 4 to 16. The CBCL is fairly easy to administer and score, and there is an extensive research base for its use. The *Behavioral Assessment System for Children* (BASC; Reynolds & Kamphaus, 1992) provides behavioral rating scales for teacher, parent, and child and allows for comparison of behaviors in different settings. The BASC also provides a structured developmental interview format that can be used for the initial interview.

Beginning the Interview

It is now the day of the initial interview, and you are expecting the parents to come. I feel it is important to arrange to meet the parents either by the front door of the school or in the front office. Many parents may not be familiar with the school layout and may have difficulty locating your office. As you meet them, try to present yourself as "approachable." This means addressing them by their formal names and inviting them to call you by whatever name you prefer. I usually asked parents to call me by my given name as an attempt to lighten the atmosphere. This is merely a matter of personal preference; I'm sure you will develop your own style as you gain experience.

As you walk to the office, it is usually helpful to chat about something inconsequential—the weather is always a good choice, as are the hall decorations in most elementary schools. Although you will probably be nervous initially, remember that the parents are probably equally nervous and unsure of what to expect. If you allow your nervousness to make you cool and withdrawn, rapport becomes more difficult to establish. I usually wait a few minutes for the parents to become comfortable and will offer coffee or tea if appropriate.

Since you made the initial contact by phone, the parents have some idea why they are there. It is important to review the reasons for the interview and to provide an overview of what will happen at this meeting.

At this point I also ask if I may take notes. It is often helpful to state that the notes are to assist in remembering our discussion. Most parents have no difficulty with this, and sometimes a parent will request to tape the interview. Consider this request carefully. If you refuse, the parents may well wonder why. Taping the interview may change your initial approach and your level of comfort. If possible, it is appropriate to ask why they wish to tape the interview. Usually it is an aid for them to remember what was said. I find that I forget the tape recorder is on after a short period of time.

As I begin the interview, I find it helpful to talk about the goals of the interview. In this manner you set the stage for asking questions and not for doing therapy. I also tell parents that what they tell me is confidential and will not be shared with anyone without their permission. It is important to clarify that the only time this confidentiality would be breached is if there is danger to the child or if a court order is in effect. (See Jacob & Harthorne, 1991, for a further discussion of ethical issues). Some students have wondered if parents will then not talk as freely. My experience has been that, for the interview at least, no noticeable holding back of information occurs. From an ethical standpoint, you need to disclose the limits of confidentiality before proceeding. If you do not address this issue up front and then later learn there is ongoing child abuse, you will do more damage to your relationship with the parents than if they were informed of their rights. If some of the information is to be used in a report which may be later shared with school staff, it is important to let the parents know and to be cognizant of their right to privacy. You may wish to edit the information for your report and keep specifics between you and the parents. This is particularly true if your report goes into a central file and you lose control of who may read it.

I also share with the parents the information that I will be asking several questions during the hour and that it is within their right not to answer some questions. Because most of us are socialized to answer questions from an "expert," some parents may not feel free to abstain from an answer. Usually you will not be asking questions that are that sensitive but by giving the parent permission to refuse to answer, you often communicate your respect for them as well as give them some feelings of control in the situation.

As you move through the questions, you should note nonverbal as well as verbal behavior patterns. Behaviors such as repeatedly talking at the same time, finishing each other's statements, or one parent being active and the other passive are significant and should be noted in your notes. It is often helpful to question both parents on some points to see if their perceptions agree. For example, when asked if their child is a follower or a leader, each parent may see the child differently. The mother may feel the child is a leader while the father may feel he or she is a follower. Both parents may well be right because they may see the child in different situations. Such information is helpful to the astute clinician.

During the interview you may find that the mother and father will disagree with each other; this is common. The mother and father frequently interact with the child in a different manner and about different items. If parents disagree in the session, it is appropriate to question each individually and to ask for examples from each parent. When a disagreement occurs, do not side with either parent but allow a discussion of the perceptions of each.

The following interview is an example of an initial contact with parents. A fourth-grade boy had been referred to the school psychologist for counseling by his teacher. He had been challenging the teacher's authority and had thrown an eraser at the blackboard in a fit of anger when told to be quiet. Both parents attended the interview and were generally cooperative. The limits of confidentiality had been previously discussed and agreed to by all parties involved.

MSC: I'm glad you could both come tonight and I appreciate your taking time off from your jobs.

Father: We care about our son and his behavior is very upsetting to us. We don't tolerate such behaviors in our house, and I don't know why he is acting this way. It may be his teacher is being too soft on him and now needs to crack down.

MSC: It may be that, but we are here today to try and provide information as to his development and you are both invaluable sources of information for the school. I hope we can work together for your son's best interest. Can you tell me a little about what is happening in his life right now?

Father: Well, it has been a hard year for both of us because of the recession—we are both in our own business and it hasn't been too good this year.

Mother: There's been a bit of fighting in the house because we are both so worried about money.

Father: You are worried about money—I feel things will come around. She's right though—there has been a lot of fighting between us and I'm sure he has heard some of it. For as tough as he acts, he's a very sensitive boy and very protective of his mother.

MSC: You sound like you like him. It's a real strength for him to be sensitive. What do you mean protective of his mother?

Father: I think sometimes he feels I'm mean to her. I try to reassure but I sometimes lose patience and then I yell. I don't mean anything by it but he has always been sensitive to loud voices.

Mother: Even when he was a baby he would cry if there was yelling around the house.

MSC: These are excellent observations and will surely prove helpful during therapy. They also indicate that his pattern of being sensitive to conflict is long-standing and may contribute to the difficulties currently experienced in his classroom. I'd like to ask a few questions about his early development. How was the pregnancy?

As you can see from this interchange, both parents are concerned and open to their son. They are willing to share information and answer needed questions. In addition, the interviewer supported the way both parents interact with the child and recognized their regard for their son.

Multicultural Concerns

When meeting with parents of different cultures from your own, it is imperative for you to have an understanding of cultural interaction patterns. If you are unfamiliar with the culture, you need to consult with someone who has experience with the cultural mores. You may also wish to secure supervision in this case in order to assist the treatment. Remember that the Euro-western view of therapy is not necessarily shared by other cultures. In some cultures, seeking help is seen as an admission of failure or of shame. In other cultures, one may go to a medical doctor without encountering problems but not to a psychologist. In these cultures, it is not unusual for the child to have been seen repeatedly by a pediatrician for somatic complaints and eventually referred to you by the physician. Resistance to therapy is apt to be present, and you must tread carefully.

One case I worked with was an Asian American family with a traditional family make-up. The father came to the initial interview and was very quiet throughout. The mother answered most of the questions after consulting the father on some of the answers. Although eye contact was poor, the parents were cooperative. The decision to proceed with the child interview was made by the father. It was important to enlist a colleague with experience with Asian American families to help me understand the dynamics of the case. In this case my family contact was the mother who relayed information to the father and then called me back to discuss his directions. The mother was able to share that the father felt shamed for his son to be having behavioral difficulties and to be seen by a therapist. My approach in this case was tempered by these dynamics and a fruitful dialogue was established with the child about his melding of two cultures.

It is not only very important to be aware of cultural differences when working with families, but also to realize that many psychological theories are based on the Euro-American-centered ethic. These theories may or may not apply in the same manner to different ethnicities (Sampson, 1988). Realizing that there are differences is but a first step. Although some counselors prefer to believe that they are "color-blind" and "class-blind," all of us carry into the sessions beliefs that have been honed on our own experiences. It is important to realize that different cultures or people with differing economic status from your own generally experience life in a different manner. When working in rural Georgia and Wisconsin, I needed to adjust my view from the midwestern, middle-class view I had grown up with, which valued school for learning and encouraged striving toward a college degree. In both of these settings the emphasis of many families was on preparing the child to be independent and to work either in the neighborhood factory or on the family farm. For many of the families, there were no goals of leaving town on graduation or even of high scholastic achievement. The goals were for the child to learn how to balance books, understand growth cycles of crops, and value hard work. Moreover, I quickly found that the African American families viewed me with suspicion as a sign of the "white" school system. Since I was generally working with children with difficulties, I was immediately suspect as trying to "get rid" of the problem, namely, their child. It was important to realize this attribution at the beginning of my interactions and to sensitize myself to their needs rather than to the needs of the school. It was not easy to arrive at a compromise that would be in the child's best interest.

Another area that may differ is the view of the self and community. Vargas and Koss-Chiono (1992) suggest that the therapist needs to be aware of the effect of family and the ethnic community on "culturally different" children. Miroshima (personal communication, 1994) suggests that Asian American children may react to anger in a different manner than white American children. He cites a situation where an Asian American boy was referred because he seemed to have anger attacks for no reason. When the child was observed, it was found that, when angered, he became very quiet before he eventually "blew up." This behavior was consistent with what is culturally expected when angered.

Another example of differences occurred when Mexican American children were felt to be unmotivated academically (Ramirez & Castanada, 1974). When the same data were reevaluated, it was found that these children were conforming to family-held goals rather than seeking individual achievement (Vargas & Koss-Chiorno, 1992). Books on culturally sensitive therapy include Fine (1992), Barona and Garcia (1990), and volume 21, issue 4 of *School Psychology Review* (GoPaul-McNichol, 1992).

Ending the Interview

As the interview progresses, you will find several areas of inquiry that are appropriate for a particular case. Just as you need to ask questions about the child's history, it is important to ask what the parent is expecting from the therapy. These questions are most appropriate toward the end of the session. If there are misconceptions, you may also wish to discuss what therapy cannot provide.

If parents have been in therapy themselves, they may have some understanding of the process but you should make it clear that children do not always have the same type of experience. For example, one mother asked me how her seven-year-old would be able to talk about her feelings for 50 minutes. It was necessary for me to describe a typical therapeutic session. In another instance I did not raise the question with a family of what therapy may consist of and they pulled their daughter out of treatment because she was "only drawing pictures." Unfortunately they quit treatment just as we were beginning to develop trust and their daughter was revealing her feelings through her drawings. This procedure was not what the father had experienced when he had been in intensive therapy and he had little understanding of the reasons behind the drawings. Because he had been resistant to therapy anyway, this misunderstanding served to justify his ending of the program.

Since that time I have attempted to forestall such problems by describing what may occur during a therapeutic session. Sometimes parents will request to sit in on the treatment. I discourage this observation by pointing out the child's right to privacy and how observation may interfere with the therapeutic process. Most parents accept this explanation. If you have a parent who is unable to accede to this request, however, you may wish to discuss the matter further and ask for the opportunity to begin working with the child alone. Fortunately, most schools do not have one-way mirrors so that parents would have to be in the immediate room which discourages their observation. In some cases, I have refused to provide services if the parent insists on being present. Further discussion of parental needs is presented in Chapter 5.

It is important to discuss with the parents the child's need for privacy in the sessions. This privacy extends to what has been said in the session. I usually ask that the specifics of the sessions be kept between myself and the child. The child, of course, is able to share whatever he or she wishes with the parents. I ask permission from the parents to talk to the child about this issue and reassure them that I will communicate with them on the general gist of sessions and progress. In this way parents are not totally separate from the treatment while I can still promise limited confidentiality to the child. Legally, of course, the parent has a right to access any information the child provides. Most parents, however, are sensitive to their child's right to privacy and as long as they are kept informed, have little problem with this procedure.

Prior to ending the interview, be sure to ask the parents if they have any further questions. If not, I usually indicate when I would like to see the child for an interview. At a clinic, the appointment is set at this time for the child interview. In a school setting, I indicate when I plan to see the child and when the parents can expect a follow-up phone call from me.

Before closing the interview, you should ask the parent how they plan to broach the coming interview to the child. They may have not thought about what they will say, and I find it important to discuss this matter briefly before the interview closes. In the past some parents have told the child that a lady will come and play games. This type of statement may be appropriate with younger children (age 3–5). Older children, however, may feel deceived when you have them answer questions or draw pictures and there is no sign of video or board games. I find it more appropriate for the parents to tell the child that he or she will see an adult who works with children who may have some problems in school. During that time the child will talk about feelings, thoughts, or anything he or she may want to talk about. With this introduction I find that children at least feel some control when they meet me for the first time. I also ask the parents to talk to the child either the night before or the morning of the first interview. Placing this discussion close to the meeting means the child has less time to feel anxious or worried about the encounter. At the end of the interview encourage the parents to call if they have any additional questions or information or if their child shows resistance to the planned interview.

3

Interviewing
the Child

Clinicians who attempt to interview a child in the same manner as they would an adult are setting themselves up for a less than informative interview. Interviews with parents are generally conducted in rooms with chairs meant for adults. The interviewees are usually there at their own request or at least have had a choice in attending the session. Adults have different communication styles and levels of language development than children. Finally, in most cases, the adults expect to respond to a series of questions. Although some of these elements are present in a child interview, they all differ in some meaningful way. Before discussing these various aspects of a child interview, you need to understand why a child interview is important.

Importance of the Interview

One of the basic questions posed by beginning clinicians is why is an interview necessary—can't treatment proceed without an interview? Of course treatment can begin without an interview—but how would the clinician know where the treatment was going? An interview allows the clinician to observe the child in a nontherapeutic setting while gathering information. Determining the issues a child is bringing to therapy and answering the question of appropriateness of therapy for the child are goals for the initial interviews. When issues that the child brings are used in therapy, the child is more involved in the process and treatment cooperation may be better (Witt et al., 1988). Conversely if children feel they have little control in their treatment, they may reveal few of their thoughts, feelings, or fears (Wood & Wood, 1983).

Finally, the interview allows you to establish initial rapport with the child. Moreover, it is during this time that you begin formulating the case and forming hypotheses as to the best treatment method. Case formulation is discussed in detail in the next chapter.

Determining Reasons for Interview

The child may bring certain expectations to the first meeting with the clinician. Some children think they are there to be tested, while others believe they are in trouble and the interview is like going to the principal's office. Whatever the child's belief, the interview is a time to sort out fears and preconceptions of who you are and what the therapeutic process is about.

It is always important to find out why the child thinks he or she is in your office. This maxim applies in a school office as much as a private office. You can learn a great deal about how the child reacts to new situations by your observations and the child's answer to "why do you think you are here?" Statements such as "because my mother wanted me to come" or "so I will behave" are as revealing about the parent as they are about the child and should be duly noted. A study by Kister and Patterson (1988) found that some children view coming to a "doctor" as an indication that they have done something wrong, even when they are physically ill. If not corrected, this misperception is likely to have an impact on your therapy goals. The child may interpret your intervention as a vehicle for finding out what she or he did wrong—not as an opportunity to explore feelings and worries. In a related study of the effect of preparation on therapy participation, Holmes and Urie (1975) found that when children are prepared for therapy (including the initial interview), there is less likelihood of treatment ending prematurely.

Appropriateness of Therapy

Another aim of the interview is to determine if therapy is appropriate for a particular child. Not all children are appropriate for individual therapy. Individual treatment is probably most appropriate for children who can communicate either verbally or nonverbally and who are able to use what they learn in another setting. Generally, if a child is very resistant to coming for treatment and to forming a relationship with you, it is likely that treatment will not succeed.

This is not to say that initial resistance indicates that you should not continue with treatment. Many children are resistant initially because of fear of the unknown. They will, however, eventually respond to you. However, there are a few children who are not willing to come and will resist any overtures on your part. In this case, individual treatment is probably not appropriate and other avenues of intervention should be explored. Ethically, it is important to respect the child's resistance.

Variables such as age, ability to benefit from individual treatment, and readiness for treatment are also important to assess during the initial interviews. These areas are discussed in the following paragraphs.

Age

Age does not necessarily preclude children from profiting from individual therapy. Preschool children who can act out their fears often profit from therapy. For example, a boy of three was referred to a school psychologist by his special education teacher because he hit other students. Because he was a large child, his teacher was concerned for the safety of his classmates. Although a behavioral program was effective with other behaviors, it did not reduce his hitting behavior. Several short sessions were utilized and he responded well to the individual attention. Using a dollhouse, the boy repeatedly acted out aggression between a small doll and a larger one. A conversation with his mother indicated that his older brother frequently hit him despite numerous attempts on her part to extinguish this behavior. When the boy came to the next session, the therapist set the stage for an intervention based on this information.

C: Ouch! You just hit me again. I feel hurt and mad.

Boy: Ha! I feel good. I like to hit you and I'll hit again.

C: You make me feel so small when you hit me.

Boy: I'm bigger and I can do what I want.

C: If you hit me, then you are bigger and more important.

Boy: Yes, you can't do anything.

The treatment continued for several more sessions but the issue of being small and insignificant loomed large for this child and hitting was possibly his only avenue of defense against what he perceived as a threatening world.

Benefit

It is also important to determine during the interview if the child is likely to benefit from individual treatment. Children who are mentally retarded may not benefit from individual psychotherapy because of limited understanding and language development. For these children an alternative, such as group therapy, focusing on social and adaptive skills would likely be more appropriate. There are also children who are unable to tolerate closeness to another person. Such closeness can be either emotional, physical, or a combination. For these children a therapeutic program may include a small-group setting to diffuse interpersonal proximity. Since individual therapy requires more investment in time and cost, group treatment may be the most expeditious and efficient method of service delivery.

Readiness

It can also be the case that the child is not ready to discuss certain problems. Some children require space in order to work through feelings before discussing or acting them out with others. It is important to respect a child's right to have input into the treatment entry. It is my experience that children who feel involved in determining treatment goals are more ready for therapy.

For example, a six-year-old boy was referred for therapy after having just lost his father to a sudden heart attack. The father was in his early 30s and the boy's mother felt it might be good for the little boy to talk about his feelings. On the surface, this request looked perfectly reasonable. During the interview, however, the boy asked the school psychologist for time to be alone. He stated that he knew he was sad and that he missed his father but he wanted to think about other things right now and needed to "forget" about feeling sad at school. He said that at home all anyone talked about was his father's death and everyone was sad. The school psychologist asked if he felt he would ever want to talk about the problems. The boy's reply was revealing. He stated that he would like to talk about his feelings after his family became more "normal." He agreed to come and talk to the school psychologist at a later point in time. He later sought out the school psychologist and began treatment approximately six months later.

The clinician may also determine from the interviews with the parents and child that the most efficacious treatment route is not individual therapy. Family system problems may need to be resolved before individual therapy can be effective. A behavioral management program may be found to be more appropriate for the child's needs than individual therapy, or group therapy may be the treatment of choice. The child interview helps you select the most appropriate treatment.

Preparing for the Child Interview

The interview of the child is generally shorter than adult interviews you have previously conducted. It is often a good idea to interview the child on a different day from the parent interview. Some models have the child accompany the parents and wait in the waiting room while they are interviewed. Although this is more convenient for the parents and the clinician, I have found that some children resent the time spent waiting, and others become very nervous about what is being said about them.

In the school setting, the parents will not often be readily available so you can avoid the problem. However, you will need to set up a mutually convenient time with the teacher for your first session. It is important not to schedule your interview during a class the child really likes such as physical education, music, art, or recess. As obvious as this seems, these are the times usually suggested for your interview. If you choose this time and the child is angry about it, your interview will be problematic at best. You may wish to allot approximately 20 to 25 minutes for the initial interview. A longer period of time may unduly interfere with the teacher's schedule while a shorter period is insufficient for information gathering.

The Interview Setting

Child interviews are generally less question-and-answer format than those with adults. Allowing children more latitude in activities and control during the interview may result in better memory and involvement in the session (Todd & Perlmutter, 1980). Child-sized furniture also helps the child feel at ease. When children are interviewed in rooms with larger furniture, they often look, and probably feel, dwarfed by the furniture with, in turn, increasing feelings of insignificance and lack of control. Allowing access to age-appropropriate activities and environments may empower the child to become involved in the process.

Many clinicians find a playroom for younger children is conducive to the interview process. A playroom may include a dollhouse, puppets, trucks, building blocks, modeling clay, and markers. For older children and adolescents the presence of clay, markers, board games, or toys can serve to break the ice. At times older children will play with toys more appropriate for younger children. They will often use them in a different way than younger children do, and these behaviors should be noted.

For example, a 13-year-old boy I interviewed preferred to play with puppets. During the interview he repeatedly had the weaker puppet being attacked and then saved by a dragon puppet. Although the play was immature for the adolescent's age, it provided an important glimpse into his feelings about himself and his relationship with others.

Some children feel more comfortable sprawled on the floor working on a project than they do sitting at a table. You need to adjust your comfort level to the child's to connect with her or him. With younger children you may wish to wear clothes that can tolerate getting marker on them or being on the floor. On days I know I am working with younger children, I adjust my wardrobe accordingly.

Observations

In the school setting, it is often wise to schedule a classroom observation prior to beginning your contact with the child. Observing in multiple settings can assist in forming hypotheses to be explored during the interviews (Martin, 1988). Moreover, observations can provide a window to the child's functioning with peers and in different environments. Observing a child in settings such as a directed activity, recess and/or lunch, a less structured setting such as art class, and in the halls can provide useful information not only for case formulation but for later use as a baseline when evaluating treatment efficacy.

Several methods of behavioral observation are available in the literature (Brophy & Good, 1970; Mash & Terdal, 1988). One of the most useful methods I have used is to select an "average" child in the classroom. *Average* is defined as a child who isn't the best or the worst in the class. The two children are then observed and behaviors tallied across situations. Although target behaviors may vary across children, it is usually a good idea to note the child's relationship with the teacher and peers. Observations to make include how the child gains teacher and peer attention, time spent on task, positive and negative comments made to the child or by the child, and how often the child interacts with others. These target behaviors are helpful in assessing the quality of the child's interpersonal relationships.

In the private-practice setting observation of the child is not as easy a task as in schools. In deciding whether to observe a child, the clinician needs to determine what information would be helpful for the particular case. If the same information can be gained through parent and teacher interviews, an observation may be unnecessary. However, if the clinician later decides it would be helpful to observe the child or to meet with the teacher, this observation should be discussed with the child. Children may feel betrayed if they see their therapist in the school setting without prior knowledge about it. These feelings may well weaken the therapeutic alliance.

For example, a five-year-old girl was seen in a private clinic for frequent tantrums and oppositional behavior. She had previously been seen by another clinician in a different clinic but suddenly had refused to talk to him any longer. The second clinician was surprised by some comments made by the girl when she overheard a man shouting in an adjacent office.

Girl: He's really angry—who's he talking to?

C: Why do you think he's angry?

Girl: He's really loud—is he going to come in here?

C: No. Why do you think he's coming in here?

Girl: My other doctor was in my school and I saw him talking to my teacher.

C: How did that feel?

Girl: I was very angry. I knew that he was talking about me and he never told me.

C: He never told you he was coming to your school?

Girl: No—and he was mad at me.

C: How did you know he was mad at you?

Girl: Because I'm bad at school.

C: You thought he was mad and so he came to school?

Girl: He had a loud voice too.

C: Were you mad because he didn't ask you if he could come?

Girl: Will you come to my school?

C: Would you like me to?

Girl: Only if you tell me first. I don't want you to be mad at me.

C: I don't want you to be mad at me.

Girl: He was a bad doctor.

C: He was bad because you couldn't trust him.

In this case a well-meaning clinician had come to the child's school to meet with her teachers. Unbeknown to him, the child had seen him in the hallway and arrived at a conclusion that was incorrect. However, she was unable to talk to the clinician about her fears and her feelings of betrayal. It is always wise to remember that when you don't want to be seen by a child, you always will be.

Children, particularly children who are often in difficulty, are very sensitive about right or wrong and if you violate their trust, it is quite likely the therapeutic relationship will be destroyed. In the above case, it would have been wiser to discuss the need to talk to her teacher with the girl and to clear up any possible misunderstanding before it could occur. This is not to say you ask the child for permission to come, merely that you let him or her know you may be in the school. In the above case, the appearance of the child's reluctance to continue with the first clinician coincided with his school visit. The long-term approach used in this case was to provide the girl with an opportunity to express her anger at him as well as a chance for a resolution of feelings.

It is equally important to observe the child during your sessions with him or her. One of the first opportunities occurs when you first meet the child. The clinical setting offers an opportunity to observe the child's interpersonal functioning, social appropriateness, and range of emotional expression. Table 3–1 provides areas for observation during the interview.

Separation Issues
The astute clinician is able to gather information on how the child separates from the teacher or parent as well as how the child separates from the

TABLE 3–1   Significant Behaviors to Note During Interviews

Separation from parent (or teacher)
Eye contact
Appropriateness of behavior
Social ease in new situations
Response to rules
Range of affect
Expressive language abilities
Activity level
Attention span
Play themes
Behavior at end of session/Separation from therapist

teacher or parent as well as how the child separates from the clinician at the end of the session. Some children require additional time to make a transition from one situation to the next. Others make such adjustments easily. As you prepare for your initial meeting, it is helpful to set the stage with the caretaker involved. Although most children are able to walk to your office with you alone, some children need a slower transition, and it may be necessary to have the teacher walk with both of you to your office. When parents accompany the child, it can be helpful to have them present for the first few minutes and then prepare the child for their departure. With other children you may need the parents to remain until the child feels comfortable. With the child described earlier, it was necessary for the mother to attend the initial sessions until the child again felt safe with a clinician.

Just as important as the initial separation from teacher or parent, is the separation from the clinician at the end of the sessions. Children can experience difficulty ending sessions. For some children the session is one of the few times they have undivided adult attention. They may resist ending the session through various delaying tactics. One four-year-old girl was known to tell her parent she had one more thing to say to her clinician. Another would have a tantrum when separating from her mother and then another tantrum when separating from the clinician when the session ended. These are important behaviors to note and to use when developing treatment goals. The possible meaning behind these behaviors is discussed in a later chapter.

Session Behavior

The behaviors you note during the session may fall into important patterns. For example, a child may be overly clingy and friendly to an adult she or he barely knows. The child may relate so quickly to the therapist that the inexperienced clinician may feel there is a special bond with this child. It may be, however, that the child relates this way with all adults, and one purpose of this behavior may be to offset fears of abandonment. In contrast, another child may be very cautious and withdrawn and may not respond to the clinician at all. Obviously treatment strategies for both of these children will differ but the underlying dynamic may be the same: fear of abandonment or separation.

Children vary in their need for control of their environment as well as their response to adult control. Some children may respond well to an initial directive to choose anything they want from the array of activities in the playroom. Other children may have difficulty with too many choices. It is also possible that one child may insist on directing the activities while another will wait for the interviewer to take the lead. All of these behaviors should be noted for future use.

It also is important to observe the different affects the child brings to the session. Most children do not show one emotional expression throughout a session. Particular activities may elicit responses that are therapeutically meaningful. For example, one child was very reluctant to draw a picture of her family. When pressed, she produced a picture of her mother and herself but left out her father. She began screaming when asked if there was anyone else in her family and claimed he was dead. This behavior was the only time she had spoken of her father. Her reaction to the activity was indicative of issues needing to be addressed. Eventually it was discovered that sexual abuse was occurring in this family.

Eye contact is another variable to be cognizant of during your sessions. A shy, withdrawn child usually experiences difficulty with eye contact. Many adults act negatively to a child who does not meet their eyes. Therefore, when misbehavior occurs, poor eye contact can be interpreted as fabricating a response. Moreover, it is not rewarding to many adults to speak to children with poor eye contact, and adults have been found to limit their interactions with these children (Kazdin, 1988).

How the child responds to the environment is important to note. If you have several activities laid out, does the child skip from one activity to the next or settle on one? Does the child experience difficulty following the rules and if so, how does the child handle the resulting frustration? Does he or she constantly test you to see how you will react? One youngster repeatedly tested the limits throughout the initial sessions. She reacted well to corrections but soon was into something else that was either dangerous or destructive. When corrected, she would repeatedly ask if the clinician still liked her. Observations of this child with her mother showed that the child frequently was able to secure her mother's attention through misbehavior. When her behavior was appropriate, the child received limited maternal response. Although behavior always has a purpose for the actor, this purpose may not be readily evident to the observer. It is important, therefore, to observe the consequences of inappropriate or oppositional behavior in order to understand the benefits derived from such actions.

Interpersonal Relationships
The interview can also serve as a window to the child's use of interpersonal relationships as well as the child's expectations of the adult reaction to them. Children organize their experiences and reason socially at different developmental ages. It is important to evaluate how the child reasons about relationships in order to begin to understand how the child perceives his or her world. Children who are behind in social reasoning skills may well have difficulties with relating to peers and to adults (Selman, 1980).

An early stage of social reasoning is that of the child as center of the universe. As the child matures, it becomes possible for her or him to take another's perspective and reason accordingly. Children at the first stage of development find it hard to understand the difference between accidental and intentional behavior. For example, one child's appointment had to be canceled because of a death in the clinician's family. The child was rescheduled but continued to harbor resentment and anger about the change. It took several sessions to explore and resolve these feelings. The child felt that the therapist should always be there for the sessions no matter what occurred.

Arrested development at this early stage can be problematic. One can see adults with this agenda who are clinically referred to as "entitled." This entitlement means that the person always puts the self first no matter what. Such behaviors are often problematic in the formation of mature relationships. If a child you are working with evidences this type behavior, it will be important for you to assess the quality of the emotional relationships in which this child is involved.

The interview also allows you to evaluate how the child relates to other adults. The child's style of language, use of questions, and understanding of your statements are all areas that provide information. A child's social skills can also be evaluated during the interview. The use of polite language or socially appropriate behavior is a clue to the child's ability to internalize adult expectations. Likewise, a child who repeatedly violates the usual standard of conduct (by picking the nose, sneezing without covering the mouth, etc.) may be at risk for social ostracism by his or her peers (Gresham & Elliott, 1989).

Multicultural Considerations

It is important to be aware of cultural differences in eye contact when assessing both this behavior and that of proximity preferences. Some cultures discourage eye contact and the child's behavior should be viewed in this light—not as abnormal. A child from a Chinese American family, seen in treatment in our clinic, refrained from enthusiastic engagement and eye contact was poor. These behaviors were also noted in her family's behavior during the initial interview. It would be inappropriate to target these behaviors as abnormal and to structure a program to change such behaviors.

Likewise, physical proximity differs between cultures. With some cultures it is appropriate to stand or sit close to the other person. One child from an Italian American family would talk only inches from the face of a clinician from a Nordic background. This clinician felt smothered and overwhelmed by the closeness and as he backed away from the child, the child moved closer and closer to him. Eventually the child complained to her parents that the clinician didn't like her. In contrast, a child from a Korean American family required additional space between him and the clinician. Such cultural differences need not only to be respected, but also recognized.

Children from different cultures may also respond differently to stress. One Asian American child was referred for consultation because he was having frequent temper tantrums that the teacher described as "coming out of nowhere." Observation of the child showed that he would experience frustration and become increasingly polite and quiet until he finally could contain himself no longer. A professor of Asian American background indicated that it was culturally normal for the child to become more polite before exploding (Morishima, personal communication, 1994). The teacher had interpreted this behavior as the child having accepted the limits offered. Subsequently the teacher changed how she responded to the child when he began to be frustrated, which in turn changed his response. Therefore, it is imperative for the clinician be aware of possible cultural differences and when in doubt consult someone who is familiar with that culture.

African American children also bring their unique experience to the interview process. Greene (1992) observes that African American children are subjected to an everyday onslaught of information which sees their differences as inferiorities or deficits rather than just a difference. African American children are asked to assimilate into the general culture while also being part of their culture, which is frequently undervalued by mainstream society. Clinicians may unknowingly ascribe to these opinions and see pathology in the African American family where instead there may be adaptation to a difficult situation (Gibbs, 1989).

African American children frequently do not have the luxury of a protected childhood. Many are subjected to a war-zone environment and economic hardship which most middle-class clinicians have no experience to understand. It is important to realize these differences and translate behaviors into the setting in which they occur. In addition, African American families do not seek therapy for their children until problems are extreme (Neighbors, 1985). They first attempt to secure assistance from their pastor, doctor, and friends. Additional information appears in Vargas and Koss-Chiono (1992) and Gibbs (1989).

The Interview

The beginning few moments of the interview will set the stage for later interactions. For most children the initial minutes of the interview are best spent letting them explore the room. Sometimes a child will just look at you for direction, and you may wish to suggest that it's OK to look around if she or he wishes. Although you may have an impulse to fill the first minutes with chatter, it is important to be as unintrusive as possible to give the child a chance to settle in. You may want to comment on the exploration that is taking place, and if the child begins to color, it may be helpful to observe the progress on the picture. Often if a child is busy doing something else, you can elicit information more readily. For example, if the child is coloring a picture of a rainbow (which is common with younger children), you can comment on the colors or ask where he or she has seen rainbows, and so on.

Listening Is Important

Sitting next to the child and sharing time will often begin the process of rapport building. Having the child immediately required to answer your questions about why he or she is here can make the interview seem like a task to be accomplished rather than the building of a relationship. Since many children are accustomed to adults asking questions and you engage in this behavior, they will assume (and quite rightly) that the purpose of their interaction with you is to answer your questions.

One of the hardest lessons for the beginning clinician to learn is that in interviewing children the most important skill to master is listening, not questioning. In fact, one of the main purposes of the initial sessions is to have the child feel safe and listened to by the clinician. In order for a child to feel safe enough to talk about scary and/or confusing feelings, it is important that he or she feels a bond with you. With some children, such a bond is easily formed and you can readily talk about feelings and concerns. With most children it takes some time to feel the relationship is safe for confidences, and you need to respect the child's timetable for such feelings of safety.

Initial Guidelines

During the initial session it is important to establish certain guidelines. First, as the child becomes settled in, it is helpful to ask why he or she is here. For example, a 12-year-old boy was brought to therapy by his mother, who expressed concern about his self-concept and self-esteem. After a few minutes, while he was playing with some animal puppets, the interview began with the following dialogue:

Boy: You have a lot of toys in here—do a lot of kids come here?

C: Yes, and there are a lot of things to do here and kids seem to enjoy playing with the toys. What do you like to play with here?

Boy: I like the puppets and the target games. Why do kids come to see you?

C: Some kids come to talk about their feelings and some are confused about people in their lives. There are a lot of reasons why children want to talk to someone. Are you wondering why you are here?

Boy: My mom wanted me to come, so I'm here.

C: How come?

Boy: She thinks I have some feelings I don't talk about.

C: What do you think?

Boy: I'm really OK—she gets mad a lot and yells.

C: And how does that feel?

The interview continued from this point with the boy talking about how he felt when the mother would yell at him and his anger at his dad for not standing up to him. When asked what he would like to work on, the boy talked about his wanting help with his anger toward his mother and father. Working on his anger was a goal in the therapy plan; both the child and his mother felt part of this plan.

In the initial portion of an interview it is important to discuss why the child is with you. Many children are confused about what they are supposed to do and it is often helpful to talk about what kinds of things you do in therapy. I generally discuss the fact that children come to see me when they are afraid, or angry, or sad and that I am there to help them. I allow children to call me by my first name so as to lessen the distance between us. Some younger children automatically call me Dr. Peg; when I worked in the schools, it was "Miss Peg." Some clinicians may be uncomfortable with this practice, you will need to find what works best for you.

The above interview ended with talking about the rules for the therapy room. With other children it may be important to address the rules earlier in the interview. Timing and the developmental age of the child both affect how you express the limits of confidentiality. Children need to know the limits and you should explicitly state them. I will generally say something like the following:

While you are with me, you can choose what you would like to do. The only rules I have are that you may not break anything in the room, hurt me, or hurt yourself. Your parents have agreed that what we talk about is between us. If you want to talk to them about our session, that's OK. I will only tell them about what we are working on together—not what you said. The only exception to this is that if I feel you are in danger, I will have to protect you. If I feel it is important to talk to your parents about something we have discussed, I will talk it over with you first. Do you have any questions?

Because confidentiality is a major issue for adolescents, it is necessary to stress its importance for your sessions. As discussed in Chapter 2, it is best for the therapeutic relationship if the parents are able to allow for this agreement. The foregoing script also shows the child that you are there to protect him or her. For adolescents you need to lay the ground rules for confidentiality clearly. Issues such as sexual activity and drugs and alcohol use need to be dealt with up front. I generally tell the adolescent that anything he or she may share with me is confidential *unless* I believe the behavior constitutes a danger to that person or others. I also tell adolescents that I will discuss with them any issue which I feel it necessary to report to others. It is important to let the adolescent know that you have to make sure he or she is protected and safe.

If you are working with a child who is aggressive or destructive, it is important to stress the sentence about no damage to the room or yourself. If the child breaks the rule, it is imperative that you call attention to it and hold her or him responsible. For example, one of my student clinicians was working with a four-year-old who cut the student's finger with a scissors. The four-year-old acted surprised when the clinician cried out in pain and he was immediately sorry for his action. The clinician discussed with him how it had hurt and stated that the session was now over. The rules were calmly repeated and the child was returned to his classroom.

The surprise that the child showed was similar to his lack of empathy for other children he had hurt. Over subsequent sessions, the incident with the scissors was repeatedly brought up by the boy and led to fruitful discussions about how others feel when they are hurt. The clinician was able to turn this episode into a corrective emotional experience as the child found that the clinician did not back away from him after the event as other people had, and he became more demonstrative with the clinician about his confusion over other feelings.

Interviewing a withdrawn and/or depressed child can be very difficult. I find that the child may not talk at all at first. It is most helpful to structure an activity to "break the ice" and to realize that it may take more than one session to interview this child. I will utilize puppets, drawing, music, and/or a sandbox to ease the child into the interview. It is important not to push the child to talk before he or she is ready to do so. You may also wish to use "sometimes" statements such as "Sometimes it's hard to talk about our feelings" or "Sometimes I don't know how I feel but it helps to try to draw a picture about my feelings."

It also helps to try to discover an area of interest a child may have and concentrate on that area rather than the child's feelings. For example, a second-grade girl was referred to me because she refused to talk with anyone in her classroom. She did talk at home but not about any concerns she might have. My first two attempts with her were futile and I was becoming frustrated. I happened to find out she was fascinated by a certain female rock star. I brought a cassette tape by the rock star and played it during our session. She spoke a bit about the rock star and I asked her to draw a picture showing me how the star looked. This vehicle was used over the next few sessions as a way of getting her to talk about the star and then eventually about what she would tell the star if she could talk with her.

Listening Behaviors

Listening is an important technique in any type of therapy. Active listening requires that the listener attend to the verbal and nonverbal content of the speaker's words and actions. A beginning clinician will often be too concerned about what questions to ask and how to ask them. These concerns are genuine but they can easily cloud your ability to listen if you are concentrating on what question to ask next. Often the question is not as important as the way the question is posed and its timing.

Since you are entering this field, it is likely that you are intuitive and responsive to other's emotions. It is important to listen with a "third ear" and see with a "third eye." In other words, it is just as important to listen to what is *not* being said as it is to what is said. For example, a child may speak about other people being mad when what the child is really talking about is how mad she or he is and possibly how scared these strong feelings make the child. If you hear words repeated or feelings attributed to someone with little or no preamble, it is likely the child is trying to tell you something.

You also need to listen to your inner emotional music. How are you reacting to what the child is telling you? How do you feel about being with the child? Does the child provoke anger, sadness, or rejection from you? These nonverbal messages that you are subconsciously picking up can assist you in directing the interview.

Question Format
As important as knowing when to question is how you ask the question. When children are asked "why" questions, they often infer that you are

asking a blaming question such as "why did you do that?" In addition, many children do not readily know why they did something, and asking them why usually gets a response such as "I don't know" or "I just felt like it." Think about your own situation. It is likely that you have had experiences where you were unsure about "why" you felt a certain way or "why" you did a certain thing; these questions are generally nonproductive.

"What" or "how" type questions are more useful. For example, a kindergarten child was referred for an interview because on three different occasions she was found eating other children's lunches in the coatroom. Her mother reported that she had eaten breakfast and she also had brought her own lunch.

C: Why were you eating Jessica's lunch in the coatroom this morning?

Girl: I don't know.

C: Were you hungry?

Girl: No, I just wanted to.

C: Why?

Girl: I don't know. Child shrugs and is quiet.

In this instance the clinician used "why" questions and the child's responses were defensive as if she thought the clinician was seeking evidence to punish her. Contrast the above interview with this scenario:

C: What happened after you ate Jessica's lunch?

Girl: I had to come to talk to you.

C: How come?

Girl: I don't know. Silence. I guess to find out why.

C: And if we know why you ate Jessica's lunch, then what?

Girl: Maybe you'll call my mother and she'll talk to me.

C: Would your mother have to come to school then?

Girl: She'll have to bring Jessica another lunch.

C: So if you eat someone else's lunch, your mother has to come to school to help you. You would like to see your mother at school. I bet you miss her.

Girl: I don't know what she does all day. I'm not there to help her with my baby brother.

In this case, the girl was trying to involve her mother in school and regain her place. School separation is often difficult for children and they may not be able to put their feelings into words. It is possible that this girl was worried about being without her mother and subconsciously she developed a method to engage her mother in the school. Following this interview, her mother was encouraged to volunteer some time in the kindergarten rooms to help her daughter with the transition.

As you may have noted in this interview, the clinician used statements that connected the behavior with the feelings the child was expressing. In some cases it is helpful for you to make an educated guess about the motivation behind a behavior. The child will tell you if you are wrong. The most important thing is for the child to know that you are attempting to understand—not punish or find fault.

Paraphrasing

Another way of pursuing a feeling or thought is to paraphrase what the child has said. In this way you can clarify your understanding and allow the child to correct any mistakes. Some clinicians believe that paraphrasing is just restating what the child has said. If you utilize this method, you will find the child can become impatient and say—"I just said that!" However, if you restate what was said as a hypothesis, the child will often clarify or expand on the thought. For example, if a child says he's angry and you parrot back to him, "I hear you say you are angry," it is likely there will be little feeling of understanding. However, if you say "Sometimes children can be angry for a number of reasons," you express understanding of the anger and your statement encourages a further explanation from the child. For example, you might say, "A child may have hurt feelings or may feel scared or worried. Do you feel any of these things?" In this way you are acknowledging the feelings as well as attempting to understand how it is to be the child.

Ending the Interview

Just as the beginning of the interview is important, it is equally important for you to conclude the interview appropriately. Younger children have a poorly developed sense of time and may not be ready to leave when you are. Older children may seek to prolong the interview to avoid other activities or tasks. As your time draws to a close, you should begin preparing the child for the ending. I find it helpful to remind the child approximately five minutes before the end of the session that our time is almost up. Some children have difficulty with separation and will fight leaving the session. It is important to be firm but gentle and state that you will see them next time but that now they need to go with their parents or they need to go back to the classroom. Other children will attempt to bargain with you and tell you they need to tell you one more thing. Often it is helpful to ask them to write it down after they leave so they can remember to tell you the next time you meet. It may be useful to reflect back to the child the difficulty he or she is having with leaving, saying that leaving is hard but that you will be looking forward to seeing the child in the future.

You need to monitor your reactions to these behaviors. If you subconsciously believe you are responsible for solving the child's problems or are the only person who can help a child, it may be as difficult for you to separate from the child as it is for him or her. You may be nonverbally communicating these feelings, thus complicating the child's leaving the session. If this is the case, you need to seek out supervision or speak to your supervisor about this issue. Other transference issues are discussed in Chapter 5.

At the end of the initial interview, it is helpful to ask the child how it felt to come to see you. I will often ask what the child liked and didn't like. If another interview is to be scheduled, it is appropriate to talk about the next appointment. Many children like to take a slip of paper with the time of the next session written on it. If you will not be seeing the child until after you consult with the parents, it is wise to tell her or him that. It is important that you have closure on the session and that the child knows what the future plan is.

The next chapter discusses case formulation issues gathered from the completed interview.

4

Diagnosis and
Case Formulation

Diagnosis may mean disparate things to different clinicians. In the context of this book, *diagnosis* refers to the gathering of data from parent, child, teacher, and other significant players in the child's life in order to develop a treatment plan tailored for the child. *Case formulation* is a process by which the clinician gathers data not only for use for diagnosis but also to aid in hypothesis generation as to the source of the difficulties experienced by the child. Diagnosis and case formulation go hand in hand. Diagnosis informs case formulation as to how the child may compare to other children his or her age and how the behavior differs from the norm while case formulation provides hypotheses for utilization of resources and tactics for intervention.

A Developmental Framework

Achenbach (1990) suggests the use of a developmental framework for understanding child psychopathology. This framework would allow for the incorporation of various paradigms into an integrated picture for understanding the dynamics operating for a particular child. Using Achenbach's model, information is gathered from sources and integrated. For our purposes, information on the child's physical condition, social-emotional functioning, behavior, family system, and cognitive abilities would be obtained and then utilized to form hypotheses as to the best intervention for the child.

In addition to information gathered on these areas of functioning, the astute clinician will place the information in a developmental context. Some behaviors which are appropriate at one age are very inappropriate at another.

It is necessary for the clinician to have a well-grounded understanding of development of the normal child before being able to understand a child with psychopathology or with problems in development.

It is strongly suggested that beginning therapists observe groups of children in various settings. It is helpful to observe how typically developing children interact with their teachers and peers, how they seek out attention, how they handle frustration, and what types of play activities and interests are favored at different ages. It will be time well-spent to observe children at various grade levels. Not only will such observations provide the beginning clinician with invaluable data, such observations will assist in determining what intervention strategies may be viable within classroom settings as well as the demands generally placed on children during their six- to seven-hour school day.

Research from the consultation area (Meyers, Parson, & Martin, 1979) suggests an "eye of the beholder" phenomenon. This phenomenon states that respondents to interviews have points of view garnered from their particular interactions with the child. Thus, parents have data on the consistency of a child's behavior in different settings as well as data on the distinctiveness of a child's response over time. In contrast, teachers have observations about how the child compares to other children the same age. Most parents do not have normative data while most teachers do not have information about the child's responses outside of the school environment. Thus, these informants would vary not only in their observations but also in what they have to compare the child to in terms of other children or life situations.

Using Achenbach's multi-modal–multi-informant paradigm for diagnosis, information would be gathered from sources in order to determine in what ways the child's behavior differs from that of other children the same age in similar situations. Since many disorders are not all-or-none, children present with a continuum of difficulties, some more severe than others. By gathering information from various contexts in the child's life, the clinician will not only form a more integrated picture of the child's functioning but will also be able to pinpoint inconsistencies between behavior and situations which are possibly related to changes in task demand.

For example, children with attentional problems often show adequate to good attention when in situations that are novel and/or rapidly changing (Frick & Lahey, 1991). Thus, a child brought into a physician's office may not appear to have attention deficit hyperactivity disorder (ADHD) because she or he is able to sit still for the examination—an examination that is generally out of the ordinary for the child—held in an office full of interesting objects. In a classroom or at home, however, this child may have extreme difficulty with attention span and behavioral control *particularly* when asked to stick with a task or complete a job. The author has experienced several incidents when, having referred a child for evaluation by a physician for possible ADHD, the child behaves "perfectly" in the medical office.

In contrast to the child who behaves appropriately in a novel situation, a five-year-old child was referred to the author for assessment of a possible ADHD by a physician who was unable to contain the child in the medical office. The teacher and parent reports indicated some difficulty with anxiety, particularly social withdrawal in new situations. Assessment of the child showed adequate attention and activity level but somewhat increased anxiety. For this child, evaluation by the pediatrician provoked anxiety and the child reacted by becoming very active and distractable. Thus, all of the informants were correct; the child had difficulty with attention in certain situations but not for reasons of ADHD. Treatment in assisting the parents and teachers help the child learn to cope with transitions and new situations proceeded very differently than if the diagnosis had been ADHD. The gathering of information from several sources allowed for a more accurate picture of this child's functioning within various environments.

Diagnostic Statistical Manuals

The *Diagnostic Statistical Manuals (DSM;* APA, 1989, 1987, 1994) were an attempt to provide a framework for information exchange between mental health clinicians and researchers. The first edition of the *DSM* was published in 1950 (APA, 1950). The emphasis of *DSM I* was on a psychobiological view of mental disorders. This view suggested that mental disorders represent personality reactions to psychological, social, and biological factors. In contrast to *DSM I, DSM II* (APA, 1968) was considered atheoretical and was linked to the *International Classification of Diseases* (ICD–8). *DSM II* provided lists of commonly associated symptoms with various mental disorders. *DSM III* (APA, 1980) broke somewhat from the *ICD* classification system and provided additional detail as well as a shift to a "multiaxial" approach to diagnosis. The multiaxial approach was designed to address medical, personality, level-of-functioning, and environmental stress factors as well as a "diagnosis." *DSM IV* (APA, 1994) has just been published and utilizes the multiaxial approach.

Prior to *DSM III-R*, the DSMs had been revised only when the *ICD* was revised. Due to a burgeoning research base, *DSM III* was revised and *DSM III-R* (APA, 1987) was published. The task force which developed *DSM III-R* utilized research findings as underpinnings for diagnostic categories whenever possible. Empirical data was utilized to adjust age of onset, review diagnostic symptomatology, and establish diagnostic reliability. The task force also emphasized using categories which showed reliability and which were useful for making treatment and management decisions. In addition and for the first time in *DSM* history, field trials were conducted to assist with the development of criteria for specified diagnoses—disruptive behavior disorders, pervasive developmental disorder and so on—(APA, 1987). These procedures were continued for *DSM IV* (APA, 1994).

The goal of *DSM III, III-R,* and *DSM IV* (APA, 1980, 1987, 1994) was to describe the behavioral characteristics that require a minimal level of inference from the observer. Personality disorders did not lend themselves as readily to this goal; more inference is needed for these diagnostic categories, with the end result being lowered reliability for these types of diagnoses. Since *DSM III, III-R,* and *IV* are not generally based on any particular theory, it is important for the clinician to provide a background for the diagnoses as well as for developing the case formulation. It is likely that theoretical stances will impact more on diagnostic categories which are more highly inferential (i.e., personality disorders) than those that are heavily behavioral in nature. Without a backdrop of theory, the use of *DSM* becomes like a smorgasbord of behaviors which the clinician sorts through until coming to a suitable label.

Quay, Routh, and Shapiro (1987) found little specificity between childhood disorders. Children with depression or anxiety disorders may show similar behaviors and for children, at least, it is not clear that these are separate disorders. Moreover, some diagnoses tend to co-occur. ADHD shows approximately a 30 to 35 percent incidence of co-occurrence with disorders including learning disabilities, depression, anxiety, and conduct disorder (Biederman, Newcorn & Sprich, 1991; Semrud-Clikeman, Biederman, Sprich, et al., 1992). When disorders co-occur, it is felt that a more severe form of psychopathology is present. Thus, it is reasonable to speculate that children evidencing comorbid disorders will have different treatment goals than those with another type of disorder. It is also likely that support systems and stresses in children with multiple disorders differ from those of children with single diagnoses.

The use of any diagnostic classification system by a clinician, whether *DSM* or *ICD,* needs to be in conjunction with an overarching theory. If not theoretically grounded, diagnosis becomes a labeling and sorting process with no tie to intervention. While this practice may be useful in some medical arenas (i.e., certain types of cancers can be tied to specific interventions), child therapy is not as clear-cut and often requires the interaction between many aspects in the child's life.

Therefore, it appears important to gather information from interviews not only for diagnostic purposes but also for developing interventions. Although diagnoses of affective disorder, anxiety disorder, or others are familiar to most clinicians and associated with *DSM,* it is important to emphasize the use of the multiaxial system. *DSM*'s multiaxial system used in conjunction with theory can provide invaluable insight into a child's presenting problem as well as areas that may be utilized in intervention.

The Multiaxial System

DSM III, III-R, and *IV* (APA, 1980, 1987, 1994) provide five axes or areas of evaluation. These axes emphasize not only diagnosis but also level of functioning. This change in classification is important as diagnosis is seen in a more ecologically valid manner. By giving emphasis to the level of stressors in the environment as well as the functioning level (or adaptive level) the client has achieved, diagnosis is placed in the context of the child's life.

For example, a child with ADHD who is functioning adequately differs substantially from a child with the same disorder whose parents are divorcing and who is failing in school and has few friends. The multiaxial diagnostic system allows for diagnosis as well as level of adaptation. The use of this multi-setting and multi-level evaluation provides for a more fully developed diagnostic structure that directly impacts on case formulation. A further examination of the various axes in light of their contribution to case formulation is presented in the following paragraphs.

Axis I consists of clinical syndromes such as schizophrenia, bipolar disorder, affective disorders, and organically related mental disorders and V codes. The V codes are conditions that are not due to mental disorder but are the focus of diagnosis. Also included in Axis I are childhood disorders including disruptive behaviors (ADHD, conduct disorder, oppositional defiant disorder), elimination disorders, and anxiety disorders of childhood (separation anxiety, school phobia).

Axis II consists of developmental disorders and personality disorders. Axis II is most often used by the child clinician. Included in the developmental disorders are learning problems, autism, mental retardation, and speech and language problems. Personality disorders are also placed under Axis II. It is possible to have a diagnosis under Axis I as well as Axis II. For example, a child may be diagnosed with ADHD (an Axis I diagnosis) as well as a developmental reading problem (an Axis II diagnosis).

Axis III allows for indication of current physical disorders or chronic medical conditions that are applicable to the development of the treatment program. The *DSM III-R* manual suggests that when "soft neurological signs" are found for children these should be noted under Axis III. Clinical experience suggests that children who are medically at risk often present with emotional and behavioral difficulties (Siegel, Smith, & Wood, 1991). Thus, the contributions of these disorders to the treatment plan are important aspects for the case formulation.

For example, a child was referred to the author for evaluation of frequent oppositional behavior as well as difficulty separating from his mother.

Parent and child interviews indicated significant feelings of sadness and anger that revolved around a physical condition. The child had been born with a short intestine that prevented full digestion of food. This child often experienced soiling and accidents due to this difficulty. Although he qualified for a diagnosis of separation anxiety on Axis II, his medical condition significantly contributed to his difficulty in adjustment and was an important addition to understanding the dynamics of the case. Treatment involved not only working on behavioral difficulties but also around feelings about the physical disorder and issues the mother had about protecting her "fragile" child from the environment.

Axis IV provides a six-point Likert scale for the severity of psychosocial stress. The scale ranges from 1 (none) to 6 (catastrophic). This measure is to provide information about social stresses that have occurred during the previous year. The manual suggests that the severity of stress is rated based on how much change the stress has made on the child's life, how much control the child feels about the stress, and how many stressors operate at one time. The scale is also divided into acute events (those under six months) and chronic or enduring circumstances. Examples of acute events include a change in teachers or schools, loss of a friend, birth of a new sibling. Chronic events may range from family discord, to residence in a crime-filled neighborhood, to abusive parenting. A more complete list is found in the *DSM* manual.

Axis V provides for clinical judgment of the child's global level of functioning. It is suggested that ratings should include current levels of functioning as well as the highest level of functioning achieved in the previous year, including at least one month of the school year. The scale ranges from a low of 0 (inadequate information) and 1 to 10 (persistent danger of severely hurting self or others) to 81 to 90 (absent or minimal symptoms). The higher the rating, the better the child/adolescent is functioning. The use of Axis V provides an overall estimate of the child's functioning in consideration of the psychosocial stressors noted in Axis IV. The numbers are approximate and provide only a ballpark estimate of functioning level.

DSM IV

DSM III-R, revised to *DSM IV* (1994), continues the multiaxial system. Some changes were made to selected diagnoses, and these changes were substantiated through field trials. The most notable changes are in the disruptive behavior categories.

DSM III (APA, 1980) had separate sections for attention deficit disorder (with and without hyperactivity), conduct disorder with oppositional defiant disorder being grouped with Other Disorders of Infancy, Childhood, or

Adolescence. *DSM III-R* (APA, 1987) placed these diagnoses in the category of Disruptive Behavior Disorders with the exception of attention deficit disorder without hyperactivity (ADD/WO). ADD/WO was placed in the Other Disorders category and renamed undifferentiated attention deficit disorder. This demarcation obscured the relationship between ADHD and ADD/WO (undifferentiated attention deficit disorder) as well as suggesting that *all* ADHD children are disruptive. Clinical experience challenges this assumption since many clinicians find ADHD children who are not disruptive.

DSM IV changes the category to Disruptive behaviors and Attention deficit disorders which will include ADD/WO. Such a change is welcome, since many children who have significant attention problems are not necessarily overactive. In addition to this change, a diagnosis of ADHD will require symptoms to be evidenced within a structured setting such as school as well as home or office settings. The rationale for this change was to decrease the number of children identified as ADHD. School psychologists will be appropriate to evaluate the presence of ADHD, and most training programs provide experience in such diagnoses. Section 504 of the American's with Disabilities Act of 1973 establishes the rights of children with ADHD to have modifications made in their school programs.

Clinicians have been concerned about overidentification of children as ADHD (Frick & Lahey, 1991). When children are diagnosed solely on the basis of office or home observations, overidentification may occur, with difficulties in overtreatment as well as consequences of this diagnosis on later development. Additional consequences are present in that a child may be treated for the wrong disorder due to difficulties in family interactions (i.e., problems in discipline, distress, marital discord) that can result in attention problems or increased activity levels. By treating the problem as an attention deficit disorder, the usual treatment for which includes medication, the difficulties these children are experiencing may be masked and not appropriately resolved.

The diagnoses of conduct disorder and oppositional defiant disorder (ODD) are also being evaluated. Some suggest that conduct disorder and ODD are related disorders and that ODD precedes conduct disorder on the continuum as well as predicting the eventual emergence of conduct disorder (APA, 1994). Field trials will assist in the determination of whether the diagnosis should be considered to be separate or on either end of a continuum. ODD would be the least severe disorder, with conduct disorder divided into moderate and severe levels. In addition, conduct disorder has been found to co-occur with ADHD or depression (Biederman & Steingard, 1989). In the *DSM IV* nomenclatures these diagnoses would be given separately on Axis I.

Use of the Multiaxial System in the Schools

Although *DSM* classifications are not directly utilized by school personnel, it is important that they be familiar with the *DSM* vocabulary in order to communicate with outside agencies. This understanding is necessary particularly when referring children for assessment of ADHD by physicians. With the *DSM IV* revision, communication between school personnel and medical practitioners will be particularly important for the diagnosis of ADHD. Not only should clinicians be familiar with *DSM* criteria for ADHD, *DSM IV* requires closer cooperation between professionals for this diagnosis. *DSM IV* and the attending research it will generate can help the school clinician become aware of disorders that tend to co-occur such as ADHD and oppositional defiant disorder or conduct disorder.

The change from diagnosing children solely from a clinical interview to a school-based assessment provides the school therapist with a special opportunity to enter into a liaison with the medical profession for assessment and treatment of children. The school therapist can provide invaluable information for the diagnosis of ADHD. Behavioral observations, behavioral checklists, teacher reports, and psychological evaluations (case formulations) are likely to be required to substantiate the diagnosis and are well within the domain of the school clinician.

For the clinician, Axes IV and V will be of greatest assistance to the psychiatrist, pediatrician, or psychopharmocologist evaluating the child. It is important to include information as to duration, frequency, and severity of the behaviors, as well as a brief summary of when the behaviors were first noticed and previous attempts at intervention. It is best to provide a concise yet comprehensive summary of the relevant information for the consulting physician.

Axes IV and V are the most relevant for the development of treatment goals and the case formulation. Placing the child's difficulty within the context of his or her environment makes the diagnosis most ecologically valid. Case formulation rests most solidly on the presenting problems, history of the problems, and treatment goals which are the variables included in Axes IV and V. The following section reviews the development of a case formulation for the setting of goals.

Case Formulation

For treatment to be effective, it is important to conceptualize its goals and methods. Case formulation meets this end and provides the clinician with a blueprint for intervention. As discussed in the preceding sections, case formulation combines diagnostic information with history of the referral questions and hypotheses as to cause. It also provides the clinician with a vehicle for assessing the intervention as treatment progresses. This is not to say that the case formulation is immutable. Good treatment includes the ability to alter goals to meet the changing needs of the client. Case formulation can assist the clinician to see where she or he has been and plot the course for future interventions.

A case formulation can be formal or informal. In some cases it is important to document a case for legal and/or consultative purposes. At times cases, which may involve abuse, custody disputes, or further assessment by other professionals, are referred to the clinician. In these cases a written case formulation is most appropriate. In instances when the case formulation serves as a working document for the clinician, an informal listing of information is appropriate. However, this listing must include hypotheses as to the operating dynamics of the case as well as treatment goals and recommendations.

The written case formulation needs to include the following sections: reason for referral, background information, medical and psychiatric history, developmental and school history, behavioral observations, diagnostic impressions, hypotheses, and recommendations. Each of these sections is discussed in the following paragraphs.

Reason for Referral

This section needs to specify the reason for the referral occurring at this point in time. In other words, this section answers two questions—why is the child/adolescent being referred, and why does the referral occur now? Usually there is a catalyst for a referral; problems generally do not begin directly prior to the referral. This section should be concise and clear.

Background Information

This section should describe the child/adolescent as far as age, grade in school, family composition, parents' education and occupation, and parents' marital status. In addition, previous interventions that have been attempted should be included in this section as well as any psychological evaluations. Review of school records can provide information about standardized testing as well as any other referrals that have been completed over the prior periods. Besides a review of records, information gathered from parent and teacher interviews should be included in this section. Information gathered from behavioral rating scales completed by parents and/or teachers can also be included here.

As the beginning for incorporating information from various sources, this section often provides hints as to possible influences on the child's/adolescent's life that have contributed to the presenting problems currently being experienced.

Medical and Psychiatric History
This section includes relevant medical history—any unusual or serious illnesses, head injuries, seizures, and hospitalizations. Additional information as to frequent ear infections or hearing and visual difficulties should be included here. This section also details the history of psychiatric evaluations or hospitalizations. When relevant to the case formulation, parental psychopathology may be included.

It is important ethically not to incorporate information about parental psychiatric history that does not directly relate to the case at hand. Examples of information which may be important to be included are disorders with a high degree of heritability (such as ADHD, learning disabilities, or bipolar disorders) or disorders that have been directly related to behavioral disturbances experienced by the child (i.e., maternal drinking or drug use during pregnancy, marital discord).

Developmental and School History
This section includes information as to the child's/adolescent's attainment of developmental milestones. There is also information as to the mother's pregnancy and delivery as well as length of gestation. Difficulties in any area of development need to be addressed, particularly as to how they may interact with later development. A child who was very ill during infancy or toddlerhood may have a developmental history that was negatively impacted. Any occurrences which may have had an effect on a child's development also need to be addressed.

It is often useful to inquire if there was anything that happened in the child's life when the difficulties were first noticed. The arrival of a sibling, a difficult divorce, or a death of a pet may have extenuating effects at certain stress points in a child's life that would not have the same effect at others. A child who has experienced a significant loss concurrent with beginning school may show separation difficulties, anxiety, or depression stemming from this early incident.

Information should also be included as to the child's school experiences. Did the child attend day care? If so, how many hours a day? Did the child attend preschool? How did that go? When did the child enter kindergarten and how was the experience for him or her? How did the child *and* the mother/primary caretaker handle the initial separation? Has the child ever been referred for special education services, Chapter 1 help, or any other type of tutoring? How many schools has the child attended? Was there any particular teacher who succeeded well with the child? Why? Conversely, did any teacher experience significant difficulties with the child? Why? What kinds of grades does the child attain? How do parents handle a poor report card? How are the child's social skills? Does he or she have friends? Do friends come over? Is the child invited to other children's homes? If an adolescent, does the child date? Is she or he sexually active? Any history of drug/alcohol use? How would the parent describe the child's/adolescent's temperament? How does the child/adolescent recover from disappointment? failure? success?

This section needs to provide a window as to the child's development both physically and emotionally. Information as to the child's coping skills and social abilities is important for the development not only of diagnostic impressions but also for the evolving of appropriate interventions.

Behavioral Observations

In this section it is important to delineate observations of the client over time. Behaviors, such as separation from parent or teacher, eye contact, language abilities (both receptively and expressively), impulse control, distractibility, reasoning skills, and ability to follow directions, are meaningful for the formulation.

A child/adolescent who experiences difficulty following conversation, appears to misunderstand statements or directions, or is unable to formulate thoughts in any coherent order may be appropriate for a referral to the speech and language pathologist for a comprehensive evaluation. Likewise, a child with these difficulties may experience problems in any talk-based therapeutic techniques. Therefore, the therapist would be well served to utilize therapy involving perceptual skills rather than language-based tasks. Role-playing, drawing, and/or modeling may be most appropriate for this child.

Likewise, a child who has difficulty with impulse control and/or distractibility will require a therapist to be more active than does a child who is able to delay responses and consider alternatives. A child with impulse-control problems will benefit from treatment which allows him or her to become actively involved in the sessions and which also relies on playing out themes and trying out various behaviors. With guidance from the therapist, insight into the results of impulsive behavior can be evaluated. The use of videotaping or observations can assist in developing awareness of situations where impulse control is most problematic. Planning ahead for these situations and choosing from alternative behaviors would be most appropriate for these children/adolescents. Group sessions for these children would be problematic as they will experience difficulty remaining seated and attentive. Until these skills are developed, individual and behavioral work are most appropriate.

In contrast, a child who finds individual attention threatening and who is guarded and resistant, may respond best to a group intervention with children with varied difficulties. Poor eye contact, reluctance to speak, and need for personal distance may signal that the client is uncomfortable with intense interpersonal interaction.

Behavioral observations should therefore set the stage for diagnostic impressions and the formation of treatment hypotheses. Recommendations for treatment stem from behaviors noted by the clinician, teacher, and/or parent.

Diagnostic Impressions

Depending on the setting, diagnostic impressions includes *DSM* diagnoses as well as information as to major stressors and level of functioning. In a clinical setting, this section includes Axes I and II with appropriate diagnostic decisions. It is very important to provide information on diagnoses which may exist but which have insufficient information for making a final determination. Such diagnostic impressions should be followed by the letters R/O (Rule Out).

In a school setting *DSM* diagnoses are not entirely helpful. However, when the school clinician has sufficient information to believe that the child would qualify for a diagnosis, it is helpful to include these thoughts in this section. For the school setting, information as to possible learning problems, behavioral difficulties, and environmental stressors should also be included.

Hypotheses

This section serves as a case summary and ties together all the information gathered in the preceding sections which directly impacts on hypotheses as to the underlying dynamics surrounding the child's/adolescent's currently identified problem. As such, this section should summarize the major points and outline the goals of treatment. It should also provide some information as to the prognosis for the case and the therapist's best guess as to the response to treatment.

Recommendations

This section provides suggestions for treatment. Information on cognitive skills, gained during the interview with the child, and behavioral observations by the clinician directly impact on recommendations. Referral for psychological evaluation or other types of assessments is appropriate in this section, and type of treatment should be developed here. Group counseling, family counseling, behavioral interventions and specific skills training are appropriately delineated in this section.

Following are two examples of a case formulation write-up. The first example was gathered from a clinical case and is written as a clinical report. Following this prototype is the same case written up for school use.

Clinical Example

Date Seen.   March 23, 30, 1993

Reason for Referral. Shawn is an eight-year-old white male who was referred for evaluation by his parents and teacher because of concerns about difficulty in paying attention in class, poor academic attainment, and lethargy. These difficulties were first noted in first grade and have continued through second grade despite the fact that Shawn began school one year later than most of his peers.

Background Information. Shawn currently lives with his biological parents and younger sister. His mother is a schoolteacher and his father is an accountant. Both parents have college degrees. Although there have been stresses in the marriage, Shawn's parents report their marriage to be strong.

Shawn has attended the same elementary school since kindergarten. He entered kindergarten when he was 6-1/2 in order to give him "additional time to develop." His parents held him out an extra year at the recommendation of the preschool teacher and because he was very small for his age. Difficulties were first noted in attention span during his kindergarten year. According to parental report, attempts at behavioral intervention were only partially successful and difficulties have continued. Shawn's parents report that he worked best when in a very small group or on a one-to-one basis.

Shawn has never had a psychological assessment. Review of school records indicate below-average progress in reading and written language skills with average skills present in arithmetic and general knowledge. Teacher reports indicate difficulties with attention span and work completion. The Achenbach Teacher Child Behavior Checklist completed by Shawn's teacher indicated significant problems (above a T score of 70) on the social withdrawal and inattention scales. No other scale was in the significant range. The Achenbach Parent Child Behavior Checklist indicated problems in inattention and depression.

Medical and Psychiatric History. When he was four months old, Shawn was referred for a medical evaluation because of a "failure to thrive." He experienced difficulty keeping his food down and digesting his food. Medical evaluation indicated no significant physical reasons for this difficulty. Various formulas were tried, and Shawn gradually began to digest the food. He continues to have periods when he doesn't eat and needs to be coaxed to take a bite. Shawn is small in stature for his age and weighs below expectations. His parents report that he is frequently seen by his pediatrician and his growth is carefully monitored. An endocrine evaluation is scheduled for the next month. He also had several ear infections when he was between the ages of 1 and 2 years. Tubes were placed in his ears twice and now his hearing reportedly is normal.

Shawn's mother reports that she has had recurring bouts of depression and has occasionally taken antidepressants. Shawn's maternal grandfather had a bipolar disorder and committed suicide when Shawn's mother was 15. No other relevant psychiatric history was reported.

Developmental and School History. Shawn was the result of a full-term pregnancy and uneventful delivery. He weighed 6 pounds 12 ounces at birth and left the hospital with his mother. Shawn's motor milestones were somewhat delayed. Reports from his pediatrician indicate concern about his nutrition and its effect on his motor skills. Shawn crawled at approximately 9 months of age and walked alone at 15 months. First words were reported to be at 6 months of age with two-word sentences between 10 and 12 months of age. His speech is clear and very understandable.

Shawn attended a preschool three mornings a week from 3 to 6 years of age. His mother reported that Shawn enjoyed the experience and although quiet participated in many of the activities. She also reported that Shawn's fine-motor skills were delayed and additional practice was provided in copying figures and cutting. Puzzles and matching of designs were also problematic for Shawn, and his basic readiness skills were reported to be below age expectations. At the recommendation of Shawn's preschool teacher, he was held out a year before kindergarten.

Shawn entered kindergarten at 6-1/2 years of age and progressed well the first semester. He was able to make friends with another quiet boy and was reported to enjoy the experience. When seatwork demands increased second semester, Shawn began to experience difficulty with attention to task and work completion. His teacher provided an aide to work with Shawn and he began to make progress. Difficulties in attention and work completion continued into first grade. Shawn was referred for Chapter 1 help in reading and written language.

He has improved in these areas since beginning this small group instruction. Continued difficulty has been reported by the teacher in attention to task. She also describes him as having periods of time when he seems "sad." These periods can last up to two weeks at a time and there is no known antecedent. Shawn's mother also reports periods of time when Shawn appears to feel sad and listless. She expressed concern that Shawn may have the same proclivity to depression that she has had.

Behavioral Observations. Shawn came to the interview accompanied by his mother and father. During the initial interview with only his parents,

Shawn was content to remain in the waiting room and color. When he was asked to come in, he separated from his mother with little emotion. Shawn is very small and petite for his age. Eye contact was poor throughout the session and he frequently required questions to be repeated. He was drawn to noises in the hall and asked if his parents were still waiting for him. When reassured, Shawn was willing to stay with the therapist. Although no signs of overactivity were noted, Shawn's attention was fleeting and difficult to contain. He was polite and answered all questions but did not elaborate on his answers. Shawn indicated that he is generally happy except in school, where the work is too hard for him. When asked what made him sad, Shawn replied "leaving my mom." He was able to name three friends and said one of his favorite activities was to play video games. When asked what he might wish for, he said "More time with my dad." Shawn drew a picture of his family sailing together and said he would like to do that more often. When asked what he didn't like, Shawn replied that his father works too much.

Diagnostic Impressions.

Axis I	ADHD: Inattentive type (R/O)
	Dysthymia (R/O)
Axis II	Developmental Reading Disorder
Axis III	Eating disorder
Axis IV	2 Mild
Axis V	70 Mild

Case Summary. Shawn is an eight-year-old male in first grade who has a history of difficulty with nutrition and growth. He is experiencing difficulty with attention span, work completion, and reading skill development. Shawn's mother also expressed concerns about his sadness.

Shawn shows several signs consistent with a diagnosis of Attention Deficit Hyperactivity Disorder. However, he also shows symptoms indicating the presence of dysthymia. While these two disorders frequently co-occur, it is important that Shawn be evaluated for each. Given his family history of affective mood disorder, he may be at risk for the development of a major depressive episode.

Shawn's early history may well interact with his attentional difficulties. Given the repeated difficulties he has experienced with nutrition and growth, he may well feel powerless to control even his own body. These feelings may well translate into sadness and hopelessness. Moreover, he appears to want and/or need additional time with his father.

Shawn's reading and written language skills need to be further evaluated for a possible learning disability. His attention difficulties may compound these problems and create additional stress in learning and in self-esteem. At the present time Shawn feels as if he is the only child experiencing difficulty and his greatest fear is that he is "dumb." An evaluation may assist in helping Shawn recognize his strengths as well as his weaknesses.

Recommendations.

1. It is recommended that Shawn be evaluated for a medication trial for ADHD and dysthymia. Referral to a pediatric psychiatrist for further evaluation will be provided for his parents.
2. It is also recommended that Shawn's parents refer him to his school's evaluation team for in-depth assessment of his learning difficulties.
3. While individual therapy does not appear warranted at this time, group counseling may be considered in the future. A group setting which provides support for children with learning problems would be appropriate for Shawn.

School Example

Date Seen. March 23, 30, 1993

Reason for Referral. Shawn is an eight-year-old white male who was referred for evaluation by his parents and teacher because of concerns about difficulty in paying attention in class, poor academic attainment, and lethargy. These difficulties were first noted in first grade and have continued through second grade despite the fact that Shawn began school one year later than most of his peers.

Background Information. Shawn currently lives with his biological parents and younger sister. His mother is a schoolteacher and his father is an accountant. Both parents have college degrees. Although there have been stresses in the marriage, Shawn's parents report their marriage to be strong.

Shawn has attended the same elementary school since kindergarten. He entered kindergarten when he was 6-1/2 in order to give him "additional time to develop." His parents held him out an extra year at the recommendation of the preschool teacher and because he was very small for his age. Difficulties were first noted in attention span during his kindergarten year. According to parental report, attempts at behavioral intervention were only partially successful and difficulties have continued. Shawn's parents report that he worked best when in a very small group or on a one-to-one basis.

Shawn has never had a psychological assessment. Review of school records indicate below-average progress in reading and written language skills with average skills present in arithmetic and general knowledge. Teacher reports indicate difficulties with attention span and work completion. The Achenbach Teacher Child Behavior Checklist completed by Shawn's teacher indicated significant problems (above a T score of 70) on the social withdrawal and inattention scales. No other scale was in the significant range. The Achenbach Parent Child Behavior Checklist indicated problems in inattention and depression.

Medical and Psychiatric History. When he was four months old, Shawn was referred for a medical evaluation because of a "failure to thrive." He experienced difficulty keeping his food down and digesting his food. Medical evaluation indicated no significant physical reasons for this difficulty. Various formulas were tried and Shawn gradually began to digest the food. He continues to have periods when he doesn't eat and needs to be coaxed to take a bite. Shawn is small in stature for his age and weighs below expectations. His parents report that he is frequently seen by his pediatrician and his growth is carefully monitored. An endocrine evaluation is scheduled for the next month. He also had several ear infections when he was between the ages of 1 and 2 years. Tubes were placed in his ears twice and his hearing reportedly is normal.

Developmental and School History. Shawn was the result of a full-term pregnancy and uneventful delivery. He weighed 6 pounds 12 ounces at birth and left the hospital with his mother. Shawn's motor milestones were somewhat delayed. Reports from his pediatrician indicate concern about his nutrition and its effect on his motor skills. Shawn crawled at approximately 9 months of age and walked alone at 15 months. First words were reported to be at 6 months of age with two-word sentences between 10 and 12 months of age. His speech is clear and very understandable.

Shawn attended a preschool three mornings a week at from 3 to 6 years of age. His mother reported that Shawn enjoyed the experience and although quiet participated in many of the activities. She also reported that Shawn's fine-motor skills were delayed and additional practice was provided in copying figures and cutting. Puzzles and matching of designs were also problematic for Shawn and his basic readiness skills were reported to be below age expectations. At the recommendation of Shawn's preschool teacher, he was held out a year before kindergarten.

Shawn entered kindergarten at 6-1/2 years of age and progressed well the first semester. He was able to make friends with another quiet boy and was reported to enjoy the experience. When seatwork demands increased second semester, Shawn began to experience difficulty with attention to task and work completion. His teacher provided an aide to work with Shawn and he began to make progress. Difficulties in attention and work completion continued into first grade. Shawn was referred for Chapter 1 help in reading and written language. He has improved in these areas since beginning this small group instruction. Continued difficulty has been reported by the teacher in attention to task. She also describes him as having periods of time when he seems "sad." These periods can last up to two weeks at a time and there is no known antecedent. Shawn's mother also reports periods of time when Shawn appears to feel sad and listless. She expressed concern that Shawn may have the same proclivity to depression that she has had.

Behavioral Observations. Shawn came to the interview accompanied by his mother and father. During the initial interview with only his parents, Shawn was content to remain in the waiting room and color. When he was asked to come in, he separated from his mother with little emotion.

Shawn is very small and petite for his age. Eye contact was poor throughout the session and he frequently required questions to be repeated. He was drawn to noises in the hall and asked if his parents were still waiting for him. When reassured, Shawn was willing to stay with the therapist. Although no signs of overactivity were noted, Shawn's attention was fleeting and difficult to contain. He was polite and answered all questions but did not elaborate on his answers. Shawn indicated that he is generally happy except in school, where the work is too hard for him. When asked what made him sad, Shawn replied "leaving my mom." He was able to name three friends and said one of his favorite activities was to play video games. When asked what he might wish for, he said "More time with my dad." Shawn drew a picture of his family sailing together and said he would like to do that more often. When asked what he didn't like, Shawn replied that his father works too much.

Shawn was observed in the classroom for three different activities. The first activity was independent seatwork. Shawn was required to complete two worksheets during the 15-minute observation. A behavioral count indicated that he was off-task three times as much as a comparison peer. Behaviors during that time were sharpening his pencil, dropping his crayon box off the top of the desk, looking out the window, and examining bits of paper on the floor. The second activity was a discussion period in the classroom. Shawn sat quietly through the session but did not volunteer any answers. When the teacher called on him, Shawn asked her to repeat the question. He was then able to answer correctly. Shawn was also observed during a recess period. He was with another child and they walked around the playground without entering into any of the games. Shawn's affect throughout the observations was somewhat flat with little variation seen.

Case Summary. Shawn is an eight-year-old male in first grade who has a history of difficulty with nutrition and growth. He is experiencing difficulty with attention span, work completion, and reading skill development. Shawn's mother also expressed concerns about his sadness.

Shawn shows several signs consistent with a diagnosis of Attention Deficit Hyperactivity Disorder. However, he also shows symptoms indicating the presence of dysthymia. While these two disorders frequently co-occur, it is important that Shawn be evaluated for each.

Shawn's early history may well interact with his attentional difficulties. Given the repeated difficulties he has experienced with nutrition and growth, he may well feel powerless to control even his own body. These feelings may well translate into sadness and hopelessness. Moreover, he appears to want and need additional time with his father. At this time, Shawn may not feel capable in any part of his life.

Shawn's reading and written language skills need to be further evaluated for a possible learning disability. His attention difficulties may compound these problems and create additional stress in learning and in self-esteem. At the present time Shawn feels as if he is the only child experiencing difficulty and his greatest fear is that he is "dumb." An evaluation may assist in helping Shawn recognize his strengths as well as his weaknesses.

Recommendations.

1. Referral to a pediatric psychiatrist for further evaluation will be provided for his parents. Shawn may be considered for an evaluation of a medication trial for ADHD and dysthymia.
2. It is also recommended that Shawn be referred to the school's evaluation team for in-depth assessment of his learning difficulties.
3. It is important to bolster Shawn's self-concept through success experiences in the classroom and at home.
4. In the classroom Shawn's teacher may wish to consider moving his seat to the center front of the room to diminish distractions and to place him closer to the teacher. His seatwork needs to be broken down into parts which are completed and then checked by the teacher or an aide. Reinforcement of completion of work should include a visual chart where Shawn is able to see his progress.
5. While individual therapy does not appear warranted at this time, group counseling may be considered in the future. A group setting which provides support for children with learning problems would be appropriate for Shawn.

5

Establishing
a Therapeutic
Relationship

The initial interviews and case formulation have now been completed and you are ready to begin treatment. Therapy is a continuing process and not a means to an end. Viewed in this manner, therapy sessions only begin a process of learning to adapt behavior and cope with everyday demands in life. When therapy is successful, the child/adolescent learns adaptive behaviors that allow her or him to function more adequately in the environment.

What happens in the therapy room is best conceptualized as a microcosm of a person's interactions in the world. How a child relates to you after the first few sessions is likely to be similar to how he or she relates to others. If the child is passive and withdrawn or aggressive and active with you, chances are good that these behaviors are frequently utilized to meet his or her needs in everyday life.

What the therapist does with these behaviors is directly related to helping the child/adolescent adapt his or her behavior and resolve issues that are blocking further social/emotional development. The client will "expect" the therapist to react the way most people have behaved in the past. Therapy occurs when the therapist acts differently from what usually happens to the client. When behavior which usually generates anger or rejection does not elicit this reaction in the therapy room, the child/adolescent may begin to experience feelings and confusion not usually allowed to surface. This "corrective emotional experience" enables the child/adolescent to begin looking at his or her own behavior and the reasons behind the behavior. This chapter presents methods to form and enhance relationships between clinicians and their clients to serve as the basis for therapeutic change.

Messages from Therapist to Child

Before a corrective emotional experience can begin, a relationship must be formed between the child and the therapist. With some children this relationship is readily formed; with others it takes a lot of hard work and time. Children are excellent readers of nonverbal messages and will respond to them. Clinicians need to be aware of their own behaviors that may be misread by children/adolescents as hostile or uncaring. For example, talking to a child without being at eye level may communicate that the child is not important or that the clinician is over the child. Thus, when greeting the child you should not look down but rather sit or stoop closer to the child's eye level. For adolescents or for withdrawn children a direct greeting may be too threatening and you are well advised to allow the client to approach at his or her comfort level.

Another message which needs to be communicated is that the child feels valued by the clinician. The pacing of the session should be comfortable for the child. If you are rushed or preoccupied, the child will pick up this message, and for some children it may confirm their fear that they are unimportant. One cardinal rule which needs to be established is that there shall be no interruptions during your session unless there is an emergency. Phone calls, people at the door, or other interruptions not only interfere with the flow of the session but they can also diminish the importance of the sessions.

One example illustrates what can happen when interruptions interfere with a session. I was working in a school district when, during one session, my phone kept ringing. I would apologize to my six-year-old client and answer the phone to take a message to call later. Eventually the child began playing aggressively with the dollhouse—more aggressively than ever before. His doll play was of a female doll telling a little boy that she didn't have time to play with him and that he'd have to play alone. I asked if he had ever felt that way, and to my chagrin he replied that I seemed to have more time for people on the phone than him.

Although this message was certainly nothing I had intended to communicate, the child internalized the interruptions in this manner. I thanked him for teaching me a valuable lesson and from then on I accepted no interruptions unless there was an emergency. Later, when working with adults in a hospital, I was required to wear a pager. Inevitably my number would be beeped in the middle of a psychotherapy session. When I would delay answering the page, my clients frequently commented on the fact that I didn't take time out from them. This feeling of being valued permeates all aspects of therapy at all ages; you need to be sensitive to how your actions may be interpreted.

The first few sessions generally serve as a backdrop for later work. It is important to allow the child to become comfortable with you. Establishing a set time and day for the session assists in setting up a routine and making your sessions predictable and part of the child's life. This predictability is important in both a clinical and a school setting. Eventually, where appropriate, the child can remember the appointment time. When I worked in the schools, children as young as six came to their appointments on time. I felt that it was indicative of their ability to take responsibility for their part of the therapy. In fact, children who were able to remember their appointments were often more successful in the treatment than those who did not keep the appointments.

Therapeutic Listening

In therapy, as in many interpersonal relationships, empathy is an important variable. *Empathy* refers to the ability to put oneself in another's place; to understand how someone else perceives the world and how these perceptions affect that person's feelings. Empathy is *not* pity or sympathy. The concepts of sympathy and empathy are frequently confused. *Sympathy* means that you feel sorry for the other person. In empathy you do not feel sorry but rather have an understanding of the person's predicament. Empathy also does not take away responsibility for the person's actions. Sympathy can mean that the responsibility of solving the problem is abdicated to someone else.

The difference between these two concepts is very important for the therapeutic relationship. If a child or adolescent feels and believes that you understand him or her and that you are his or her ally, then you can bring up issues that may be painful or threatening without losing the relationship. However, if the child reads you as feeling sorry for him or her, you become a ready target for manipulation or dependence. Your ability to put yourself in the child's place and understand how he or she is feeling will assist you greatly in developing treatment plans. Empathy provides the basis for how you listen to the child and the resulting understanding.

Active Listening

Active listening includes the ability to process what the child is saying as well as the feelings underlying the words. The beginning clinician may be so worried about what to say next that he or she will miss important nuances in the child's conversation. You should force yourself to listen and then respond. Active listening means you are totally there for the client—your mind is not on what you will say next, what you are having for dinner that night, or what classwork is left to be finished. This type of listening takes discipline, as it is easy to let your mind wander. If you find your mind wandering, it may be that the material at hand is not important and the client is using a lot of talk for a smokescreen. Sometimes clients will fill up the time by talking about very little. You need to examine whether this is indeed happening. If so, it is important to bring out this observation.

If, on the other hand, you are having attention problems, then it is necessary to refocus your attention to the task at hand. It is particularly problematic to have too many things on your mind (as many students often do) and to try to concentrate on what is being said. One method I find helpful is to really focus in on the words and to try to interpret them subvocally into feelings. You may also wish to change the activity so that you are more involved in the situation. Sometimes it can be appropriate to shorten the session so that you can attend to pressing matters. It is better to shorten the session than to give the client the impression you are not engaged in her or his concerns.

As a beginning clinician you need to remember that what you say is not as important as how well you understand the child and communicate this understanding. If you hear the feeling behind the words even if you are unable to frame your thoughts eloquently, the child will come away from the session feeling understood—perhaps one of the few places he or she has experienced such a feeling.

Active listening includes techniques such as reflection, clarification, paraphrasing, summarizing, and interpreting. All of these techniques rest on the therapist's ability to understand what the child/adolescent is attempting to communicate, as discussed in the following paraphraphs.

Reflection includes statements that reflect back the feeling underneath the words. It is possible to use the same words to express quite different feelings. For example, the same statement can convey sarcasm, anger, or relief depending on the tone of voice. The following example illustrates the use of reflection.

C: That was a dumb test.

T: You didn't like the test?

C: Why should we learn that stuff anyway—I'll never use it?

T: You really sound angry—I wonder if you feel disappointed in how you did?

In this case the child was angry at himself over how he had done on the examination but directed this anger at the test—a safer target (and probably more healthy)—rather than at himself. However, this anger deflected at the test would not allow him to change his behavior so that he could do better next time.

C: I am angry—it was a dumb test!

T: You might be right, it was a dumb test—but you have another test coming up in two weeks—what do you plan to do?

C: I don't feel like studying for it—it's just memorization anyway.

T: Mmm.

C: Maybe I should start earlier learning the stupid dates and events.

T: It might help you to do that to learn the facts and not have to do it all the night before.

C: How did you know I only studied the night before?

T: Just a guess. But with your new plan you may not get so angry next time at the situation or yourself.

The second part of this example shows the use of *clarification*. As the therapist explored the options, she provided clarification for the child as to the end result of not studying. The therapist also took a risk in suggesting that the student had studied the night before the test. In this case the educated guess was correct and opened up thinking about what strategies the child could utilize for the next test. Clarification can help the child/ adolescent look at the plan and also provide an opportunity for the clinician to determine if he or she has understood the child's feelings correctly. *Paraphrasing* is similar to clarification. Paraphrasing seeks to rephrase the child's words. The emphasis is not so much on specifying what the child has said as much as restating the child's words to demonstrate understanding as well as to keep the client on track.

C: I don't feel like learning all of these dates and events the history teacher thinks are so important.

T: So learning those dates is not important to you? *(paraphrasing)*

C: No—I don't see how they are useful.

T: But the teacher asks you to do that? *(clarifying)*

C: Yes—it's so unfair.

T: I can see how you could feel frustrated about this problem. *(reflection)* What do you want to do about it? *(clarifying)*

C: I don't really want to learn them but I need to pass the course.

T: So you have two choices—learn the required dates or hope to do OK on the test with little studying. It seems you have a decision to make. *(summarizing)*

The last part of this model shows an example of *summarizing*. Summarizing can be used to pull together information that has been provided over time. Because many interviews or sessions can range over many topics, summarizing helps to keep the client on track as well as to integrate information. Summarizing does not generally include interpretations of the child's behavior; rather it serves as a method to help integrate information for both the client and the clinician. Summarizing can also be used to tie together themes or patterns which are presented during the session but may initially appear unrelated. A session I conducted with a six-year-old girl tied together a number of statements she had made during the 50-minute session. An excerpt of the session follows.

C: I can hear that man yelling—he's mad at someone.

T: He's pretty loud isn't he?

C: He's really scary—do you think he can get in our room?

T: I wouldn't let him hurt you. His yelling is really frightening you, isn't it?

C: *(Child plays with clay, hitting it and making round patties.)* I used to see a man doctor, you know.

T: Tell me about him. *(This was the first-ever mention of a male therapist the child saw for over a year six months prior to this session.)*

C: I didn't like him. He came to my school once and told on me to my teacher. I saw him and ran away.

T: You didn't like him to be at your school so you ran away? *(Child continues to play for several more minutes without talking.)*

C: I don't like men. I'm glad you are a lady.

T: Men can be scary for you. You were mad at your other doctor and your father was mean to you too. Then you heard the man next door and had the same scary feelings. It's hard to trust men to keep you safe.

C: I don't want to talk about my father—I told you I don't have a father *(now yelling)*.

The last segment in this excerpt by the therapist was a summarization mixed with an interpretation. *Interpretations* generally need to be used very sparingly and should be carefully delivered. In this case, the girl had all along refused to talk about her father who had yelled and been abusive. However, she was beginning to talk about other men in her life and transferring her feelings about her father to them. The interpretation was an attempt to help her see this transference. As the therapy commenced, references would continue about men and their "scariness." Therapeutically, the girl's asking the woman clinician if she would protect her was a good step since her mother had been unable to keep her safe from her father. The child's ability to remain in the room with the clinician's reassurance was a good step. Prior to this session, if someone started yelling, the girl needed to escape from the area. In this instance the interpretation was heard but not absorbed. However, the child's response set the key for further sessions about trust.

Interpretations which are given too early or prematurely in clinical work are not successful. If an interpretation provokes a strong reaction, it may be on target but too painful to be attended to at that time. Painful interpretations are more easily borne once the relationship is well established. For the child in the above excerpt, no discussion of any feeling was allowed the first four months of weekly sessions. Her ability to tolerate any discussion of feelings during the illustrated session was a major step forward.

If no reaction to an interpretation occurs, the client may not be ready for your hypothesis or it may be incorrect. You must always be vigilant to how the interpretation is received. If you are convinced your hypothesis is correct, then try to rephrase it again at another appropriate time. You may also wish to ask the client how he or she felt about what you said. For example statements such as "I wonder what it means that you didn't say anything when I said . . . ?" or "I'm confused by what just happened. I said something that you didn't respond to but I noticed you tightened your fists (moved in your chair, or any behavior which indicates discomfort)." Interpretations can include reflections of feelings as well as summarizing what happened earlier.

All of these techniques should be used sparingly and should never interfere with the flow of the session. Beginning therapists may overuse these strategies or fall into a habit of using catch phrases such as "You seem to feel that . . . ;" "I hear you saying . . . ;" and "How does that make you feel?" These pat statements not only are artificial but after a short period may alienate your client as seeming inauthentic as well as stilted.

The timing of your statements is another important variable. Do not attempt to use a reflective or paraphrasing statement to fill in silences that are uncomfortable for you. Let silences happen and wait to see what happens if you do not speak. Silences may indicate that the child/adolescent is searching for something to say or censoring something that eventually needs to be explored. By jumping in too quickly the therapist "rescues" the client and fills a silence that may have been productive. It is important to realize when the silence is uncomfortable for *you* and when you need to fill it.

Practice these skills with someone with whom you feel comfortable enough to experiment. Like any other skill, active listening abilities need to be practiced. Exercises that can help you develop your abilities are provided at the end of this chapter.

Therapist Self-Awareness

It is very important for you to assess your own reactions to a case. Just as the interaction between the clinician and the child has its own cadence and rhythm, you will sometimes find yourself reacting to the child in ways that are difficult for you to understand. You should examine these feelings because they are often a sign that something more is occurring. Clinicians bring their own issues to the sessions; as clients needs touch on these topics, the clinician may find himself or herself responding in an unprofessional manner.

The client may remind the clinician of some of his or her own struggles or experiences. For example, a counseling student I supervised had been adopted as an older child and had experienced difficulty fitting in with the natural siblings in her new family. She began working with a child who had been adopted by a family and the adoption had failed. The child was now being placed with another family. The student became overinvolved in the case. She called the family frequently, met with the student additional times that were not clinically indicated, and generally lost her perspective during supervision. In this case, the student clinician's issues became an important part of the supervisory hour. She had difficulty in keeping boundaries established between her feelings and the child's. Although she meant well, the clinician needed to deal with her own issues, which were beginning to get in the way of the treatment. She "felt" too much for the child to really provide assistance for the client to examine the issues objectively. The student was referred for counseling to assist her in evaluating her issues and arrive at some resolution. If you find yourself losing perspective or over-identifying with a client, ethically the child should be referred to another professional.

In addition to monitoring your reactions to clients with problems similar to issues you may have experienced in your development, it is important to realize that topics may arise about which you may feel uncomfortable. Ethically, you need to be aware of the types of clients with which you feel unable to work. Situations may arise where you find yourself sitting across the table from a parent who has been convicted of physical or even sexual abuse of his or her child. As a school clinician, you are still required to provide information to that parent. However, you may not feel comfortable working with that parent on parenting skills. In this case it is appropriate for you to refer the parent to another source.

It is therefore important not only to pay attention to what is happening to the client during the session but also to read your own reactions. If a certain child engenders feelings of anger in you, examine if it's the child's behavior, your reaction to the child, or something that strikes a chord from your own life. The competent clinician listens to all of the people in the session, the child and himself or herself.

Multicultural Issues
Clinicians should be aware of differences in culture and their effect on the establishment of a therapeutic relationship. There are currently no empirical indications that therapy delivered by a clinician from a different cultural or ethnic background differs from that delivered by a person from the same background. What can make a difference is the extent to which the therapist understands differences in background and is sensitive to these differences.

As the United States becomes more of a multicultural society, emphasis is increasingly placed on people's differences rather than on their similarities. It is important to recognize that individuals are more alike than they are different. Basic needs, such as belonging, love, and nurturance, are shared by people from diverse backgrounds. When working with a person of a different ethnic origin or a background with which you are unfamiliar, it is most appropriate to consult with professionals familiar with this ethnicity or culture while simultaneously evaluating your competence to work with this individual. I find it most helpful to seek out a person from a similar background and ask questions about his or her beliefs and values. Important questions to have answered include how much and how often eye contact can be made and be acceptable for this culture; how emotions are generally expressed within the culture; what information about relationships between men and women family members the culture discusses; and what the expectations are for girls and boys within the culture.

A child who was referred to me for therapy came from a family whose father was Caucasian and whose mother was from Singapore. It was helpful for me to talk with a fellow clinician whose family was Asian and Caucasian. The experiences the child had are different from those of children whose parents are both of the same ethnicity; she needed to come to grips with the varying cultures and ethnicity melded into her family. The clinician I consulted helped to sensitize me to the pull that the child felt in trying to blend her family's cultures without feeling she had betrayed either of her parents.

For my therapy case it was important for me to realize that the girl was struggling with her mother, whom she saw as ineffectual and without power because she deferred to her husband. As this girl reached puberty, she rebelled against her mother's insistence that she be obedient to her father and to teachers. One of the therapy goals was to help the child accept her parents' way of adapting and to empower her to develop her own method of adaptation. Therapy included her parents in a three-way discussion around the conflicts that are usually experienced in adolescence and that overlaid the girl's need to develop her own identity.

Another case, which was referred to me by a school district for an assessment, involved a child who had been adopted from a Latin American country at age 14 by an American family who were fluent in Spanish. He was 17 when referred to our university clinic for assessment of a possible learning disability. His mother reported that his Spanish was problematic and was immature in its grammar and style for his age. He was assigned to a student of mine who was fluent in Spanish and who had extensive experience with children from Latin American backgrounds.

My student's interview with this young man indicated that his previous school experience had been marred with significant problems. In his Latin American country he had not begun school until age seven and was then placed in a kindergarten class. He reported he had felt so bad about being much older than his classmates that he often did not attend school. This state of affairs continued until he was adopted and moved to the United States. He was reported as highly motivated but experienced problems with learning to read in either Spanish or English. Further evaluation revealed that he had learned Spanish as his second language—a native Indian language had been his first language. This young man not only had attempted to merge his Spanish background with his new American experience but also to incorporate his identity as a native Indian.

This case shows how complex cases which may look fairly straightforward on the surface can be. The varied and complex background of the young man proved a challenge for diagnosis and certainly contributed to the difficulties he experienced in the United States. Consulting with professionals familiar with such cultural differences is the minimum step you need to take. Realizing the level of your own knowledge in this area and taking steps to gain further knowledge is very important for you as an ethical clinician.

The First Therapy Session

Even if you have interviewed the child/adolescent at a prior session, it is important for the child to be introduced to your change in roles. This switch must be acknowledged or the child/adolescent will believe that his or her job is to answer questions. It is a good idea to review the limits of confidentiality and to emphasize again that you will be sharing general information with the child's teacher and parent. Remind the child to tell you if he or she wishes to share something with you but wants you to keep it confidential. Together you can decide how to share information you feel is important for the child's parents and/or teacher to know. If I wonder about what the child wishes me to share, I check it out.

Explain what you will be doing together, including a discussion of the goals that will be set for the therapy. Because children may be surprised when you introduce the idea of setting goals for the therapy, be prepared to provide examples. The following dialogue illustrates how a first session may begin.

T: It's good to see you again.

C: Mmm.

T: Last time you were here we talked a lot about how things were going for you. I also met with your mom and dad to talk about things at home. Did they tell you about our meeting?

C: Yes. Mom said you talked about school and my work.

T: Mmm. Go on.

C: *(long pause)* I guess they want me to work harder.

T: And how do you feel about that?

C: OK, I guess.

T: You've told me what your parents and teacher want you to do here. What would you like to work on with me?

C: What do you mean?

T: Sometimes kids who come to talk to me have things they want to work on. I wonder if you have anything you'd like to talk about during our time together.

C: I'd like to have more friends. Kids call me names and won't let me play in their games.

T: So you'd like to talk about making friends. Can we make a list of things we could work on together?

C: Sort of like an assignment notebook.

T: Yes, except we will make the assignments ourselves. Let's see now, the first thing we can put on our list is talking about how people treat you.

C: Mmm.

T: Can we also put on the list working in class?

C: OK.

T: Why don't you write the list?

C: OK, but I don't know how to spell some of the words.

T: I'll help you. We will meet every Tuesday at this time—is that OK with you?

This example of discussing the goals of the treatment involved the child in the decision process. The therapist also checked out what the child understood about the previous meetings. The session would go on to talk about how the child felt about being teased.

Setting Goals and Gathering Data

It is a good strategy to have the child/adolescent write down the goals with you. In this way the goals can be reviewed at a later time and progress can be evaluated. If the purpose of therapy is to assist the child/adolescent in monitoring his or her behavior, then the client needs to begin to assess his or her own progress.

The goals you develop with the child should be consistent with your case formulation, the wishes of the adults involved and what the child feels he or she needs. When there is a conflict between the goals envisioned by the parents and/or teacher and the needs and wants of the client, it is important for you to arrive at a compromise. If treatment is to be at all successful, the child's needs should be addressed initially. Meeting with parents and teachers and reframing their needs in terms of the child can often clear up any misunderstandings.

Many children are referred for counseling because of behavior problems of one sort or another. Because self-esteem or self-control is often given as the reason for counseling referrals, one of the tasks of the early sessions is to specify what behaviors are involved. Problems with self-esteem can translate into difficulty with school work, paying attention, making friends, or other problematic behavior. Most children or adolescents do not come to the first session and say "I want to work on my self-concept." Most often they will tell you they are having trouble getting their work done or getting along with other kids, or they aren't sure what's wrong.

Knowledge or Performance Deficits

In addition to specifying what behaviors and feelings will be targeted for the sessions, you need to determine if the problems lie in a knowledge or performance deficit. If difficulty is present on both of these levels, it will be important to teach some basic skills. If the problems lie in execution of known skills, then practice in the skill is necessary as well as assistance in performing the skill in the classroom and/or at home.

One way to determine if problems exist in knowledge or performance is to teach the child how to monitor his or her behavior. With younger children you can use a chart system like that in Table 5–1 to help them keep

TABLE 5–1   Chart for Counting Behaviors

Class	Monday	Tuesday	Wednesday	Thursday	Friday
Reading					
Morning recess					
Math					
Lunch					
Language					
Social studies or science					

track of their behavior. Both negative and positive behaviors can be charted. It is important to stress that the child will not be disciplined for the number of marks made on the chart. I usually tell the child I want to see just what it is like to be in her or his classroom.

Have the child use hash marks or numbers of times he or she observes the behaviors occurring. The classes can be changed as necessary; for some children times can be specified instead of class names. It may also be helpful to have the child tape the chart on his or her desk to remind him or her to fill in the boxes. The teachers may help the child monitor his or her behavior and remind him or her to fill in the boxes. You can use the numbers generated in such a table as a baseline for the behaviors chosen as targets.

In the office you can generate a master chart showing the increase of appropriate behaviors and the decrease of inappropriate behaviors. If the chart is used to keep track of inappropriate behaviors, then it is important to provide reinforcement for appropriate behavior. My experience has shown that more attention is often paid to misbehavior than appropriate behavior. I prefer to have the child track how many times he or she behaves appropriately. In this way attention is paid to the behaviors you wish to increase.

Once you have the baseline you can begin to chart the appropriate behaviors. Children like to watch the chart in your office grow in numbers of appropriate behaviors. Many times the chart can be a reinforcement in and of itself. Teachers can also be assisted in reinforcing attempts to change behaviors. Although I prefer to keep school business at school, children may decide to bring the charts home for parent approval. Often children have kept their charts and shared them with parents.

As the child develops the needed skills, you can be instrumental in helping her or him develop self-monitoring behaviors so that the chart can eventually be discontinued. As you faze out the chart, encourage the child to reinforce herself or himself and support the teacher in encouraging the new behavior.

The chart is merely a vehicle to assist in discussing feelings. Consequences for the behaviors being charted need to be delivered in a natural setting, *not* in your office. This distinction is important since you should not be placed in the role of disciplinarian. Your role is to support the child's attempts and help him or her explore alternative options.

A chart can be used for adolescents to keep track of their behavior and of what happened before the behavior as well as its results. Because this tracking of behavior can be work, I generally contract with the adolescent for one class that is particularly problematic. The chart needs to include space for the adolescent to write the situation that occurred and the action he or she took. Behaviors that may be charted include pushing, hitting, talking out in class, not paying attention, and failing to complete work. A useful type of chart is presented in Table 5–2.

This chart provides a place for the adolescent to look at the behavior as well as how he or she felt about it. The chart provides a record of events that occur between sessions. Rather than attempting to reconstruct the week from memory, the chart reminds the adolescent of events, allows for the discussion of alternatives to what occurred as well, and gives the adolescent a chance to look at cues in the environment that presage a behavior problem. Assisting the adolescent identify those environmental cues can be proactive for preventing the problematic behavior from occurring. Helping the child/adolescent to *act* and *not react* to her or his environment instills a feeling of self-efficacy leading to the development of a healthy self-concept. The data gathered from these charts set up the counseling contract and are used for evaluation of the treatment plan.

TABLE 5–2   An Example of an Adolescent Chart

Behavior	*What happened before*	*What happened after*	*How I felt*
Hitting	Joe called me a name.	I lost my computer privilege.	angry and confused; Joe didn't lose any privileges.

The Counseling Contract

It is important to lay out the ground rules for the counseling sessions and thus make explicit what the sessions are designed to accomplish. This accountability is for the benefit of both child and clinician. By setting out the goals and responsibilities for the sessions, improvement can be measured. If these measurements are not acceptable, then treatment changes are made.

The contract also delineates who is accountable for which actions. Because the contract is between two people, the child holds responsibility for the sessions just as does the clinician. Having the contract written, or at the very least verbalized, formalizes the process and commits both parties to participating. The child decides which actions he or she is willing to work on while the clinician commits her or his time and skills.

In addition to establishing accountability on the part of both parties, the counseling contract also specifies the amount of time, duration of treatment, and length of session. It is important for the treatment to discuss with the child, parent, and/or teacher all of these variables. Setting a realistic time limit may make sessions more fruitful. Therapy outside of the schools is frequently restricted by financial and time variables. Given the ever-increasing needs for counseling of children and parents in the schools and clinics, it is important to provide the most efficient support.

If the contract limit expires and work still needs to be accomplished, it can be renegotiated and a revised timeline established. This procedure allows the clinician and the client to review their progress as well as to evaluate what further steps are needed. Generally a review should occur after at least six weeks of meetings. Specifying the timeline in the beginning of the treatment sets up expectations for the work done together.

Ending the Session

At the end of the first session, you should briefly summarize the session, checking with the client that decisions which have been made are understood by both of you. In addition, it is often helpful to ask the child how he or she felt about the session. I also ask how the child feels the session went and clarify the time and day of the next session. By asking these questions at the end of the session, you can determine how the child feels about coming and establish an agreement about coming to the next session. It also helps to find out if any misconceptions remain as to what the sessions may involve.

A teenager was seen in our clinic by one of the student clinicians. He was brought for the session by his parents and initially was not in favor of coming. When asked at the end of the session how he felt, he stated that it wasn't as bad as he had expected. He had thought it would be like going to the principal's office. He then agreed to come the following week. This information provided three clues. First, the adolescent felt coerced to attend the session. Second, he felt that the session would be one of discipline and discussing what he had done wrong. Finally, he agreed to come again and give the clinician another "chance." These clues were only provided at the end of the session. The clinician had not known that the parents had put her in the position of being a disciplinarian. By discussing the teenager's statements, the clinician was able to tell him that he had a say in what would transpire in the session and could reassure him that she would not serve as a stand-in for his parents. She was able to indicate nonverbally to him that she was his ally. In this sense, this teenager had a new experience with an adult in a joint problem-solving situation. In the past, the teenager had been told what to do by the adults in his life. He rebelled against these strictures. By being sensitized to his typical way of responding, the clinician provided him with another model of relationships with adults and of problem solving that included his point of view.

It is always a good idea to provide a transitional period for the end of the session. Approximately ten minutes before the session ends announce that there are ten minutes left in your time together. Encourage the child to help you clean up. A four-year-old child I saw for an initial session refused to leave the session and then refused to help in cleaning up.

T: It's time to go home with your mother in a few minutes.

C: Mmm. Just a few more minutes.

T: We need to start picking up our toys.

C: I don't want to go. Let's play with the dolls.

T: *(more firmly)* It is almost time to go home. We need to start cleaning up now.

C: *(Doesn't move)*

T: I know it's hard to leave some place when you are having a good time. I don't like to go when I am having fun. But it is time to go, and we can do this again next week.

C: No.

T: *(Begins to clean up and encourages the child to help)* Here is the castle you made of blocks. Should we put that on the shelf for next week?

C: Will you let anyone else play with it?

T: No, it will wait here just for you.

C: OK.

This child needed reassurance that the clinician would remember her and keep her castle safe. The action of setting the castle apart helped the child feel that there would be some continuity and that no one else would play with her creation; that is, that the clinician would keep her as a special person.

Transitions to the end of a session can be difficult for many children. You need to reassure the child and set the stage for the following session. Use a firm but gentle tone of voice. It is easy to be cajoled into allowing additional time. This practice is to be avoided as it only delays the inevitable and rewards manipulative behavior. The end of the session should lay the foundation for the following sessions as well as the beginning of the therapeutic relationship. The next chapter discusses methods for furthering this relationship.

Exercise 1

An important exercise you may wish to use is to interview others in your class about issues in your life. Pairs of students can choose a topic with one acting as the clinician and one as the client. Topics for discussion may include the hardest thing you have ever done, a frightening experience, or anything that may lend itself to discussing feelings. Critique the role-play as to how it felt on both sides, note questions or observations that could have been rephrased to be more effective, and identify anything more that could have been asked. Then switch roles and role-play a similar scenario. This exercise will help to begin to develop listening skills.

Exercise 2

Another useful exercise is to talk with a child you know relatively well about a topic he or she chooses. (Ask the child's parents for permission before doing this activity.) Tape record your conversation, letting the child know this is homework for a class. Most children are glad to help out with an adult's homework. Then go back over your tape and note the questions and observations you made. Besides noting what you may perceive as mistakes, note the questions and observations you made that you like.

6

The Relationship
Is the Thing

In any relationship there are expectations based on the participant's previous experiences. These expectations apply to the therapeutic relationship as well as social relationships. The relationship evolves as the clinician meets with the client in the same manner as with other environments. The therapeutic relationship is structured by both participants and has a history built on previous sessions. As you relate to the client, you will find that experiences the client has had in other relationships will intrude on the therapy. The client may replay behaviors which have been perfected in other relationships and will expect similar reactions from you. By exploring these behaviors in a caring and honest environment, the client can find ways to understand his or her actions and facilitate changes as desired.

Importance of the Relationship

The relationship is a necessary but not sufficient condition for therapy to occur. If the relationship is structured on trust and respect, it can withstand the explorations of painful and emotion-laden experiences. It is important, however, for the beginning clinician to realize that establishing the relationship is but the first step in the work of therapy. The work of therapy, and it is work, begins as this relationship is established. Within the framework of the relationship, the clinician can begin to gently confront the child or adolescent with behaviors which are maladaptive or unconstructive. Such confrontations proceed as the client shows readiness for such awareness.

Experience teaches the clinician when and how to begin such confrontations. Because all clinicians are in the process of learning, they may make a mistake as to when to begin a confrontation. The relationship which has been built on previous sessions, however, can withstand such errors in judgment. An example of such an error is the following interview with a 15-year-old girl who was experiencing significant school problems. The therapist had begun confronting the girl with insights as to her own part in the problems she was blaming on teachers and parents.

C: I missed you last week. Can you tell me what happened?

Girl: I just forgot to come. No real reason, I guess. *(She is moving around in her chair, looking very uncomfortable.)*

C: Well, I missed you and wondered what you were doing. It felt like maybe you were mad at me for something I had done.

Girl: Mad? I just forgot that's all.

C: Well, it seemed like what often happens when your teachers or parents do something you don't like and you ignore them or do not go to class. *(silence for 20 seconds)* I thought maybe I had done something that disappointed you.

Girl: *(long pause)* I just had other things that came up.

C: Well, I am glad you came today. I think it's important for us to continue working together on what's happening in school right now. Now, how is it going in English?

The session before the missed appointment, the therapist had moved too quickly. They had been discussing her part in the "unfairness" of adults, and on reflection the therapist realized that she had fallen into the trap of acting out the role of the "unfair" adult in the girl's mind. Because the relationship had been built on other occasions when the therapist had been "there" for the girl and helped her through some traumatic experiences, the girl was able to come back to the sessions. If the relationship hadn't been built as strongly and if the therapist hadn't read the signs that there was a relationship between the girl's behavior and the previous session, therapy would not occur and it is highly likely the girl would have dropped out of therapy.

This example illustrates the work of the *good-enough* therapist who has built a relationship with a client that can sustain therapy through rough episodes. A good-enough therapist is one who has been with the client through other difficulties and one whom the client can trust to be there. Rather than accepting everything the child/adolescent does, the therapist understands the motivations behind behaviors. The good-enough therapist is experienced by the client as understanding and caring for the client.

Mistakes will be made in the therapeutic process. A beginning clinician may believe that experienced therapists do not make mistakes. The difference is that the experienced clinician is able to realize the mistake and take corrective action. For example, the good-enough therapist may attempt to move faster than the client wishes, which can produce therapeutic conflict. An astute clinician will search earlier sessions to determine where the strategical error had occurred and correct the problem. The relationship can provide the backdrop for such corrective action. Without the relationship, corrective action will not occur as the client will have left therapy.

A good-enough therapist is "there" for the client to the extent that he or she will trust the therapist to be there most of the time. In such cases mistakes in timing or interpretation are forgiven and therapy can proceed. The beginning clinician must realize that mistakes will be made. These errors, however, should serve to assist the clinician in searching for what went wrong and how to avoid such difficulties in the future. Therapeutic errors often will not result in the end of therapy if you have taken the time to build a good relationship. If the therapy is discontinued, you owe it to yourself and future clients to explore the part you have played in the therapeutic failure. Often the reason for a discontinuance will be a relationship that was not fully established or a therapist who did not recognize his or her errors.

How to build a sustaining relationship which can hold painful emotions is something you will learn and perfect over years of practice. The beginning steps are outlined in the following sections. Suggestions for avoiding common therapeutic mistakes and for realizing when such mistakes have been made are also discussed. First, the variables which may interfere with relationship building will be explored.

Developmental and Family Variables

Although most parents want their children to grow up to be independent and psychologically healthy adults, the child's attempt to individuate from the parents can be threatening to some caretakers. At certain developmental points, it is normal for children to challenge parents and teachers for independence. How the push for independence is handled by key adults in a child's life sets the stage for later development.

Attachment

Children who are securely attached to their parents have been observed to keep their parents within their reach when faced with ambiguous or new experiences (Ainsworth, 1979). They will approach a fearful situation and then retreat to their parents for reassurance. In this manner the child learns he or she can approach things that are scary and yet be protected by the parents. The child's trust in parents allows him or her to explore the environment. As these children grow, they begin to internalize the parental reassurance and incorporate it into their schema of themselves. In such a way the child is enabled to try new experiences, build feelings of self-efficacy, and develop feelings of self-esteem that can withstand experiences which are hurtful or destructive.

In contrast, children who are insecurely or too tightly attached to caretakers will not approach new situations, will cling to parents and be unable to separate, and will fuss when the parents are not available. As such children grow, they may well experience difficulty trying new activities, developing a sense of themselves, and accepting responsibility for their actions. Some of these children will construct self-schemas which are either grandiose or self-defeating.

Separation Problems
The grandiose child will believe he or she can accomplish anything he or she desires with no conceptualization of realistic evaluation of his or her skills. The difference between this child and one who has developed in a healthy manner is the inability to cope with failure or frustration of desires. The grandiose child expects the world to provide what he or she wants when it is wanted. Because the caretakers have provided everything as wished for, the child believes this state of affairs will continue indefinitely and that he or she is "entitled" to such events. Belief in such entitlement creates significant problems in development as the child comes up against world demands that do not provide such support. Grandiose children/ adolescents may develop a coping style which lays blame on the person or situation provoking a response. In this way they can argue that they are not responsible for problems that arise. After all, the problems are the fault of the person demanding unreasonable actions (such as work) from them.

We all know people who fall into this category and with whom it is notoriously difficult to deal. When such cases present themselves to you as clients, it is a real challenge not to react to them as would many in the world outside of the therapy room. To react in such a way is to invite rejection of the therapy; thus, no therapy will occur. Even when these clients are referred at a young age, they present a real challenge to developing a therapeutic relationship.

Enmeshment
One major roadblock to establishing a relationship is the caretaker. In many instances the caretaker may not allow for a close relationship to be established between client and clinician. If you are not aware of the enmeshment between the child and caretaker, you may unwittingly threaten the care-

taker by becoming too close too quickly to the young client. In this instance you should involve the parents with the treatment as much as possible. It is also important to be very cognizant of unspoken boundaries the caretaker establishes in order to maintain the enmeshment. The following example concerns a 16-year-old girl and her mother. The girl had been referred for treatment by her mother because the girl cut classes and had frequent bouts of crying. Her mother had been very concerned about the girl's sadness following a break-up between the mother and a long-time boyfriend. The girl and her mother had lived together since the father deserted the family when the child was born.

Girl: We went driving by his house last night. It made me so sad to go there and know he was inside and not with us. If my mother hadn't had me, there wouldn't be any problem. She could live with him and his daughter wouldn't hate me.

C: You feel they aren't together because of you?

Girl: Well that is why—his daughter hates me and told him that if he married my mother, she'd never see him again. So he broke up with her. I have always gotten in her way.

C: So she lost her boyfriend and you feel you were responsible. Is that how you got in her way?

Girl: Yes and before with my dad.

C: With your dad?

Girl: Yes he left because she decided to have me and keep me.

C: So by being born you were responsible for your dad leaving. And now you caused her boyfriend to leave you.

Girl: I'm just in the way. She's so sad now and it's all my fault.

C: You see your mom as being sad?

Girl: She doesn't smile like she used to—I'm worried about her.

C: Did you know that she's worried about you for the same reasons?

Girl: We are the same in many ways. We only have each other. I'm not sure it will ever change for us. We've always been like this—it's probably no good for me to come here to talk.

C: The real question is do you want anything to change?

Girl: Would I come here if I didn't?

C: What do you want to see happen?

Girl: I want my mother to be happy and marry her boyfriend.

C: If she did that, could you then do what you want in your life?

Girl: It would be better for both of us.

C: I wonder if your feelings of responsibility toward your mother have anything to do with the fact that you often skip school.

Girl: I love my mother.

C: It's OK to love your mother but still want to make your own life.

Girl: It's all mixed up for me. I don't know what to feel or do. She needs me.

C: So it's important for you to be there for her?

Girl: I can't leave her to be all alone.

C: Do you see any relationship between your cutting school and your need to be there for your mother? What would happen if you went to college?

Girl: I want to go to college.

C: I know you want to go to college but you seem to be doing your best not to graduate from high school.

Girl: It's not my fault I can't graduate—if they didn't have all those requirements that I really don't need.

C: So you aren't responsible for your failing grades?

Girl: You are just like them—I am doing my best.

C: Am I just like your teachers in that I think you can do the work but can't because you would have to grow up then?

Girl: Yes—don't you see, I can't. It's not my fault—they should just let me be.

   In this example, the girl cannot separate from her parent. To even begin discussing such a separation is anxiety-provoking for the girl. She is not prepared to deal with the basic feelings of guilt over her mother's difficulty with her love-life and the very fact of her existence contributing to the father's rejection. Her mother was asked to come in for a joint session to talk about these issues. The following dialogue was taken from that session.

C: Sharon has expressed her concern about how you are doing.

Mom: Why should she be worried about me? I'm worried about her.

Girl: You don't have your boyfriend to take care of you anymore.

Mom: I can take care of myself.

Girl: But you don't go out and do things anymore.

Mom: I am doing fine. I'm worried about you not going to classes. If you keep this up, they won't let you graduate in a year.

C: I'm confused about why Sharon hasn't been going to class.

Girl: I told you. I can't get to class—I intend to go and then something comes up and I do it instead. I can do the work if they would just give it to me and then I could pass the classes—I don't really need to sit there.

C: So if your teachers would give you the work, you would be able to do it without even going to class?

Girl: That's right.

C: I need you to help me understand this now—you tell me that you can do the work without going to class for the teacher's explanation and yet you have failed almost all of the tests you have taken. How can this be?

Mom: You know, if they would just give her a little extra time, she would be fine. Sharon has always been smart. If you could call them and explain that she has some emotional problems right now, they might let her do the work at home.

C: So you would like me to call them and have them change the rules for Sharon. Could you talk a little more about the emotional problems?

Mom: I've talked to you about her crying and her need to be at home more now that our lives have really changed. She feels that he left me because of her but I wouldn't have married him without her being part of the family. She is the most important person to me.

C: Could it be, Sharon, that it is hard for you to think of leaving home now that your mother is alone.

Girl: I've told you before I really want to go to college.

Mom: I want nothing more for her than that she goes to college and has a good life—better than what I have had. We need to have your help to get the school to listen to us.

C: I am concerned that Sharon feels that she isn't able to follow through on her responsibilities and wants extraordinary consideration in order to graduate.

Mom: She only wants what she needs to have in order to graduate. I don't think we are being unreasonable.

C: What would it be like for you if she were to graduate from high school?

Mom: It would be fine. I would continue at my job and she would go to college.

C: Is it possible that Sharon is concerned about how you will be if she should go to school and she can't bring herself to leave you?

Mom: I don't really think that's the problem. The school is just not helping us very much.

Girl: I can do it if they will just bend their stupid rules.

As you can see, the session was not going well, neither the girl nor her mother would allow themselves to see a connection between their relationship and the girl's inability to attend school. They also felt entitled to special treatment by the school system and were unable to see any problems with their demands. This case continued for several more sessions with both the mother and the girl, to no avail. Therapy was discontinued when the counselor refused to write a letter excusing Sharon from school on the basis of emotional illness. The illness, which was present, was enmeshment and to participate further in this dysfunction was felt to be antithetical to treatment. In this case the mother and girl were so intertwined that they were unable to separate their feelings from each other. Each felt the other was depressed. Moreover, although it is likely that the mother was not conscious of her desire to keep her daughter from graduating, she was giving out signals to her daughter that to graduate would be a type of abandonment.

Difficulties also arise when a child who has been tightly attached seeks to stretch those bonds a bit. Parents may react very strongly to such attempts at independence, which are a part of growing up. As they clamp down, the formerly tractable child may become more and more rebellious and angry. This type of difficulty often brings child and parents in for treatment, either privately or in the school. An example of this type of problem is taken from a case of a 15-year-old boy. He was referred by his mother because of his "disrespectful attitude." His performance in school was slipping from a straight A average to Cs and Ds. His mother reported that he would challenge her on her requests, and these challenges often escalated to screaming matches between them. When the boy was nine, his father had left the family to marry another woman. The mother described the father as frequently putting her down in front of the son. Recently the father had been decreasing his contacts with his son. The following session occurred in the midpoint of the therapy.

Boy: Things are really getting bad at home. She thinks she can tell me everything to do and gives me no time to do what I want.

C: So it is feeling like she is taking up all of your time.

Boy: She just keeps talking at me constantly and won't let me alone. I tell her I will do what she wants but when I want to do it. I really wish she would just leave me alone!

C: You sound very frustrated.

Boy: I am angry. I can make her life so difficult she will finally leave me alone.

C: So in the end you will do what you want.

Boy: I can't wait until I am old enough to get out of there. She just stays home all day and doesn't try to do anything to make herself better. She's just lazy like my dad said.

C: You sound pretty disappointed in her. Have you always felt like this?

Boy: No, I used to really like her. We would have lots of fun but she's changed. I thought when I got to high school she would go back to school and get a life. She just stays home and I think she'll always want me to be there. I sometimes feel like running away.

C: What would you like to do about this problem? It sounds like you are really fed up.

Boy: I'd like for all of us to sit down and talk about these problems. Maybe she will listen to you.

C: So you feel that I may be able to help you talk to her and change some of these problems. It may mean you will have to think about some of the things you do too. Will that be OK with you?

Boy: At least maybe she'll change some things too.

The session ended with a joint appointment with mother and son for the following week. The clinician felt that it was important for both players to be present since issues about independence and growth were being explored. In the joint sessions issues continued to emerge about respect, abandonment, fear of loss, and individuation. The mother eventually was able to give the son some growing room. She joined a support group and eventually enrolled in a local community college training program.

In this case the boy forced the issue of enmeshment and began acting out his concern. In the earlier illustration, the girl was unable to separate from her mother and the enmeshment was hampering her ability to individuate and develop into her own person. Although there was a good therapeutic relationship in both cases, therapy was successful only in the case where the adolescent was able to use the relationship to break free. In the first case, the girl wasn't able or willing to separate, and the unfortunate result was one of continuing difficulty. Long-term treatment would have been needed, which would have moved very slowly, utilizing both mother and daughter in all sessions. This type of treatment is often beyond the scope of most school systems and is appropriately referred to a private practitioner or clinic.

The Poorly Attached Problem

Another type of attachment problem which can translate into difficulties in later adjustment, is that of a child who is poorly attached to his or her caretakers. In this instance the child does not feel connected to the caretakers and may react to this lack of relatedness by withdrawing or acting out in ways similar to the child in an enmeshed relationship but for a different reason.

A poorly attached child may be so because of parental psychopathology, parental illness, or unexpected parental absence. In this case the child may grow into an adolescent who is unsure of his or her loveability as well as his or her ability to return love. As demands for ability to relate to their peers increase, difficulties can arise in how the child/adolescent copes with these new challenges.

An example of developmental concerns which can arise from poor attachment is the case of a 20-year-old male college student who was failing. He was originally referred because of an inability to concentrate on his work and complete class assignments. At the midpoint of therapy, he began talking about his relationship with his mother, who was very domineering and who had engineered his life prior to his move to another town for college. The therapist had reflected on the student's ability to leave his mother's shadow and cast it as a moment of strength.

C: How does it feel to hear that you may be stronger than you feel?

John: (very quiet—all of a sudden begins to cry, increasing into sobs)

C: Sometimes it's hard to hear good things about yourself.

John: I never have been strong. I felt that I would die if I hadn't left—I never really felt cared about from my mother or father. There didn't seem to be any warmth in them—I just seemed to be something they had to deal with.

C: What were the tears about?

John: I'm not really strong like you said—I just ran away. I can't respect myself. My dad never respected me or felt that I could do anything right. I never was good enough for him to care about me.

C: So you felt that there was something missing from you and that you needed that something in order to gain your dad's love.

John: I tried hard to get him to respect me—I don't think he ever will now. My mother tried to help me but she wanted me to be like her and I just wasn't good enough to do that either.

C: So you were a failure in your eyes?

John: Yes *(crying softly)*, and here I am unable to do my work in school.

C: So that proves it again that you are a failure. It seems to me that you have done something very difficult in leaving them and trying to establish your own life.

John: But I'm not doing it very well. I had trouble in high school too and then suddenly in 11th grade I had a teacher who thought I was really smart. I then found all my classes to be easy and I did well until my sophomore year in college. Now I can't do it anymore.

C: What do you think sparked this change?

John: I'm not really sure. Maybe because the work is now too hard.

C: Why would that happen all of a sudden in your sophomore year and not before?

John: I'm not sure.

C: How's it been with your father recently?

John: Well he's been sick lately and I really haven't talked to him much about anything.

C: This is the first time you have talked about him being sick.

John: Well I didn't think it was important—is it?

C: When did he get sick?

John: Maybe six months ago.

The co-occurrence of his father's sickness (which was a heart attack) and John's inability to function in college at about the same time was more than a coincidence. John continued to have difficulty talking about his father's illness. He was eventually able to explore the link between his fear of his father's death (the ultimate abandonment) and his inability to function. Once these feelings were explored, he slowly began to be able to work on his own life and take charge of his responsibilities. His slide into nonachievement may be conceptualized as an attempt to go back to dependency on his parents and establish connections which had never been forged with his father before his father died.

Attachment issues thus can be important to explore, particularly with adolescents and young adults. For younger children and adolescents issues of parental attachment can surface in the therapeutic framework. Enmeshment can significantly interfere with the work of therapy unless this issue is identified and addressed, and attachment issues can bring conflict into the therapy session. The techniques for establishing a therapeutic relationship capable of managing such conflict constructively will be discussed in the following section.

Fostering the Relationship

In order for the therapeutic relationship to handle conflict, strong emotions, and the work of therapy, it must be fostered throughout the therapy sessions. You must not be afraid to provide support for the client even when things are said that may be upsetting. The old maxim of "I like you, I don't like your behavior" is very appropriate for you to remember. It can also be difficult to apply in some situations.

One of the attributes most necessary to foster a relationship is that of positive regard (Rogers, 1961). Positive regard does not mean that the therapist accepts everything the client says as accurate or valid. It does mean that the therapist embraces the personhood of the child/adolescent and sees the possibilities within that child/adolescent. The therapist then works to free up those possibilities so that the child can continue on her or his journey of development. If a client does not feel accepted by the therapist, it is doubtful that change can occur. Therapy is work and change is hard. In order to change the client has to believe she or he can change; the major change facilitator, the therapist, must also believe in this ability. All therapists have cases with which they do not connect. It is ethically important to realize the limits of your connections and act in the best interest of the child by referring him or her elsewhere. To force working with a child/adolescent with whom you are unable to connect is likely to end in failure. A more sobering fact is that you are the representative for future therapists in this person's life and a negative impact can have potentially damaging results.

The first few sessions should be devoted to getting to know each other. Conducting a mini-interview about the child's or adolescent's history is important to gaining an understanding of his or her particular interpretation of the world. This interview also serves as a format for asking questions about important occurrences, which may be useful in later sessions when exploring feelings and situations occurring in the present. This interview can also set the stage for establishing goals for treatment.

As you mature in your practice of therapy, you will find that skills addressed in Chapter 5 will become second nature. In the beginning stages it is helpful to tape record your sessions so that you may go back over them looking for openings that were missed or for failures in empathy and support. I have found it helpful to utilize a relatively informal approach where the child or adolescent can address me by my first name and has an equal say in what we do. Many of my clients call me "Dr. or Miss Peg." I feel it helps them to see me as closer to them than as an authority figure. This form of address has also encouraged them to talk with me about how it feels to be with adults who direct their daily lives.

I have also found it helpful to provide time for play within the sessions. Even older adolescents often feel more comfortable doing other tasks while talking rather than sitting face to face. These tasks can range from board games to walking to drawing pictures together. The type of activity chosen is not as important as the opportunity you provide the child or adolescent to decide what he or she wishes to do. Some will want to play and some will enjoy just having an adult's attention to themselves.

Process in Therapy

Process in therapy is the meat of what is happening in the sessions. It is not the words that are used as much as the emotional dance between the therapist and client. What goes on in the therapeutic exchange involves much more than the words; it is how the emotions present in the therapy room are utilized for therapeutic change.

You need to *see* what is happening with your third eye. The *third eye* is the ability to understand what is happening emotionally in the sessions and utilize the information to further the therapy. If you are "in tune" with the client, you can read the emotions both by the client's words and by your reactions to them. It is very important to read your reactions to the information provided by the client. For example, if the person in your therapy room is resisting your suggestion, you may find yourself trying to convince him or her. You may leave the session feeling very tired, frustrated, and perhaps angry. Go back over the session to try to discover what happened that led you to these emotions. Perhaps you began a discussion prematurely or possibly you missed some important cues from the client that signaled they had another agenda in mind. Your ability to analyze the emotions flying around the room will assist you in your therapy.

At times I have observed my student's sessions through a one-way mirror without the sound on. I have then played the videotape for the class without sound and asked my students to describe what they feel is going on in the session. What is important to remember is that your feelings are genuine and you are reacting to something in the room. The problem is for you to isolate just what is sparking your reaction. As you gain experience, it will be easier for you to decipher such experiences at the time they are occurring and take action at that point.

The limbic system governs the body's reaction to emotion and stress. A type of "limbic music" between both participants occurs in therapy (Cassem, 1991). This limbic music informs the therapist as to the congruence between what the client is saying and feeling. When words and emotions are not congruent, the astute therapist will react to the emotions and explore what variables are accounting for the discrepancy. In some cases the client may not feel comfortable discussing an underlying feeling. In this situation, the relationship needs to mature before the client can disclose feelings that may be shameful for him or her. In contrast, other clients may not be aware of the disparity between emotions and words. For them the therapist will need to move carefully when exploring the difference. At times the client may react with resistance, anger, or denial. These reactions are defenses constructed against the anxiety provoked by the experience of feelings the client may perceive as shameful or disgusting. There have been times when I have been discussing painful episodes in a client's life only to have the client smile. Pointing out such a discrepancy may assist the client in reviewing his or her behavior.

For example, a student of mine was experiencing significant problems relating to her clients. She came across as removed and cold, and her clients picked up on such behaviors. She would discuss areas that were painful for them and smile while she was doing so. When we met in supervision, I asked her why she was smiling throughout the meeting. She had not noticed her behavior prior to this point and was surprised to see how often she smiled while discussing painful topics. It became clearer to her why her client was reacting with defensiveness and frequently canceled their sessions. Self-exploration revealed that my student was uncomfortable with strong feelings and her smiles were really signs of anxiety—not pleasure at the client's pain.

Dealing with Defenses

In some cases beginning therapists may view defenses constructed by their clients as maladaptive. Contrarily, defenses are a way of defending against emotions the client feels incapable of dealing with alone. As such, they serve as a coping mechanism that helps the child/adolescent deal with daily life. You are advised not to take these defenses away prematurely. When defenses are challenged, you will find that conflict will arise in the session. Such conflict (discussed in the following section) can assist in therapeutic change when the therapist can assist the client in examining their defensive structure.

Do not assume that all defense mechanisms must be stripped from the client in order for health to occur. Most people require defense mechanisms to function in the world. Defense mechanisms prevent the individual from being flooded with emotions. As such, they are adaptive in nature as long as they do not prevent the individual from growing and living. In treatment you must determine which mechanisms are healthy and adaptive for the individual and which ones are preventing the child/adolescent from growth and development. The more destructive mechanisms are generally those that are used to justify inappropriate and/or unconstructive behaviors.

When defense mechanisms interfere with healthy development, challenging them will provoke conflict. You can use such conflict constructively within the treatment session to promote growth and change. The relationship allows you to help the child/adolescent sort through her or his behaviors within a safe and nurturing situation.

Conflict in Therapy

One of my students was discouraged because she felt that the 13-year-old she was seeing in therapy was not bonding to her. He was very quiet and reserved during the sessions. He would hesitantly speak about the conflicts between his parents, both parents' difficulty with alcohol, and his feelings that the family was spinning out of control. It was evident that he was feeling at a loss in dealing with his feelings of hopelessness and futility. Moreover, he felt ashamed of his fear of losing any stability in his life and had an overwhelming fear that life would not improve.

The sessions were painful for my student because she felt the long silences in the sessions meant that he was not connected to her. She also experienced his feelings of helplessness and belief that nothing could be changed that permeated the sessions. In this manner, my student began to empathically understand how the adolescent felt and what it was like for him to live day to day in this situation. What was important to the boy, however, was that she was able to tolerate these feelings and continued to be "emotionally available" for him. Although my student wanted to solve the problems her client was experiencing, it was most appropriate that she helped him deal with his feelings as she explored other alternatives.

Too often we may assume that we have to "solve" the client's problems in order for our therapy to be effective. This misconception may provoke the beginning therapist into moving too quickly as a way of handling their own emotions rather than doing what is best for the client.

Not being able to assist a client who is in a bad situation can be anxiety-provoking for you. Being able to tolerate ambiguity and not having closure on a problem are important lessons for you to learn. The goal of treatment frequently lies in assisting the client to modulate his or her reactions to an unpleasant situation. You should accept the fact that the best assistance you can provide is to support the child/adolescent in learning additional coping strategies in order to adapt to a difficult situation.

At times in a therapeutic relationship it is important to be able to tolerate very painful feelings and to provide an outlet for them. There are times when clients feel their emotions are so destructive or scary that they cannot be tolerated. By remaining in the room and sharing in the feelings, you can mitigate some of the fearfulness of these emotions. In the earlier case of the 20-year-old, his sobbing was later explored as to the combination of sadness and rage. He was able to talk about his fear that the therapist would not be able to "handle" his emotions and would leave the situation. Although these feelings may seem irrational to objective observers, the intensity of feelings can be very intimidating to both the client and the therapist.

By withstanding the onslaught of strong emotions, you provide a model for handling these emotions. In social situations strong emotions are discouraged and people find themselves saying "It will be all right—don't cry." In contrast the therapeutic situation doesn't say "don't cry" or "it will be all right," but rather sits with the client through the emotions.

As the family problems in the above case became clearer, it was apparent that family counseling was the most appropriate course of action, with additional support provided for the boy. In time the family was referred for therapy with a family counselor. Although the family did not continue in the joint sessions, the boy called my student and asked to continue with her.

This case aptly shows that a bond can form when you are just "there" for the student emotionally. The boy felt my student was the only person who would really listen to him even when he could not talk directly about what was bothering him. By sitting with him through the emotions he was experiencing, the therapist provided him with enough support to seek out help when his family was willing to pursue the recommendations that had been made. In this manner my student showed a willingness to tolerate the turbulent emotions the boy was experiencing.

Table 6–1 presents an outline of the concepts which occur in therapy and which are described in the following paragraphs.

Resistance
As the relationship matures, it is important to begin exploring feelings and situations that seem to be a pattern interfering with the adjustment of the client. You may find the client will resist your attempts to bring up these patterns, and conflict can arise. It is important to recognize resistance when it occurs and adjust your treatment appropriately.

Resistance can be manifested in many ways. It can take the form of missing sessions, abruptly changing the subject, zoning out during an interchange, and becoming angry. When you come up against resistance, a natural

TABLE 6-1   Concepts in Therapy

Concept	Potential Problems	Possible Solutions
Resistance: Feelings and situations that interfere with therapy	Pushing against resistance causes more client resistance	Pull back; acknowledge disagreement
Interpretation: To make sense out of patterns of behaviors and feelings	Incorrect or premature interpretations	Revise interpretation; reserve for future use; present as a hypothesis
Re-enactment of Issues: Behaviors similar to those the client does outside the therapy room that are acted out in the session	Therapist reacts the same way as others do; loss of rapport and damage to the relationship	Recognize the client's need to repeat actions; provide a different experience through your reaction

tendency is to push against it even harder, to repeat what you have said more loudly or in other words, and to become angry yourself. Although understandable, none of these reactions is constructive or useful in therapy.

Again, it is important to recall that therapy is different from social interactions. You are providing a *corrective* emotional experience for the child/adolescent. The reaction you will provide to resistance will vary from what the individual has experienced in the past. Resisting a force often produces an equal amount of resistance from the opposite player. This is as true in therapy as it is in physics. In therapy, however, continuing to push against resistance will not be helpful and may in fact hurt the relationship since the client feels misunderstood.

When resistance is found, it is most constructive to acknowledge that it is present and to begin thinking about why it has happened. One of the most common reasons for resistance is that you are moving too quickly for the client and making leaps in interpretation for which the client is not ready. An equally possible situation is that your interpretation is incorrect and the client is reacting rightfully to it. In either case, the strategy is the same. Since resistance will increase when you push against it, if you pull back, resistance will dissipate. Therefore when resistance is encountered, it is usually helpful to acknowledge that there is disagreement and to begin to explore where the discrepancy lies. By being open to a possible difference of opinions, you provide an instance where the client feels heard and respected. By exploring the reasons for differences, you provide a model for solving problems and disagreements rather than just pushing for the client's opinion. This reaction is different from what is usually experienced by the child/adolescent and helps you evaluate the reaction the client shows to exploring his or her feelings.

Interpretation

Interpretations are attempts by the therapist to make sense out of patterns that occur in the client's behavior or feelings. Used sparingly, interpretations can help the client link up patterns that have been problematic in the past to feelings and perceptions. A groundwork for the interpretation must be carefully laid before an interpretation is *offered*. It is important to understand that interpretations are subject to discussion with the client. When you make an interpretation that is rejected by the client, you need to ascertain whether the interpretation is premature, resulting in the client's being unable to understand it, or incorrect. Either way, you need to respect the limits set by the client and forestall the interpretation for revision or for later use.

Beginning therapists are often tempted to use interpretation freely as a therapeutic method. Unfortunately, an interpretation can be formulated prematurely or is presented to the client before he or she is ready to "hear" them. Premature interpretations can block progress since they may explain away areas too quickly and too patly. If the client accepts the interpretation, then the buttressing work that is needed to put the interpretation into practice is missing. If the interpretation is incorrect, the client may feel he or she needs to accept the interpretation (after all, you are the expert!). The result can be that the client will not appropriately resolve troublesome areas and difficulty will again arise at another time. In contrast, if the interpretation is incorrect, the client may reject it, which some therapists will interpret as resistance or denial, resulting in a loss of connection. Carried to its extreme, this scenario can result in the ending of the relationship.

The following example illustrates an interpretation carried to an extreme. A 19-year-old female was in treatment for difficulties with depression, suicidality, and acting out behaviors. Treatment was proceeding well on issues of vulnerability, boundary setting, and fear of abandonment. During this period the client experienced failure in college. Her school history indicated problems in learning from the primary grades. It was decided to refer the client for psychological testing to rule out a learning disability and/or attention deficit disorder. The client usually dressed quite flamboyantly, with several earrings in each ear and many rings, necklaces, and bracelets. She was assigned to a psychologist for testing and was motivated to find out what if any difficulties might be underlying her problems.

The psychologist to whom she was assigned wore button-down shirts, suits with a matching tie and socks, and looked very "professional." She went into the testing with an open mind but quickly resisted the testing and refused to continue after half of the assessment was completed. The psychologist interpreted her behavior as "narcissistic" and concluded that the testing had challenged her ability to cope with frustration and failure. This psychologist felt his behavior had been fair and even-handed but that the girl was in denial and would need to be confronted with her problems.

The following dialogue is from the session after the failed psychological assessment.

Girl: How could you have sent me to him—he hated me? He was always frowning at me. I felt like I couldn't do anything right.

C: What made you feel that way?

Girl: He didn't like me at all. I felt like he was judging everything I did.

C: So with his frowning and judging it became very hard for you to stay there with him and finish the tests.

Girl: Yes. I felt horrible—I almost didn't come today because I thought you'd yell at me for leaving.

C: So that experience made you wonder about our relationship?

Girl: Yes, it brought back all my feelings of not being good enough.

C: So it became necessary for you to regress back to failing like you have in the past when you felt vulnerable?

Girl: I didn't do it on purpose—you are just like him—making it all my fault.

C: You're right—I'm sorry, that was unfair of me. You must be disappointed in me for not recognizing how strongly you felt.

Girl: I really got scared that you would be mad at me.

In this instance the girl felt judged by the psychologist and later by her therapist. She was very sensitive to any indication of being rejected and interpreted it as failure on her part if she was not totally accepted by an adult. When the psychologist was perceived as being judgmental and negative, the client's performance deteriorated. When the client sensed disapproval by her therapist, she felt rejected and abandoned. These feelings were manifested quickly and threatened the relationship so carefully forged in the treatment. It was important for the therapist to acknowledge the disappointment the girl felt in her and to apologize. This step does not mean the interpretation was incorrect; just that it was premature.

Reenactment of Issues

The above example exemplifies the process of reenactment of issues within the therapy session. The session is often an arena where similar behaviors, which occur naturally in various situations the client encounters, are acted out. The client described above was very sensitive to any sign of abandonment or rejection. When she felt threatened, she inevitably became angry and rejected the person before any feared rejection could occur.

When an issue is hot, delicate handling is necessary to prevent flight or damage to the relationship. Hot issues can be identified by emotions that appear to be more intense then would be expected. When these instances occur, it is important for you to move carefully and slowly. In the above example the client needed to hear the therapist apologize for her error. The therapist's willingness to admit an error reassured the client as to the therapist's commitment.

This change in tactics by the therapist does not mean abandoning the idea of the client's sensitivity to rejection. Rather, exploration of the concept was delayed until the client signaled readiness. This opportunity arose several sessions later and is illustrated in the following excerpt.

C: It has been a difficult couple of months for you. You have shown a willingness to try new things and explore feelings which are pretty scary. You have succeeded in the class which was most difficult for you because in the past you perceived the instructor as disliking you. You found out that he did care about you but didn't like how you disrupted his class. How does it feel for you to hear me say these things?

Girl: It's still scary for me. I guess I feel that I will disappoint you.

C: You can't disappoint me—only yourself. I'm here no matter what.

Girl: That has helped me to do this. But I still get afraid of losing you.

C: Do you remember the time I asked you to be tested by the psychologist you disliked? Do you remember how you felt?

Girl: I remember being so scared that you would give up on me and that nothing could ever help me.

C: So your problems were so terrible that no one could help?

Girl: Yes—that's how it felt. When you said that I was looking for him to reject me, I thought you were talking about you and me.

C: It takes a lot of courage for you to face up to these scary feelings now. What is different for you?

Girl: I know that some of my problems are because I look for people to reject me and I find they do. It's hard for me to admit it and I still feel it will happen. But now I try to wait until the feeling passes and try it anyway.

Through several sessions between the testing incident and the preceding session, the client practiced examining her fear of rejection and looking at what could happen if she went ahead and did the feared action anyway.

This change in behavior took courage and was possible because of the relationship built up over several sessions. The therapist was able to demonstrate to her that she would not be abandoned if she made a mistake or was less than perfect. As sessions continued, she became stronger and more able to tolerate imperfections in herself and others.

Conclusions

This chapter outlined some important components of the process of therapy. While no book can provide you with examples for every occasion, the basic tenets are present in any therapeutic relationship. The beginning therapist can make many mistakes in the words that are used but as long as the child/adolescent knows the relationship is intact, these mistakes can be rectified.

Therapy is work for both the therapist and the client. If you find yourself becoming bored in a session or having your attention diverted from the task at hand, it is likely that the work is not progressing and a roadblock has been established. It is important at that point to shake up the process and find out what is occurring in the session. The therapeutic relationship will take the treatment only so far. After both parties feel fairly secure in the relationship, the real work begins through the use of interpretation, confrontation, and working through conflict. Therapy is a process that only begins in the session. You know the process is continuing beyond the session when your client begins to think about what you have discussed. Helping the child/adolescent understand that this process takes time and will take hard work often assists in helping them through the false starts that can occur.

This chapter focused mostly on adolescent treatment. The next chapter discusses techniques that are useful with younger children. Some of the techniques can be successfully modified for older children.

7

The Use of
Play and Games
in Therapy

Play and board games can assist in the work of therapy. The needs of the child determine the type of activity selected. For some children treatment can be directly through exploring feelings and concerns by talking. For most children additional techniques are needed to help the child discuss problematic areas. These techniques include the use of dollhouses, puppets, drawings, role-playing, and board games. Some of the techniques can be adapted for use with both younger and older children while others are most appropriate with one or the other age group. This chapter discusses the use of these various play materials within the therapeutic context.

Play

Play has been defined as an activity that is motivated solely by a desire to have fun (Erikson, 1950). As such, play has no purpose other than pleasure. Play can include an element of "make-believe," which allows for fanciful distortion of reality to express feelings that are not generally accepted in everyday life. In contrast to many activities children engage in, play is not structured by an outside authority. It is directed by the child as he or she invents the activity. Play also follows a developmental curve in that very young children may unknowingly blur the lines between reality and fantasy while older children are easily able to distinguish between the two. Moreover, as children develop, their peers become more and more important in their play activities (Semrud-Clikeman & Hynd, 1990). In fact, healthy development requires the child to make the leap from individual to cooperative play.

Play is frequently used by children to act out developmental steps. For example, a child may pretend that to be leaving home is going to "work;" or the child may act out feelings of curiosity through the common childhood act of playing doctor. Basic developmental tasks, such as separation-individuation, mastery of anxiety, and environmental exploration, have been suggested to be resolved through play (Berlin, 1986). Because play is such a large part of a child's life, it is a useful therapeutic technique. While play is particularly useful with children who are unable or unwilling to discuss their concerns, it can be helpful with any child. Therapeutic play can include the use of puppets, a dollhouse, clay, and drawing.

Play as an Ice Breaker

When selecting an activity, the clinician needs to be aware of the child's needs. For some children a direct-face-to-face encounter with an adult can be anxiety-producing. The use of a game or play activity can take the anxiety out of the situation and allow the child to relax enough to enter into conversation. Many children/adolescents may have difficulty opening up during the first session. Others will not want to be at the session, and the person making the referral is often someone other than the client.

For example, a student of mine was seeing a 14-year-old girl who was brought to treatment by her mother. The daughter frequently challenged the authority of the mother, skipped school, and was making friends with girls the mother considered to be "problems." The girl came to the first session very sullenly and responded to the overtures made by the student clinician with one-word answers. This uncomfortable situation continued until the student offered the girl a chance to draw. As she drew pictures, she was more willing to share information about herself. Midway into the session the girl volunteered that she really enjoyed dancing. The student clinician picked up on this interest and the girl agreed to bring some cassette tapes to the next session to help teach the clinician to dance. Not only did this action help the girl to talk about herself, it provided a vehicle to engage her in the treatment and assist her in coming to the next session.

Play as Self-Expression

For some children play can be most helpfully utilized to assist them in playing out their feelings. Because there is an "as if" quality to play, feelings that would not ordinarily be acceptable to express can be played out. Feelings of intense anger, destruction, or fear can be expressed because they are "pretend." Feelings of insecurity and anger were present in an 11-year-old client seen by the author. His mother had a diagnosis of "borderline personality disorder" and had been reported to Child Protective Services several times for temper outbursts toward her child. His father was ineffectual and unable to shield the son from the mother. This child experienced significant feelings of anger toward his mother, feelings that were not safely expressed. He also had a bravado which made it difficult for him to admit any weakness to the therapist. The following excerpt is from a session conducted during the middle of the Gulf War.

Child: I'd like to kill that Hussein! He's really bad. I'm going to take the wolf puppet and shoot him—pow pow.

C: That will teach him. How does it feel to shoot him?

Child: Really good. He's evil and should be killed. I hate him. Pow Pow.

C: You are tougher than him—it must feel good to be powerful.

Child: Pow Pow. I'm going to cut off his head and wipe him out. Bush should go over there and teach him a lesson.

C: So President Bush is going to give him what he deserves?

Child: Yes—you be Hussein and I'll be Bush and shoot you.

C: AAAAAH! That hurts—you shot me.

Child: Yes you deserve it. I'm going to trample on you. Take that! *(He pushes the puppet's head down and beats on it.)*

C: He's a bully isn't he?

Child: Yes, I hate bullies.

C: Bullies are people who try to beat up on you and don't care how you feel.

Child: Take that Pow Pow.

C: How does it feel to beat up on that bully?

Child: I like it. I'm going to twist off your head now.

C: OOOOW! Please don't hurt me anymore. I'm afraid of you.

Child: It feels good to hurt you—I'm not going to stop.

C: Please don't. I can't fight you now. I'm just a child—you shouldn't hurt me.

Child: Why not? I'm bigger and stronger.

C: So people who are bigger have a right to hurt you?

Child: Yes. You have to have someone there to help you and you are weaker than me. *(Here he has switched from being the person beating up the bully to the bully himself—there is real confusion for him as to which he feels like being.)*

C: How does it feel when someone bigger than you hurts you?

Child: I don't care—it doesn't matter.

C: When someone who is stronger hurts me, I get pretty mad at them—sometimes so mad I wish they would die.

Child: I feel that way too sometimes. But then I just go play with my action figures.

C: It's hard to be mad at someone who is supposed to take care of you. Sometimes it feels worse than the hurt they give you.

In this case the boy was torn between anger at his mother and the feelings of love he believed he should have toward her. Moreover, he felt let down by his ineffectual father. The puppets allowed him to express all of these feelings and he was able to tolerate some beginning attempts at interpretation of the feelings. Puppets can often provide an opportunity to begin exploring areas which would otherwise be untouchable for a client.

Puppets

Puppets are frequently used in therapy; children as young as three use them in fantasy and storytelling. Puppets can range from manufactured ones to hand-crafted ones made out of socks or paper bags. Children often enjoy making the puppets with you, which can be of therapeutic value. Old tube socks painted with fabric paint can be used for puppets. These puppets can be made to fit the child's own life story. As in the case above, some children may prefer to use animal puppets to act out their plays. You need to be willing to join in the play and let the child direct the action until the time is appropriate for you to introduce some reality into the game. If you attempt to introduce this reality prematurely, the child will either ignore your attempt or disagree. Neither of these occurrences is a problem, as you can move back into the play and continue as if there were no interruption.

Puppets can also be used to help the especially shy and withdrawn child to begin talking. Some children are very fearful of new experiences and will cry during the first few sessions. They may be afraid to separate from their parents and a puppet can be used to draw them into the session without directly confronting them. One such instance was a three-year-old girl beginning therapy at the order of the court. She had found her mother shot to death in her bed. The girl had been experiencing nightmares and an inability to separate from her grandmother.

The girl came to the first session with her grandmother and refused to come with the therapist. She also refused to let her grandmother accompany her to the therapy room. Fortunately, the therapist was able to utilize the waiting room since it was empty at the end of the day. Puppets were brought into the waiting room and the clinician selected a puppy puppet.

C: Bow-wow. I'm here all alone and looking for a friend. Have you seen a little girl here?

Child: *(sniffling)*

C: I'm looking for my friend. She was here a little while ago? Have you seen her, Grandmother?

Grand: I saw her in here.

C: Here's a little girl. *(approaching the little girl)* Will you be my friend?

Child: *(snuggling close to her grandmother)*

Grand: See the little puppy—he wants to be friends—can you be his friend?

Child: MmMm.

C: Oh good—Do you want to pet me?

Child: OK.

C: Oh, that feels good. Would you like to hold me? *(Hands the puppet to the little girl and takes the lamb puppet.)*

Child: Ruff. I'm a little puppy.

The session continued in the waiting room. For the next session, the clinician came with both puppets and the girl took the puppy. They began talking about taking a walk together and during the third session the girl was able to come with the clinician to the therapy room with the grandmother. After a few more sessions, the child was able to come to the sessions alone.

Dollhouses

Virginia Axline (1947) was one of the first therapists to utilize play and toy materials to stimulate fantasy in therapy. Since that time dolls and dollhouses have become increasingly popular in treatment. Dollhouses which have

movable furniture and dolls of various ages and sexes can provide sufficient flexibility for children with differing needs. While dollhouses large
enough to be used as the therapist and child sit on the floor are most life-
like, smaller dollhouses which are on a table can be helpful. The most important ingredient is that the child and therapist can join together in the
fantasy. The therapist needs to be able to play act with the child and leave
some of his or her "adultness" behind. It is important to allow the child to
play with the dollhouse and not to get too caught up in interpreting the
child's play. It may take several sessions before the child will be able to
tolerate any type of interpretation or questioning of the play.

A four-year-old boy was referred to the author because of concerns about
his adjustment. He was unable to play cooperatively with his peers, actively defied his parents and preschool teachers, and had developmental
delays in fine-motor and language skills. He was enrolled in an early childhood special education program at one of the author's assigned schools. A
large dollhouse with a mother, father, brother, and small boy doll was presented to the child during his first session.

C: You can use any of the dolls you want as long as you don't wreck any
of the toys. Now which ones do you want?

Child: All.

C: Tell me their names.

Child: OK, here's mommy, daddy, Chipper, and Bud. You take Chipper and
mommy. *(Child's name is Bud.)*

C: Where are you Bud? Mommy wants to see you.

Child: I'm playing up here—wheee—*(slides down the roof).* I'm sooo tall. Come
on up here Chipper.

C: I'm coming. We are so high up—I'm scared to be up here.

Child: It's OK. They won't find us and we can see so far!

C: Here comes Mommy.

Child: She's dumb—I've got the power in my eyes and she can't see us yet.

C: Are we invisible?

Child: Yes, we can do anything we want.

C: What's going to happen now?

Child: The house is going to blow up. BOOM! There it goes.

The sessions continued throughout that quarter. The child continued to
blow up the house with Chipper and him outside of the house. As the sessions

continued, it became evident there was a lot of fighting in the home and the child literally felt that the house could blow up at any time. Conferencing with his parents brought these conflicts to the surface and they became more aware of how their conflicts contributed to the boy's difficulty with behavioral control and challenges to their authority. Paradoxically, the boy was attempting to so focus attention on himself and problems he was provoking that his parents wouldn't concentrate on their own difficulties, thus preventing a split. Although the child was most likely unaware of what divorce is, he was picking up on threats to his own stability and family unit.

The dollhouse provided the therapist with cues to the source of the child's discomfort. Parent interviews had not provided information as to the state of their marriage or of an impending divorce. At the follow-up conference, both parents began coming to grips with thoughts they had individually been having about divorcing and the family was referred outside of the school for marital treatment.

Planning the Session

When selecting the type of play activities to utilize for the session, it is important to conceptualize your goals. Ask yourself questions such as the following: What is my purpose for the session? What is my goal? What types of materials may facilitate the accomplishment of that goal? These questions will help you sketch out your session. If the child has themes of aggression, providing him or her with materials which will bring out such themes can allow exploration of the child's feelings within the therapeutic setting. If the difficulties include faulty relationships with parents, teachers, and/or peers, then setting up a storyboard or dollhouse which can provide a backdrop for these problems will be helpful. The goals set forth in the case formulation should direct the therapy and provide direction for each session.

Role-Playing

Role-playing allows the child to take on a role without the use of puppets or dolls. Some children are readily able to pretend they are someone else or somewhere else. This technique is not appropriate for children who are very self-conscious or shy as they are not readily able to enter into the make-believe. For children who are able to play-act, this technique can be used to help them practice skills, try out new skills in a safe place, and take on other people's roles.

Role-playing is particularly useful in helping a child see what it might feel like to take another person's place. For example, a child who has difficulty complying with adult direction can role-play the adult while the therapist plays the child. Not only does the child begin to experience the frustration the adult has with him or her, the child can also see what he or she looks like when thwarting the adult. Sometimes this self-realization can assist in change as the therapist and child role-play another way to react. The therapist can model a different way of behaving when the child gives directions that are not followed. The therapist may express his dislike of the direction verbally rather than acting it out as the child has done in the past. The child's experience as the adult can also be discussed in terms of what the child would like the adult to do. In addition, the therapist can mirror the child's typical behavior and help the child explore how it feels to see himself or herself. By mirroring the behavior the therapist may assist the child in finding alternative ways to react to the adult's directions.

In addition to being used as a mirror for the child's behavior, role-playing can be used to help the child practice for a particularly difficult confrontation. For example, if a child needs to request help from a teacher and is unsure how to ask for it, the clinician can help the child formulate what he or she wants to say and then practice. One child seen by the author needed help to plan out how to ask his teacher directions when he didn't understand the assignment. He was afraid to approach the teacher because he thought the teacher would think he was "stupid." He was told to think of different times when he might need help and ways to go about getting help. The clinician practiced with the child and coached him on ways of approaching the teacher. With the child's permission the clinician also approached the teacher and briefed him on the goals the child had set to change his behavior.

The use of role-playing can also be utilized for a child to practice a new skill such as asking another child to play a game. In this scenario the clinician may role-play how to ask someone to play. Different situations can be presented and the child helped to solve the problem. What can he or she do if the other child refuses? What could be behind such a refusal? What does the child do then—ask someone else, play alone, get mad, etc.? In each case the clinician can help the child select appropriate alternatives. The following example illustrates a role-playing activity. A 14-year-old male was referred for therapy because he was having significant difficulty with his peers. His behaviors at times were inappropriate and he did not appear to understand how they would alienate other children.

P S-C: Let's try something a bit different today. You said some kids in your class have been calling you names and giving you a hard time at the lunch break. Why don't I play you and you act out how they treat you.

Joe: Do you want me to do the same things they do?

P S-C: Yes, just like it happened yesterday during lunch.

Joe: OK.

P S-C: I'm walking along the hall chewing gum.

Joe: Here he comes again—he looks just like a pig.

P S-C: What did you say to me?

Joe: I said you are a pig—you eat like a pig and look like one too.

P S-C: Oooh! You're a pig too. Why don't you just shut-up.

Joe: Make me!

P S-C: I don't have to. Just leave me alone. Why do you keep bothering me?

Joe: I don't like being near you.

P S-C: So stay away. Don't bother me and I won't bother you. OK now, let's talk about this. What was it like to be the kids bothering you?

Joe: It hurts—why can't they let me alone?

P S-C: I think they like to bother you and you contribute to the problem in some ways by how you eat. I observed the lunch room the other day and what do you think I saw?

Joe: I don't know—what were you doing—spying on me?

P S-C: No, I wanted to see what was going on. Some kids are really mean and I'd like to help you figure out what you need to do to avoid such problems since they won't go away.

Joe: Oh. Well, what did you see?

P-SC: You were eating with your mouth full and spilled some things down the front of your shirt.

Joe: The food must have been messy.

P S-C: Well, that's true but let's think together about what would make this problem improve.

Board Games

Games are a type of play and generally involve an aspect of competition (O'Connor, 1991). Successful game-playing requires a child to be able to delay impulses, take turns, and understand the rules of the game. As such, board games require a certain level of maturation. Children begin learning games that can be played without teams such as Red Rover Red Rover or Duck, Duck, Goose and graduate to games that require more cooperation such as baseball and dodge ball.

Some believe that game-playing is a teaching tool for later social development (Sutton-Smith & Roberts, 1971). It has been hypothesized that through the playing of games children learn socially acceptable ways to handle winning and losing as well as cooperative skills such as taking turns and working toward a common goal (Serok & Blum, 1982). Children who are adept at game-playing may more readily succeed in social interactions because they are able to anticipate others' actions and adjust their reactions to fit the situation.

Recess is a time which can be the most difficult part of the school day for some children. In fact, some children I worked with would deliberately misbehave or not complete their seatwork in order to avoid going outside for recess. Recess was so aversive for these children that they would find almost any excuse, including being sick, for not going on the playground. For some of these children the reason they did not succeed at recess was because they either didn't have social skills or if they did, didn't know how to put them into practice. These social difficulties will be discussed in a later chapter. Other children lacked basic playing skills such as taking turns, learning the rules of a game, or inhibiting their impulses.

The use of board games in therapy can help break the ice, begin a therapeutic alliance, and assist children in learning basic interpersonal skills. Games incorporate many of the skills needed in relating to others. They provide a microcosm of society in dealing with competition, authority, rule-governed behavior, development of strategies, and impulse control. Different games can touch on varying behaviors. Some games require strategy and skill for success while others are games of chance and luck, thus diminishing the advantage the adult may have.

Games such as checkers, *Stratego*, and *Monopoly* require strategy and foresight in order to win. Other games, such as *War, Candyland, Sorry*, and *Trouble*, have more to do with luck than with skill. These differences can help with different children. A child who feels he or she cannot win no matter what he or she does will not relate well to an adult who chooses a game requiring skills above the child's developmental level. Likewise a child who picks up on an adult's boredom with a game will seek to end the interchange and come away from the session without feeling valued. Therefore, it is important not only to choose the game to fit the situation but to also be *available* to the child during the game-playing. Some adults will allow the child to win a game. This strategy can easily backfire and if caught in the deception, the clinician will need to reestablish trust with the child. My advice is to play the game loosely and when the opportunity for winning is obvious, then you need to win and deal with the end result.

One eight-year-old the author worked with preferred checkers to any other game even though she was not able to win. Since she insisted on playing this game, the author believed she had a need to master her concern about winning as well as issues concerning authority. By mastering these anxieties in game format, she was practicing dealing with these concerns for later opportunities in her daily life. By the author's mirroring of winning with grace, the child was able to deal with her feelings of inadequacy. Teachers reported that she was improving in her need to boss other children around in games and in helping other children not as adept at playing a game. Some of the comments the author would make during their game-playing were later observed when the girl was playing with other children. Statements such as "you sure are trying hard" and "that was a good move" replaced such former statements as "that was a dumb move" or "you sure are stupid!"

In another case a boy of 15 was referred because of problems with respect toward his teachers. He would put them down in front of the class for any type of error committed in the classroom. Because he was very bright, he often found mistakes that other children might miss. He was reluctant to talk during the sessions so the clinician brought the game *Stratego* to the second session. This game was not one the clinician was particularly adept at and she believed the boy would do very well at this task. In this manner it was hoped that she could set up a true situation where the boy would triumph over her and yet see a different way of handling failure. It was hypothesized in the case formulation that the boy rejected any type of failure or weakness in others for the very reason he was subconsciously afraid that he would fail or be weak. He saw adults around him as "weak" if they were unable to stand up to him. Such weakness was a sign to this boy that the adult wouldn't be able to "take care" of him; a fear he harbored since he had been abandoned by his father. The clinician hoped to show that losing (failing) wasn't necessarily bad or a sign of weakness.

The boy won the first game easily and crowed over the clinician. He asked the clinician if she had allowed him to win. When reassured that she indeed had tried her best, he gloated even more. The clinician pretended to be hurt and teased him about his putting her down: "After all I'm the adult and I should win!" "Yes, but you didn't—I won." "I guess that makes you stronger than me." As the sessions continued, the clinician would use humor during the sessions when she would win. She would also provide self-soothing statements to herself such as "That wasn't a good move, but I know I can do better next time." When the clinician finally won a game, the boy was able to provide support about the win and give her congratulations.

Cheating

There is always a question about how to handle a child's cheating at a game during therapy. Children often check out reality and boundaries by trying behaviors they *know* are not acceptable. If the adult colludes with them on ignoring limits, the child may feel a loss of comfortable structure or he or she may feel too much in control of a situation. I feel it is always proper to bring attention to the behavior—not to correct or punish but to talk about it. The following excerpt illustrates a way to handle cheating.

Child: One, two, three, four, five. See I moved five spaces.

C: Mmm. I count only four spaces.

Child: Well, yes but this is a better place to be.

C: Yes, that's true and I'm sure that's where you would like to end up. What do you think we should do?

Child: We could pretend I only had a four on the dice.

C: Yes, that's true. On my turn then can I pretend to get any number I want?

Child: No—that's not fair.

C: It's fair for you but not for me?

Child: OK, I'll move five spaces.

In this case the child was gently confronted about the breach in rules. While the rules were not strictly enforced, the child was confronted with the change he made to the rules as well as the issues of fairness and feeling for the other person's point of view. Another child dealt with this dilemma in another way.

Child: I'm going to move here and you go here.

C: Mmm—I'm confused. Why would we do that?

Child: Well, let's make up our own rules. I think you should go two spaces and I'll go two spaces this way. I think that would be a good way to do it.

C: OK, will we always play it this way?

Child: Yes—you go two and I'll go two.

For this child, the need for autonomy and choice was paramount and could be easily accommodated within the therapeutic setting. There was no need to impose other rules into the session as both parties agreed on the new rules. When the child attempted to change the rules to fit a new situation, the clinician was provided an opportunity to talk about choices and how hard it can be to stay with a choice made.

Thus, cheating does not need to become an issue unless you attempt to enforce rules as would be done in the outside world. The therapeutic alliance is all about changing behaviors and expectations and that applies to rules as well as to feelings. By empowering the child/adolescent to develop her or his own rules, the therapist allows her or him the freedom to explore other options to the ways they have behaved in the past.

Board games can be utilized to help children deal with conflictual feelings within a safe environment. Issues, such as winning, losing, and testing one's mettle, are life dilemmas that need to be faced and resolved throughout life. Developmentally, it can be just as problematic for a child who is always seen as failing as for a child who is always seen as winning or never given the opportunity to fail. Struggling with these questions within the therapy session can enable the child/adolescent to seek answers when similar situations present themselves in everyday life. You need to resolve for yourself how you react to failure and success before assisting your young clients to deal with these opportunities for learning in life.

Board games can serve as a background for discussion of feelings. There are therapeutic games available such as the *Thinking, Feeling, and Talking Game* and *Conversations*. These games can be useful for some clients but for many children they are transparent attempts to get at feelings some children are not willing to disclose easily. For other children, these commercial games can provide models for talking about feelings. You may wish to utilize one of these games and observe how the child/adolescent reacts to such devices. The following section discusses the use of word games to try to evaluate a child's feelings and fantasies more subtly.

Informal Games

Word games provide an opportunity to explore feelings that may be too painful or not available for expression by the child/adolescent using traditional methods. Word games can be introduced to the child as games of imagination. Many children enjoy playing these games, particularly when the clinician joins in. While some of these games are more appropriate for older children, most of them can be adapted for younger children with the clinician serving as the scribe. The following paragraphs describe different types of word games I have used. You may well want to adapt these games to your own purposes or come up with your own ideas. The most important tenet is that the child provide the majority of the ideas with appropriate prompting from the clinician.

Scribble Games

Winnecott (1971) developed a scribble game for use with children and adolescents. The concept of his game is to initially have the child draw a scribble and then fill in the scribble by making it a picture of something. For instance, a scribble that looks like a circle with lines inside can be made into a face. Then the child completes a scribble the clinician provides. Winnecott suggested that what the child sees and makes of the scribble may provide clues to material that is anxiety-producing for the child. The clinician can then talk about the scribble with the child, using gentle probes about what the scribble may represent for the child.

This scribble game was used with a five-year-old African American girl referred for treatment. Concern had been expressed by her kindergarten teachers that she was very impulsive, clingy to adults, and requiring great amounts of reassurance. Her mother was divorced and described her ex-husband as abusive to both the mother and the girl. There was a restraining order in place preventing any contact. The little girl was very open to coming and bonded immediately to the clinician. She hung on the clinician, demanding attention at all times. She was coaxed to sit down and play a scribble game. The girl complied, giggling all the time and stating that she wasn't able to scribble at school on her papers.

Child: This is fun! How do we play?

C: First you draw a scribble and then I'll make a picture.

Child: OK. *(She draws a circle with squiggles on either side of it.)*

C: Let's see now—what could this be? Mmmm. I think I could make these squiggles look like pigtails and the circle could be a face. What do you think?

Child: Yes, it's a girl like me. Can you make her look like me?

C: Sure—what color should I make her hair?

Child: Well, black I guess.

C: What should I make her mouth do?

Child: She can be mad.

C: Can you draw it for me? OOO that looks mad. I wonder why she's so mad.

Child: She's not mad—she's happy.

C: Maybe she's mad and happy too. I'm confused. What should we do with the eyes—can you draw them for me?

Child: OK, I'm going to make them really big. See her face—her mouth is mad but her eyes are smiling.

C: That must be hard for her. I wonder if you ever feel confused like that. *(long pause)* Sometimes kids can feel mad but can't let other people know they are mad. Do you ever have that happen?

Child: Uh-huh. Sometimes I am really mad when my teacher tells me what to do.

C: What happens then?

Child: She's mad at me and yells—sometimes I have to leave the room.

C: How come?

Child: Don't know.

C: Mm. Well, let's do another one. I'll make the scribble this time and you make it into something. *(Makes a scribble that looks like a long road or curvy snake).*

Child: I know what this is—it's the hall at my school. See here I'm making doors and here are the coats.

C: Yes, I can see it just like you said. What is this little dot here?

Child: Oh that's me—I am out in the hall.

C: All by yourself?

Child: Mmm. Here's my face, and my hands, and my legs.

C: I see it. What's your face doing?

Child: These are the tears here—I'm all by myself.

C: It must be hard to feel like you are all by yourself. Sometimes when kids feel all alone, they will try to have an adult pay attention no matter what.

This child was so in need of attention and reassurance that she would go to any lengths to get them. She often misbehaved in order to get her needs met and yet the price she paid for the misbehavior served to reinforce her unspoken belief that she wasn't worthy of attention (and love). Eventually there was an opportunity for the clinician and girl to explore her feelings toward her father's leaving as well as the concurrent emotional loss of her mother while the mother struggled to deal with her emotional issues and her need to work full-time. One of the goals established in the treatment was to help the teacher and mother understand the crux of the child's misbehavior and to provide reassurance and attention when signs were raised that the girl was feeling stressed.

Scribble Stories

As the girl became more comfortable in the situation, we moved into using scribbles to tell stories. Since she couldn't write at this point, she would draw scribbles and then the clinician and the girl would translate the scribbles into language. These scribbles were put together into a small booklet the girl would ask for on subsequent sessions. The booklet eventually was given a cover which the girl decorated.

Child: Can we do a story today?

C: Sure—here's your book. Do you want to start or should I?

Child: I'll start. Let's see—*(she begins to draw looping scribbles and talking as she draws).* There once was a little kitty and she was walking in the forest all by herself. She was happy and smiling and singing.

C: Why was she so happy?

Child: Well, it was her birthday and her mom and dad were baking her a cake and had lots of presents for her.

C: So she was looking forward to her party.

Child: Mmm. They'll all be together and hug and kiss.

C: That's a nice story. What happens next?

Child: She gets home and finds her daddy is missing. Now she's crying.

C: What happened to her daddy?

Child: I don't know—I don't like this story any more—let's do something else.

C: OK—in a minute—I'm wondering how it felt to lose her daddy and not know why?

Child: The kitty was scared—she was a bad kitty. Bad, bad, bad. She should be sent to her room with no cake.

C: Ooh—she was a bad kitty then—did her daddy leave because she was bad?

Child: Maybe—he's gone and she's all alone.

C: I'll bet she felt sad and scared too—maybe a little bit mad because he left her all alone.

Child: Mmm. He's not coming back.

C: What the little kitty is is really really good.

Child: Oh she can't be good—she's a bad kitty. I don't want to do this any-more—let's play this game.

Several more sessions were needed to help the child begin to explore her feelings of abandonment. The stories continued and she enjoyed having them written down so that she could look at them on some sessions. Sometimes she would ask the clinician to tell her the story again. As she grew in her ability to handle some of these painful feelings, the clinician began to introduce incomplete stories into the treatment program.

Incomplete Stories

Incomplete stories can assist you in setting the stage for exploring areas you believe are important to the child or adolescent's treatment. Structuring the stories in such a way so as to evaluate hypotheses contained in the case formulation can assist in the treatment.

This technique requires the child to complete a story the clinician begins. They may take turns adding details to the story and the clinician can ask questions to assist in steering the stories in helpful ways. The following excerpt was utilized with the above child.

C: Once a girl lived with her mother in a big apartment building. The girl went to school and had friends. Her name was Keshia. Her mother worked a lot and Keshia couldn't see her very much. One day Keshia was at day care and her mother was very late in picking her up. What happened next?

Child: Keshia waited and waited and still no mommy. She started running around the room and yelling. Her teachers were really mad at her and told her to stop it. "No, no . . . I want to go home—call my mommy and tell her to come and get me." Keshia started to cry and her teachers just got madder and madder.

C: Why did Keshia think her mom was so late?

Child: She didn't know—why don't the teachers call her mom and find out. *(The child becomes more and more animated at this time and begins roaming around the room. Eventually she settles down and sits on the clinician's lap.)*

C: It's hard to have to wait. Sometimes when people are late, I wonder if they are coming at all?

Child: Mmm. What if she fell into the subway? Maybe she'll never come.

C: Then what would happen to the little girl? She'd be all alone—first her dad leaves and then her mom.

Child: Mmm. She's really getting scared.

C: Let's pretend her mom comes in the door just now—what does the girl do?

Child: She runs to the mom and hugs her as tight as she can.

C: Then what happens?

Child: The mommy pushes her away—"Don't hug me so tight, girl—let me sit down—I'm tired." Keshia just holds on tighter.

C: So her mommy doesn't really know how scared she was. Let's pretend that Keshia can now tell her how she feels. What would you like to see happen?

Child: I'd like the mommy to hold Keshia in her lap and tell her it's OK.

This information can be utilized to assist the mother and teachers understand why the girl is acting out—understanding that her need for high activity is a reaction to the anxiety of being alone and abandoned. These areas of concern for this little girl were brought to the fore every time she imagined something might have happened to her mother. After all, her father had disappeared—why not her mother?

Incomplete stories can help to shed light on areas of concern as well as assisting the child to use fantasy to cope with some of the fears. By exploring these areas as well as assisting the child to imagine a different outcome, the clinician can model coping methods. In the example the clinician helps the child explore what it would be like for her need for reassurance to be met. In other sessions the clinician can assist the girl in thinking about how she can soothe herself as her anxiety mounts. The clinician can alert the mother and teachers to the girl's need to act out her fears, thus framing her needs in terms of emotions rather than willful misbehavior. Such a change in emphasis helps adults tolerate a child's needs and provide support to the child in need.

Incomplete Pictures

Just as incomplete stories can be utilized to help a child, incomplete pictures can also serve a purpose. You can provide a drawing with missing elements and have the child complete the picture. Another option is to have a magnetic board on which you can put figure outlines and background. Either one of these methods is effective. The drawing allows you to save the picture for later reference. I generally introduce the game to the child as a way of finishing a picture I started. With some children it is possible to work together while other children prefer to complete the picture themselves.

The first picture is often easily completed by providing stick figures without faces and having the child complete the expressions. You can ask the child to fill in the background as well as have him or her introduce activity into the picture. In all cases the child should be encouraged to make a picture of his or her own. This approach is more structured than the following technique of figure drawing.

Figure Drawing

A technique which has a long history is that of figure drawing (Martin, 1988). This method has been used in the past as part of a diagnostic process. Psychometric validity has been elusive for this technique and it is best used in conjunction with self-report or as a rapport builder rather than the basis for a diagnosis. In therapy, this approach is better conceptualized as a vehicle for adding dimension to the child's therapy and for exploring emotional areas of concern.

The beginning clinician may well be tempted to over-interpret the drawings provided by the child. Some projective drawing manuals interpret various actions as reflecting emotional conflict or problems. In therapy the best explanation for many of the pictures is the one the child gives you. It is, of course, important for you to explore the pictures in more detail than just having the child tell what is happening in the picture. I generally have children/adolescents draw me a picture of themselves, their best friend, their family, and finally something the family does together. Each of these drawings is done with little comment by me until all are completed. Then I ask about the picture: How is the child feeling? What makes him or her feel that way? What is the child doing? What happened before the picture and what will happen next?

The following example shows the use of drawings in therapy. A boy of 13 was referred to the author to determine whether individual or family therapy was appropriate. He was often oppositional and resisted any restraints placed on him by his parents or teachers. He had recently begun staying out after curfew and refused to tell his parents where he had been. He was willing to talk with the author but expressed concern that she would "just take his parents' side."

C: I'd like you to draw me a picture of your family doing something together.

Child: This is stupid—Why do I have to do this?

C: I think it will help me to understand how things are for you. I'd like you to try to do this for me. I will share with you any ideas I have after we are all done. Does that sound fair to you?

Child: All right—but I still think this is stupid. (*He begins to draw a picture with his parents and younger brothers sitting on a couch watching television.*)

C: Where are you in the picture?

Child: I'm in the other room—behind this closed door here—do you want me to draw that too.

C: If you would.

Child: OK *(He draws a picture of him sitting on the bed reading a book.)*

C: That's good. Now I'd just like to ask you a couple of questions about your picture.

Child: Why?

C: It will help me to see things the way you do. How are the people on the couch feeling?

Child: Oh, they are OK—bored, I guess, but they like watching the TV. They have to watch what Dad likes—I guess Mom isn't too happy watching football but she'll go along with it anyway.

C: How come?

Child: Don't know. I guess she doesn't care anymore.

C: It must be hard for you to watch her feel that way.

Child: It just makes me really mad at him. He gets his way on everything.

C: And then you are in the other room. How come?

Child: I don't want to be near him—I have no say in watching the television and I just can't be quiet like the others when he starts to boss everyone around.

C: So you decided to be by yourself and do your own thing?

Child: It's easier. I can't wait until I can leave home—I only have a couple of years left and I can go away and not have him come after me.

C: So you are just trying to survive living there until you can legally leave home. What do you imagine you might do then?

Child: I don't know but at least I wouldn't have to put up with him anymore.

C: Would you draw me a picture which could show how you would like your family to be?

Child: That's hard—I've never really thought there was any way they could do anything else.

C: Can you try? *(Child begins drawing a picture of the family sailing on a boat together with everyone having a different job to do.)*

C: I wonder what it would be like to live like that?

Child: It won't ever happen.

C: Maybe not—but it won't happen if you never give your parents a chance to know how you feel.

Child: (becoming very angry) I knew you wouldn't understand—I've tried to tell them and they never listen.

C: It's a real risk to tell that what you would like and then have them ignore it—it might cause some boys to want to act out in anyway they could.

Child: It doesn't make any difference.

C: I'd like to share this drawing with them and see what their reaction is—would you like to be with me.

Child: I don't want to talk.

C: You wouldn't have to—just be there and listen.

Child: OK.

The family conference happened two weeks later with the boy attending. His parents were noticeably upset by the picture and his feelings. This session set the stage for work on communication skills. The boy's acting-out behavior continued for several more weeks. However, he continued to come to the sessions. When he was asked to draw another family picture a few months later, he had moved into the television room albeit next to the door. This change in the picture was interpreted to represent his cautious start at taking part in his family.

The use of drawings can serve a twofold purpose. They can work well to further session work as well as provide a record of changes throughout the therapy span. One case seen in our clinic involved a seven-year-old girl who was experiencing daytime soiling. Her parents had recently separated and she was experiencing stress over the change in her life. Although upset by the change, the expression of strong emotion was frowned on in this family so she actively denied any concerns. However, her drawings were of people smiling with tears rolling down their faces. When asked to describe these drawings, the girl was unable to tell how the people were feeling. Eventually she was more able to describe her feelings. Concurrent work was necessary with her mother to assist with her ability to deal with her daughter's feelings. Drawings during this period of treatment involved crying rainbows, suns, and fluffy white clouds; all objects generally thought to represent happiness in many children's drawings. Eventually the child's drawings began showing rain clouds and thunder and lightning; perhaps reflecting her own feelings of sadness and anger.

Ethical Considerations
The best policy is usually to be clear about sharing such drawings with parents and teachers. The first session that drawing is introduced is when

disclosure of these drawings should be discussed with the child/adolescent. It is appropriate to advise the child that the drawings will be kept within the sessions unless the clinician believes the child is felt to be in danger or likely to hurt others. In all other cases I let the child know that disclosure of her or his drawing will be done only *after* such sharing has been fully discussed with her or him. It is always good practice to discuss these ground rules with parents and secure agreement from them also.

Conclusions

This chapter discusses some techniques that can be utilized in therapy with children. Many of the techniques can assist with children who are reluctant to talk or who are unable to discuss their feelings. For further information about play therapy, the interested reader is referred to books by Virginia Axline (1947) and Bruno Bettelheim (1972). *Game Play: Therapeutic Use of Childhood Games* (Schaefer & Reid, 1986) is another good source of information concerning the use of games in therapy.

The use of storytelling, scribbles, and projective drawings can further the treatment when combined with dialogues from the child built around the pictures and stories. It is most important to be careful not to over-interpret or interpret too early what the child is expressing. Once the relationship is established, the child can handle your observations which may be off the mark. You must decide whether the child is not ready to hear the interpretation or if the interpretation is incorrect. If you can adopt a hypothesis-testing approach developed from the case formulation, then observations can be made to confirm or disprove goals developed for the treatment.

Many school and private clinicians have offices in different places. I find it helpful to put together a portable "therapy case." Such a case allows you to transport your materials so that they are handy for use. There is nothing more frustrating than finding some important items are at your other office. Your case can include markers, plain paper, puppets, a felt storyboard, and construction paper. You may also wish to bring games such as checkers, *Trouble, Connect Four, Candyland, Battleship,* and *Sorry* to selected sessions.

8

Termination
Issues

As with all good things, therapy must end. For some clients this realization is difficult while for others it is liberating. For any client, termination is as much of a process as treatment. It is important to prepare as carefully for the ending of the therapeutic relationship as for the sessions. Some of the difficulty in ending the relationship may have to do with your own difficulty with endings while other problematic areas are the client's concern about loss. For some children and adolescents you will have been one of the few adults who really listened and cared about them. When termination is appropriate, the client will have established other methods for dealing with his or her concerns.

Reasons for Ending Therapy

Sometimes treatment ends because the child moves to another school or is in the process of a natural transition from elementary school to middle school, and the school psychologist is not in both places. In the case of mental health clinics, treatment may end because insurance no longer covers services or because transportation to the clinic is problematic. For my graduate students, treatment may end for their clients at the end of the counseling practicum. Each of these reasons for ending can provoke different feelings in the child/adolescent and must be dealt with appropriately. Thus, each of these scenarios is briefly discussed in the following paragraphs.

Natural Transitions

Vacations

Therapy within the school system usually conforms to the school year. This means that each spring a natural transition is required for children in treatment to begin the summer vacation separate from the clinician. It is important to prepare the child for these transitions as carefully as you may for a child who is ending sessions because the work is complete. Many children have concerns about the change in their routine and require reassurance that you will remember them over the summer. It is important to build in at least four to six sessions to talk about the transition to the summer months. Helping the child to plan strategies to assist with problems that may arise during the summer is an important activity for these final sessions.

Discussions of feelings of loss and abandonment are also important for both of you. It is important to be aware of your own feelings of loss as well as those of the child. It is not uncommon for the child or adolescent to feel this loss even for naturally occurring vacations such as winter and spring breaks. Sometimes for the two weeks before summer break and the week before spring and winter break, students experience significant emotional problems stemming from their loss of routine and in some cases, the only stabilizing force in their life.

You are in a unique position to assist in sensitizing the school staff to commonly seen problems before vacations. Because many adults are also under stress prior to vacations, their tolerance for misbehavior may be at a minimum. It was a common experience that the Thursday and Friday before a major school break were often highly charged, with children and adolescents showing their feeling of stress with acting-out behavior. It made you dread the days preceding a vacation.

For some children and adolescents the vacations that most of us look forward to either were frightening because they would be in a dysfunctional setting 24 hours a day or there would be no adults available to them. For either of these problems, it is important for you to assist the child in planning alternative activities during the break. An astute clinician can find summer camps that can provide a respite for both the child and parents. Organized summer activities can also be brought to the parents' attention and the parents can be assisted in finding the most appropriate activity for their child and schedule. For parents without financial means, organizations, such as the Lions, Rotary, and other clubs, can be contacted for assistance with fees.

For adolescents, employment may assist with the long days of summer. It is important to assist some clients in thinking about their options for employment. You not only can assist in selecting places to apply for employment but also can discuss issues ranging from their manner of presentation to how to complete an application form. While helping the client plan for the vacation, you should begin talking about what it will be like for client and clinician not to see each other for a time.

For children where such cessation of services is not in their best interest, it is important to provide additional service either through the school system if the child qualifies for related services to special education or through community mental health clinics or private practitioners. If none of these options is available or viable, then you need to assist the parents in finding support for emergencies either through local hospitals or mental health workers. A last resort, and one which should be used sparingly, is to provide the parents with a person to call within the school system who works on an extended contract.

School Changes

There are two types of school changes—those caused by moving to another school system and those relating to natural changes from elementary to middle school or middle school to high school. We will first deal with the changes caused by a family move. In this case the child is losing not only his or her contact with you but also his or her peers, feelings of belonging, and participation in community activities. Moreover, the child's sense of security is challenged when a move requires changes in residence. Particularly problematic is when the child moves into another geographic region. Not only does the child need to change his or her home, he or she also may be moving to a place with different customs and climate.

One child seen by the author had moved over five times before her fifth-grade year. She was referred for counseling because of feelings of low self-esteem and inability to make friends. Sherry was able to talk about her feelings concerning the move and the need to start a fifth new school. Her affect was generally sad but resigned to what she felt was inevitable. She shared her conviction that it was a waste of time for her to make new friends as her family would move again in the near future. When asked if she had talked about her concerns with her parents, Sherry shared that they had enough to worry about without her adding to their problems. When the author asked her permission to speak with her parents, Sherry was hesitant but eventually agreed. The following excerpt is from the parent conference.

Mother: We are concerned about Sherry—she has always had friends before but now she can't seem to find anyone she likes.

Father: Sherry has always adjusted to the moves well and I don't know what is different this time.

C: What does she say about this school?

Mother: She just shrugs and says don't worry—I'll be OK.

C: Can you describe for me her reaction when you told her you would be moving?

Mother: Well, she didn't say much of anything. She just kind of sat there and said OK.

C: What had she done before other moves?

Mother: Well she cried and was difficult to handle for a while but then she would adjust, make new friends, and things would be OK.

C: How did she seem to you this time?

Father: She was very quiet and just started packing up her bedroom. We had a good-bye party and all her friends came to it.

C: Tell me what it's like for you here—it's a lot different in the midwest then in South Carolina.

Father: (laughing) Well we have had to buy new winter coats as it's so much colder here. Things cost more money too, so we have to watch our budget a little bit more closely than before. But we are adjusting to it I think.

C: How's it for you?

Mother: I think it's been harder for me because I don't meet people as easily staying at home. I haven't really gotten very involved in school activities, Campfire girls, or anything quite yet.

C: Have you been able to make friends yet?

Mother: Not really—my days really revolve around the girls and finding new doctors, dentists, and things like that.

C: It sounds kind of lonely.

Mother: (tearing up) It is. I had to leave my friends too and it's so much different here.

Father: I didn't know you were feeling so sad about it.

Mother: Well, you have enough to worry about, but with the holidays approaching I am feeling homesick at times.

C: I wonder if Sherry feels the same as you—that is, she doesn't feel able to grieve about her move because she senses how hard it has been on both of you.

Father: You mean she's protecting us?

C: It's possible—but she's also protecting herself from more hurt. She has decided it's safer not to make friends because you only leave anyway.

Father: I had no idea that she felt that way.

C: It seems that everyone in your family is protecting everyone else instead of talking about the natural feelings of loss and fear of new situations. I wonder what would happen if you allowed Sherry to see that you are sad but that you will be OK. In that way she may feel permission to grieve.

Father: My job requires moves in order to be promoted. I wonder now if I have been selfish about it.

C: It sounds like you have done the best you can. Maybe when the next move comes along, I can help with the transition planning.

It is important to engage in such transition planning when one of your clients is moving. I find it helpful, with parent permission, to contact the receiving school and to pave the way for an easier transition. I also find it helpful to imagine with the child what it will be like to be in the new school, meeting new friends and teachers. It is just as important to assist the child in saying good-bye to his or her friends and teachers. Such changes are easiest when accomplished at the end of the school year. When the change comes during the school year, then the child needs help to say good-bye. It is very appropriate to discuss feelings that often occur when leaving a place, such as sadness or, for some children, relief. I will, as appropriate, give the child a gift; sort of a talisman for the child to hold onto when feeling insecure. Some children ask to write to me and I give permission, providing them with the school address.

Moves within the School District

When children are due to move to the next school up, the clinician is provided with an opportunity to help with the transition, as well as provide the child with an opportunity to say good-bye. I encourage parents to take the child to the school for a visit before the end of the school year. Seeing a new school in the summer when no one is about gives the child a whole different feeling from seeing the school when it is inhabited. When the child visits the school, I have set up a meeting with the receiving therapist and arrange to be there for the introduction. In this way, I can serve as a bridge to the new school and the child has an idea of whom he or she will be seeing.

Following the visit, meetings with the child can include discussions as to what was different from expectations and what was the same. It is also possible to begin gently discussing the last sessions you will have with the child and to provide a framework for the work of termination. It is important that you terminate your relationship in order to allow the child to form a new relationship with the receiving clinician. Further discussion of the termination work will follow later in this chapter.

Artificial Causes

Some terminations occur because of forces that feel arbitrary to the client. In cases where children are seen in practicum classes which generally end after one or two quarters/semesters, it is the ethical responsibility of the clinician to find continued services if needed. It is also prudent for you to discuss the time-limitedness of the clinical contact at the *beginning* of the treatment with both the parents and the child. Reference to the number of sessions is important throughout the treatment not only to keep treatment goal-oriented but also to keep the fact of termination within the therapeutic work. Such time-limitedness can be therapeutically helpful as issues can be prioritized in terms of importance. If the child and/or parents are not provided information about the length of service, it is reasonable for them to expect the contacts will continue indefinitely.

In any case it is important to provide an estimate of how many sessions will be required for working on problems. Part of the case formulation should include an idea of working time needed. This time span may be adjusted, of course, as treatment proceeds. For children who are involved in practicum-based treatment, it is particularly important to discuss how many sessions will be involved. In addition, discussion should be pursued as to what procedures are in place if the child needs to continue in treatment after the practicum ends.

For children seeing a private practitioner, it is important to clarify with the parents how many sessions are covered by insurance. Moreover, discussion needs to be pursued as to what plans can be made if the child requires additional sessions. In this way all parties know the overall plan for payment. When the decision is for the treatment to be contained within the number of sessions provided by the insurance coverage, it is imperative that goals be adjusted to fit into the time span.

If best clinical practice requires additional sessions beyond the insurance coverage, then the need for these sessions should be explored with the parents sufficiently before the last session. It may be that sessions can be continued at a reduced fee or other accommodations can be made. In any case, you have an ethical responsibility to find a clinician to take over the case if you choose not to provide services at reduced fees. If these considerations are resolved prior to treatment beginning, there will be less turmoil and conflict added to an already emotion-laden situation.

The next section discusses how to determine when termination is appropriate and the procedures utilized for such a process.

The Process of Termination

Termination is as much a part of the therapeutic process as the relationship, therapy work, and interpretation. It is also the area of the process most overlooked by many beginning clinicians. Termination is an inevitable part of the process and in some sense begins during the first session. As mentioned earlier, the duration of therapy should be negotiated at the beginning of treatment. This part of the therapy contract can be renegotiated as appropriate as therapy continues. If termination is not discussed in the early stages of treatment, the client may assume the therapy is ongoing and has no end. This assumption is not helpful to the therapeutic work since emotionally needy clients will hold onto the sessions and not develop self-sufficiency.

Clinicians who collude with their clients in continuing sessions indefinitely may be promoting feelings of dependency and helplessness for clients (Koocher & Keith-Spiegel, 1990). If the goal of therapy is to assist the client in developing coping skills, then overdependence on the clinician is counterproductive. You need to be aware of your need to help. Although in many ways having a client dependent on you provides a rewarding feeling, it is important to continually assess whether the dependency fulfills client or *clinician* needs. This assessment is particularly important with children, who are dependent by definition. If unsure, you should consult with a colleague as to the nature of the therapeutic relationship.

The Timing of Termination

It is important to review periodically with the client the progress of the treatment. This review is appropriate for children as well as adolescents and adults. Such an examination can serve to move therapy forward as well as help determine if termination is appropriate.

If no natural break precipitates termination, then the clues will come from the therapy work itself. Obviously if all goals have been met, termination is appropriate. Unfortunately, this state of affairs rarely is that obvious. Hints of the appropriateness of ending the therapy are often present in the therapy sessions themselves. Some clients may inquire as to how many more times they will come to see you while others will bring fewer areas of concern to sessions. It is important to discuss at this point how much longer both of you feel treatment should continue.

At times the client may have made enough progress for the time being. It may be that time is needed for the client to consolidate the coping skills he or she has developed. For most clinicians and clients it is not possible for the treatment to continue until *no* problems in life are left. If the child/ adolescent has developed enough skills to function adequately, then it is time to discuss dismissal from treatment. One client of mine phrased it as needing a "vacation" from therapy. She was correct that it was time for her to try to live without the sessions and see how she would do.

Sometimes it can be as frightening for the clinician to let go as it is for the client. The clinician needs to periodically reassess where the child/adolescent is and how much longer the treatment needs to continue. The bond between therapist and client is bi-directional and can be as difficult for the therapist to cut as for the client. It is important to have insight into how your needs play into the continuing of treatment as well as the client's.

Clinician Initiated

For some clients even bringing up the topic of ending the sessions can provoke anxiety or even in some cases anger. If these emotions emerge, it is imperative that you examine them with the client, opening up a dialogue about what it will be like to not see you anymore. This process should be completed even when it may be premature for termination because it brings up the time-limited nature of the therapeutic relationship. For some clients, even discussing the loss of therapeutic relationship can bring up other situations where they felt loss or abandonment. However, even for these clients, you need to give the clear message that the client eventually will no longer need therapy.

You need to broach the idea of termination gently throughout the duration of treatment. It is important to explore how the client sees himself or herself functioning without the treatment. One of the most important signs that termination may be appropriate is the client's recognition of growing competence in evaluating life situations and arriving at solutions. For children and adolescents you need to evaluate their competence in coping compared to their developmental age.

If the client is not ready for ending the relationship, signs will be readily apparent in her or his reaction to even a suggestion for such an occurrence. Agitation, anger, and anxiety are normal reactions to termination and should be explored to determine if they are due to a fear of loss of the relationship or whether termination is truly premature. If the child/adolescent is unable to picture continuing without the therapy, then termination is probably premature. As treatment continues, you need to encourage the child/adolescent to imagine a time when she or he will no longer come to see you.

Client Initiated

At times termination is initiated by the client and may be abrupt. Such termination may be due to client dissatisfaction with progress, feelings of disappointment with the clinician, and/or extraneous circumstances. It is helpful for you to contact the client and parents to ask for a meeting to discuss the ending. Generally there are hints in the treatment that the client may be pulling back from the therapist or conversely that the therapist has become too close to the client, thus threatening the caretaker. An astute clinician will "pick up" on these hints. If these hints are not recognized until the client terminates the sessions, then the clinician needs to review the sessions in order to reconstruct hints provided as to the client's discontinuance of treatment. The following example is a case where the client laid down hints that were not picked up by the therapist until the client canceled her later sessions and terminated treatment. This client was a 16-year-old female in high school who was being seen in a private clinic for assistance with her relationship with men and her mother. This excerpt is approximately four months into the treatment.

Client: I went over to my friend's house the other night and she had forgotten that we had made plans. She had someone else there. I just left and when she called me I didn't answer the phone. I still haven't called her back.

C: You were very disappointed in her. She let you down.

Client: Yes, and when people do that I tend to write them off. I know that's cold but if I can't count on them, they are out.

C: So there's no chance of forgiveness for a mistake.

Client: No. I just don't talk to them again.

C: That's one way to protect yourself from getting too involved with anyone. Everyone must have disappointed you at times.

Client: Almost. For a while I think they really care but then in the end I find out that I don't matter.

C: So her forgetting your date translates into meaning that she doesn't care about you.

Client: Yes. Everyone in my life has disappointed me.

C: So you must wonder when anyone you are close to will follow that pattern and disappoint you.

Client: Mmmm.

For this client any disappointment caused her to leave the relationship. The clinician needed to have pursued this opening and applied it to the therapeutic relationship. At the time of the above incident the client had indicated she held the clinician in high regard. An astute clinician would have known that it was only a matter of time before the clinician would also disappoint the client. This situation, of course, occurred in the course of events. The clinician became ill and tried to call the client to cancel the appointment. The client never received the message and showed up at her appointed time. She canceled the next appointment. When the clinician called her, he could only reach her answering machine. The following day the client called the clinic and said she was discontinuing treatment. When the clinician finally reached the client at work to ask for one more session, the client was distant and would not discuss the possibility.

This case readily illustrates a client who terminates treatment for the very reason she sought treatment—her inability to tolerate any imperfection in a significant person in her life. The best solution would have been for her to return to treatment and to discuss what had occurred. As it stood, she would most likely seek out another therapist who in turn would disappoint her, thus starting the cycle over again. The best defense against such occurrences is to realize that past experiences described during treatment will reappear during the course of therapy.

Beginning to Say Good-bye

With children I suggest the ending as a type of "graduation," thus making the point that termination indicates success not just loss. Planning the graduation can make the ending more palatable as well as real. As the ending of your sessions is broached, you need to determine a date for the final session. By making the deadline unambiguous, you assist the child/adolescent in making the ending real. It is important to talk about how many sessions are left and to allow the client to express her or his feelings and thoughts about the process.

It is often beneficial to discuss how the child sees relationships after a person moves away. With younger and with less emotionally well-developed adolescents and adults, termination may touch on their fear of not existing for you in any existential sense. For these clients, you may find it helpful to provide reassurance to the child that he or she will continue to be important to you and part of your memory.

During your preparation of the child for the final sessions, you may be asked if the child will ever see you again. If you work in the school, you can certainly reassure them that you will continue working and they can stop and say hello. This feeling of continuity is helpful for many children, particularly those who are afraid of changes. Even adolescents I worked with who had moved on to high school seem to respond to such reassurance. They have come back to their previous school to say hello and touch base.

Many children and adolescents will initially say that it is fine to end the therapy and may even seek to end the treatment immediately. At this point you need to point out that termination is a process and that it is important to take time to say good-bye. It is tempting for children who are resistant to talking about feelings to seek to avoid experiencing the intense emotions that commonly accompany a loss or change in their lives. Just as you established a contract for the treatment, it may be important for you to establish a contract for the ending sessions.

For one 16-year-old girl who I worked with for over two years it was a very painful experience to say good-bye. I was completing my clinical internship and moving away. She had a history of leaving other relationships without discussing her feelings. When my impending departure was broached with her, she said that was fine and that she didn't need to come to any more sessions. The following dialogue followed the second session discussing my leaving the clinic.

Girl: I don't see why I need to come anymore—I know you are leaving.

C: I'd like to see you so we can discuss how this feels for you and for me.

Girl: I already know how I feel—it's so hard I don't want to talk about it. *(Begins crying.)*

C: It's hard to have someone leave you. It's hard for me too.

Girl: Then don't leave—why can't you stay?

C: I have a different job. I know you want me to stay. I would like to see you continue to work as hard as we have. I wanted to talk to you about another therapist I found whom I think you might like.

Girl: I don't want anyone else. I'm not going to meet her.

C: I wonder if you have any fantasies about my leaving?

Girl: Well—you'll think it funny.

C: Go ahead, try me.

Girl: Sometimes I think if I don't see you these last times, then you can't go because we haven't said good-bye.

C: So is that part of the reason you have canceled several of our last sessions.

Girl: Maybe.

C: You know it would be nice if you could control things by wishing them away like that—it must feel like you have no control over what's happening now.

Girl: I don't. You are going to do it anyway.

C: That's true. Sometimes when kids feel they can't control something or someone, they can feel real angry.

Girl: I can't be angry at you—you aren't going to be here much longer.

C: It's OK for you to be angry at me. I'm leaving and you want me to stay. We have gotten to know each other really well, and it must feel like you have to start all over with someone new.

Girl: I can't do it again.

C: It may feel like that now and maybe it will take some time for you to want to try again. But I'd really like you to try to come to our last two sessions even though it will be hard.

She was able to come to the final sessions and express her mixture of sadness and anger. Although it took her six months to be ready to work with another therapist, she was able to pick up from where we left off and completed her treatment that following year. Other attempts at therapy had ended suddenly at her instigation.

Booster Shots
Another case did not end quite as smoothly. A five-year-old girl the author had seen for six months had made an excellent adjustment and dismissal from services was broached with both the girl and her single mother. Both agreed to end the treatment and the final sessions went very well. A few weeks later the teacher approached the author with concerns that previous misbehaviors were reappearing. The author checked back with the mother and she reported no particular difficulties at home. With parental permission, the author sought out the girl and talked about the teacher's concerns. Placing the behaviors into the framework of having the author come back into the girl's life helped the girl see that the author still cared. It was agreed that the girl could check in with the author as needed. At first she checked in weekly but eventually she was able to move to monthly visits and finally was able to tolerate longer and longer periods of no contact.

In this case, the girl needed a "booster shot" of our contacts. Clinicians based in schools are in the best position to provide these boosters but it can be managed in a clinic setting with parental cooperation. Checking-in by phone is another way of assisting the transition process. It can be reassuring for both the client and clinician to have this type of check-in, particularly when the termination process is difficult.

Reemergence of Old Problems
It is common to find that you will revisit old areas of concern that had been resolved during the treatment. This occurrence is quite normal and helps both the client and the clinician move beyond the treatment. In a sense, such regression allows for a replay of the therapeutic process. Some clients will seek to bring up old problems in an attempt to forestall the termination process.

An example of such a ploy is illustrated by a 17-year-old male seen by the author for six months of treatment. He was somewhat resistant to termination although all treatment goals had been met. For the second-to-the-last session he reported having difficulty completing his homework—one of the problems which had formerly been resolved. He again reported difficulty concentrating because he was afraid he would not be able to complete the work adequately. The author drew a parallel, connecting his sudden difficulty with completing the homework to his fear of ending our sessions. Although this revelation brought a spate of angry words from the young man, he did not deny the connection. For the final session, he reported he no longer had difficulty but was feeling very sad about the ending of our sessions. The author shared her sadness about the ending but also her pride in the young man's progress and coming future.

It's not uncommon for such regression to be the client's way of acting out his or her concerns about the end of sessions. Providing an interpretation to the client can help as well as allowing the feelings to come into the session on both the client's and the clinician's part. If the client shows no feeling about the ending, it is appropriate to discuss this lack of emotional response. One client refused to deal with any of his feelings about the ending of the sessions. Two weeks later his mother contacted the psychologist and asked her to talk with her son, who seemed to be more angry than would be expected at everyday incidents. When the psychologist met with the student the following week, he initially refused to talk with her. As he began to talk, he expressed his anger at her for not seeing him any longer. The reasons behind the anger were explored and the termination process continued for two more sessions. After these sessions ended, he showed no further difficulties with unprovoked anger.

The Final Session

As you approach the final session, you will have mentioned the number of sessions left for the client at the beginning of the session. This countdown can feel painful but it is important to keep the ending at the forefront of the client's consciousness. It is easier but not constructive for the client and clinician not to discuss the ending at each session. The following dialogue was taken from the second-to-last session of treatment for an 11-year-old boy who refused to discuss his feelings about the ending.

Child: I want to play *Trouble* today.

C: OK. But first I want to talk a little bit about our last session, which is next week.

Child: Mmm.

C: We need to plan out our last time together. We can have treats and special games or go on a special trip.

Child: Do what you want.

C: What would you like to do?

Child: I don't want to talk about this.

C: I know, but it's going to happen anyway you know. It's hard to say good-bye and you don't seem to be giving me a chance to say good-bye. I wonder how it feels that I'm leaving you.

Child: I don't care.

C: If you did care, what would you say?

Child: I'm tired of this—can't we do something else.

C: OK. *(Bringing out the game)*

Child: I'll really beat you this time! *(He begins popping the dice cup and pops it more and more violently.)*

C: I almost wonder if you wouldn't like to do that to me for leaving you.

Child: Pop, pop, pop. I'm really strong—I could break this if I wanted.

C: I know you are strong. Strong enough to say good-bye without showing me how much you feel, I'll bet.

Child: I'm not going to cry you know.

C: Maybe not. But I'll feel like crying because I'll miss you. Sometimes kids will feel sad but not show it—they like cry inside of them or when no one is watching.

Child: I'd really like to have some pop and ice cream in the cafeteria for our last session.

C: OK. That's what we will plan.

This boy was confused by his feelings and believed he had to be strong enough to end the sessions without showing any emotions. He responded to the clinician's acknowledgment that he was strong but that she knew he was sad too.

The last session can be hard for both of you and tears are certainly appropriate for either of you. Some children and adolescents will want to know if they can talk to you if something comes up they can't handle by themselves. I generally will have cleared this with the parents before reassuring them that they can come again. At the very least, I will give them permission to call me. Just this amount of comfort seems to provide them with enough solace as well as continuing the connection.

Ending Unsuccessful Treatment
One of the harder issues to deal with is when you are unable to work with a client. For every clinician there are clients who hit us in spots and with whom we find it almost impossible to work. It is important you recognize which clients these are and find appropriate treatment for them. It is naive to believe that you can work well with all clients. The ethically responsible clinician will have enough insight to know when he or she is faced with such a client. It is in the client's best interest for him or her to be provided with appropriate treatment.

How to explain such a termination requires finesse and honesty. These issues can be discussed with the older child or adolescent, but for all clients the parents should be part of the decision to refer the client to another therapist. Discussing the remaining concerns and the lack of progress in treatment should be pursued without laying blame on either the parents or the client. When these treatment failures occur, it is tempting to lay blame on the client for not working hard enough. Another frequent excuse is that the client "wasn't ready to change" yet. Both of these reasons may be correct. However, you then need to evaluate whether there is a mismatch between client and clinician or whether it is true that therapy should be discontinued and perhaps begun at a later date.

It is unethical to continue treatment when there is no improvement in functioning or when the treatment appears to be stagnant. Seeking consultation, supervision, or assistance on the case are all appropriate steps prior to referral to another professional or discontinuing treatment. In addition, the experience you provide as to what therapy is is something the client will carry with him or her throughout life. In this way you are representing the profession. Admitting a mismatch provides a model for the client of how to handle situations that do not work out satisfactorily.

Conclusions

Termination is important and when handled well can assist the child or adolescent in learning how to say good-bye and to deal with the feelings that accompany such situations. As you work through the termination stage, you will be revisiting previous sessions and providing a cohesive integration of the areas of difficulty that have been resolved. Talking with the client about where he or she started when therapy began and relating this start to where he or she is now can assist the client in evaluating the work that has been done.

This review was particularly helpful for one client. She was initially referred following a suicide attempt when she was an 18-year-old senior in high school. She was involved with a young man who frequently was emotionally abusive. He would tell her she was fat and ugly and that no one else could want her. She was an excellent student and had prided herself on her intellectual ability but could see little about herself as lovable. She came to the first session dressed in dark clothes with her hair pulled severely back from her face and with no makeup or jewelry.

Girl: Well, we only have two sessions left.

C: Mm. I wonder if you remember what you looked like when you first came to see me.

Girl: Not really—nothing special I guess.

C: Well, try to imagine a mirror here with a line dividing it into before and after. I'll describe the before section and then you describe the after.

Girl: OK.

C: The girl I am seeing has on a navy blue dress. She has pulled her hair back from her face and has no makeup or jewelry on. She doesn't smile very much and has dark circles under her eyes. She moves slowly and looks either sad or mad. I'm not sure which. Does this person sound like anyone you know?

Girl: Did I really look like that—I have forgotten. I think I was both sad and mad. I just couldn't see any other way out of being with him and I thought I was only smart—nothing special.

C: And now?

Girl: Well, I have on a red skirt with a patchwork vest and lacy blouse. My hair is cut short and is curled. I have on earrings and a bracelet and a little makeup.

C: And how would people say you feel?

Girl: I guess I look softer—maybe more happy—I certainly feel more together than before. It really has been a change for me.

C: You worked hard at what you did—we uncovered what you had kept covered up for so many years.

Through reviewing the change for this client, it was readily apparent what changes had occurred. This review also provides a summary of the feelings and concerns that were uncovered during the sessions. It is a history that the client and the clinician share and will retain after the sessions end. This history provides a backdrop for later experiences for each of the players. You have also provided a view of what a therapist is for the client that he or she will carry to any future contacts with the helping profession.

9

Two Case Studies

This chapter presents descriptions of two cases that were in treatment with the author. These cases have not been presented elsewhere in this book and are meant to provide the reader with a glance inside the therapy room over a number of sessions. The first case was referred while I was a school psychologist. The second case was referred in a private clinical setting.

Case 1

Doug

Doug was in fourth grade when he came into my school office and announced that he needed to see the "shrink."

Doug: I need some help. I heard that you talk to kids and try to help them with their problems.

P S-C: Yes, I do that. I must first ask you if your parents know you want to to see me.

Doug: Yes. I told my mom I wanted to come in and talk to you.

P S-C: And what was her reaction.

Doug: Didn't she call you? She said she would give you permission. She never does anything she says she will now.

P S-C: She didn't call but if it's OK with you, I'll call her now.

Doug: Go ahead—you have to get her at work. Here's the number.

The phone call is made and Doug's mother gives permission for him to see the school psychologist. She agrees to sign the formal permission form that I will send home with Doug. We make an appointment to speak at greater length later that day.

Doug: See I told you it would be OK.

P S-C: I was sure you were right. It's just important that I have her sign a paper that gives me permission to work with you. I'm glad you decided to come and speak to me yourself. Can you tell me a little bit about why you wanted to come here?

Doug: I'm really mad all the time—now it seems that I'm in trouble in school and I've always done well here.

P S-C: It sounds like you feel everything is going wrong.

Doug: It is—today I lost my temper at my teacher and I threw an eraser across the room.

P S-C: You said you are mad all the time—talk a little about what that's all about?

Doug: It started this year when my parents split up. I thought it would be OK but I just *(starts crying).*

P S-C: It really looks like things are pretty hard for you right now. Sometimes it may feel like it will never get any better.

Doug: It feels like my whole life is upside down. I can't do anything right and nobody is around to help.

P S-C: Can you talk a little about your parent's separation?

Doug: My dad moved out this October—around Halloween. I didn't know anything was wrong until then.

P S-C: Do you feel you could have done something about it if you had known?

Doug: Maybe—at least it wouldn't have been such a surprise. I haven't been able to sleep at night because I think about what I can do to bring them back together.

P S-C: Sometimes kids will feel angry when things in their life happen that make them feel helpless.

Doug: They didn't even give me a chance—they should have stayed together for me.

P S-C: I wonder if you are really upset that they didn't think about you when they broke up—is it possible you could be sad about this instead of just being mad?

Doug: I'm both.

P S-C: I'm wondering if you felt that if they had really loved you, they would have stayed together.

Doug: Yes. I wanted them to stay together. Now I have no family.

P S-C: We have to think about stopping now because it's almost time for school to end. I'd like to make another appointment with you for next week—is that OK with you?

Doug: OK. I don't want to miss math or reading.

P S-C: Well, what would be a good time?

Doug: How about during independent reading at 10:00?

P S-C: That will work fine for my schedule. I can meet with you for thirty minutes. I would like your permission to speak to your teacher. I won't tell her what you have said, but I would like to share that you are under some stress now because of your parents' separation. Is that OK with you if your mother agrees?

Doug: You won't tell her what I say about her?

P S-C: No. Only some reasons why life is hard for you right now. It will help her understand your actions, like throwing the eraser.

Doug: All right.

P S-C: I will be talking with your mother tonight. Is there anything special you want me to talk to her about?

Doug: Just how I feel. I don't want her to feel bad. She cries a lot right now.

P S-C: I'll just share with her generally what we talked about. So I'll see you next Wednesday at 10:00?

Doug: OK.

The following selection is from the phone call with Doug's mother that same evening.

P S-C: I'm glad you could take this time to speak with me. What concerns do you have about Doug?

Mom: He's really having trouble with our divorce. In some way I think he feels responsible. He goes from crying to screaming at me over very little. It has been very hard on him. He is close to his dad and hasn't seen him very much since October.

P S-C: Why do you feel he thinks he is responsible for the break-up?

Mom: Well, we tried very hard to not fight in front of him and I don't think he knew anything was wrong until we sat down and talked with him about our separation.

P S-C: What did he do when you talked with him?

Mom: He just sat there and didn't say anything. Then he asked me if I was OK.

P S-C: So he was worried about you?

Mom: Yes. I think he still is.

P S-C: What makes you think that?

Mom: I guess I've been crying a lot and I think he hears me at night. I try to hide it but it's hard to be smiling when you feel as if your world is falling apart.

P S-C: So you haven't really let him see how you are feeling?

Mom: Is that wrong? I thought it would be easier on him.

P S-C: I think you have really tried to make this whole thing easier on your son. It isn't that something is right or wrong as much as how it feels to you or to him. Do you think he knows how you really feel when you are smiling?

Mom: I think he knows I'm sad. He tries to make me smile.

P S-C: How do you think he feels?

Mom: I think he's confused and doesn't know what to do. I almost think he feels that maybe we'll get back together or something.

P S-C: Will you?

Mom: No. My husband is with someone else. It's done.

P S-C: Doug may be very confused about what to feel. He may swing from mad to sad and back again. Sometimes kids will act out in order to have their parents attend to them. It's almost a paradoxical attempt to get them to pay attention to the kid instead of themselves. It may be hard on him to see you smiling when he feels you are very sad—it may also give him the message that it is not OK to show how sad you are. I wonder if you feel comfortable enough to talk about your feelings with him?

Mom: I can do that—I just don't want him to be sadder.

P S-C: It may help him to feel something with you rather than behind his closed bedroom door. I would like to see him for the next couple of months on a weekly basis. Is this OK with you?

Mom: He can come as long as he wants to.

P S-C: I would also like your permission to keep Doug's conversations with me between him and me. I will provide you with the general ideas and thoughts about what occurs. This helps him to feel safe enough to talk about anything.

Mom: That's fine.

P S-C: I'd like to talk with you now and then and maybe we can meet in the next month or so about Doug's progress. Will you be talking with his father about Doug's therapy?

Mom: Do you think I should?

P S-C: How does it feel to talk with him about this?

Mom: OK, I guess. We look like everything is OK when someone sees us, but I feel incredibly angry whenever I see him.

P S-C: Well, why don't you think about it. Doug may decide to talk with his father about this matter anyway. How do you think Doug's father will feel about my seeing him?

Mom: Oh it will be OK as long as he doesn't have to be in therapy too. He cares very much about Doug and I know wants the best for him.

P S-C: So I will call you in a couple of weeks. If you have any concerns, please don't hesitate to call me. You can call Doug's school if you wish to talk and they will give me the message. Thank you for your time. I'm looking forward to working with you and Doug.

A consultation with Doug's teacher indicated that she was sensitive to Doug's moods and had noticed a major change in his behavior in the past month. We agreed to keep in touch as to Doug's progress. She also agreed to monitor his moods and let me know when he seemed more upset than usual. It was further agreed that when she felt Doug's frustration or anger was building up, she would distract him with a different activity. Doug was seen on two more occasions before the following session occurred.

Doug: My mom talked to me last night about the divorce. She now uses that word instead of just saying they are separated.

P S-C: Go on.

Doug: Well, she told me she was very sad about dad moving out. She said she cries a lot and asked me if I had known that. I said I had heard her cry and I didn't know why if dad had just left for a while.

P S-C: It sounds like you were really confused about what was happening.

Doug: It's good to know what's going on. I told her I was really mad that she didn't tell me the truth before.

P S-C: So you felt like you had been lied to.

Doug: Yes, they always smile when dad comes over and it's like we are all pretending that everything is the same.

P S-C: But it's not, is it—no matter how much you might wish it. Do you ever think about how it used to be?

Doug: I used to all the time. Sometimes I couldn't sleep and that's what I would think about.

P S-C: So now that mom has finally told you what's going on, how do you feel?

Doug: Sad I guess. I used to be mad you know. Now I just feel sad and tired.

P S-C: It's hard to try and deal with all of this when you are only ten years old. Adults have trouble with it you know.

Doug: Mmmm. I still hope they will get back together and we can be a family again.

P S-C: Do you feel as if you have no family?

Doug: Kind of. We don't have a family like other kids.

P S-C: It's really a loss—your feelings are normal you know. It's OK to feel whatever you feel. Whether it's sad or mad or just tired.

Doug: Then why does my mom not want me to see how she feels?

P S-C: Maybe she's worried that seeing her cry will make you feel worse.

Doug: So she's doing it for me?

P S-C: Maybe. Why don't you ask her?

Doug: We made a plan to talk about our feelings every Friday night.

P S-C: That sounds like a great plan. Have you seen your dad lately?

Doug: I see him this weekend. It should be fun—we are going golfing.

P S-C: Do you talk much when you see him?

Doug: Not much. He always has his friend with him.

P S-C: His friend?

Doug: Mm. Her name is Sue.

P S-C: Oh. How is that for you?

Doug: Well, I wish she would stay at home. We always have to have her with us.

P S-C: Can you talk with your dad about how you feel? That you want some time alone with him?

Doug: Do you think he'll listen to me?

P S-C: I don't know—can you try and see?

Doug: Sure.

P S-C: Our time is almost up now. I'll look forward to hearing about your visit with your dad next week.

Doug was next seen the following week after a visit with his father over the weekend. He was quiet and withdrawn during the initial portion of the session. He stated that he really didn't feel like talking about his weekend and so I decided to have him draw some pictures instead. He chose to draw a picture of a big mountain with people climbing up the sides.

P S-C: That's an interesting picture you are making. What are the people doing on the sides of the mountain?

Doug: They are climbing up it. They have to be very careful because they could fall. It's very hard to climb on and lots of people have died there.

P S-C: I can see that it would be hard to climb. I wonder why they are climbing up the mountain if it's so dangerous.

Doug: (*Shrugs and continues drawing, adding people at the bottom of the mountain who seem to be lying down.*)

P S-C: What are those people doing at the bottom of the picture?

Doug: Oh, they fell off the mountain—they are dead. (*He continues to draw for some time, adding details to the mountain and to the people.*)

P S-C: What do you suppose those people who are on the side of the mountain looking down at the ones who have fallen down are feeling?

Doug: Scared I guess. They are pretty high up.

P S-C: The mountain looks slippery too.

Doug: Yes. They have to watch every step.

P S-C: It must be hard for them to always have to watch out so they don't fall.

Doug: I guess.

P S-C: Do any of the people have names we know?

Doug: Here's a boy at the middle of the mountain, and this is his dad at the bottom.

P S-C: So his dad fell off the mountain.

Doug: Mmm. He fell because he was all alone. He didn't want any help from the boy.

P S-C: I wonder how the boy feels?

Doug: He's really scared because now he is all alone on the mountain, and there's no one there to help him.

It would be two more sessions before Doug was able to talk about his weekend with his father. He refused to go with his father on the weekend before the following session.

P S-C: Your mom called me this morning—she's real worried about you.

Doug: What did she say?

P S-C: Well, she told me that you have been very quiet and stay by yourself and that Friday you refused to go with your father for the weekend.

Doug: *(Shrugs and is very quiet for a good minute.)* I didn't want to go with him.

P S-C: Can you talk about it?

Doug: It's so hard—he has a girlfriend now. She lives in his house.

P S-C: Is that what you found out when you were at his house last time?

Doug: *(Nods.)*

P S-C: Tell me about that visit.

Doug: We were going to go to a baseball game Friday night—I thought just me and dad—and then she came too.

P S-C: So he didn't ask you if she could come along?

Doug: No. She sat next to him and kept talking to him.

P S-C: It sounds like you didn't get much of his time. That must have felt bad. It sounds like he let you down.

Doug: Yes. I was really mad. It was our time and he brought her.

P S-C: Then what happened?

Doug: We went home and I found her stuff in his closet.

P S-C: Was that the first time you knew she stayed there?

Doug: I knew she visited but now she lives there.

P S-C: Sometimes kids whose parents have split up imagine they will get back together. Then when it doesn't happen, they get sad and sometimes even mad.

Doug: It wasn't fair—he didn't ask me and then all of a sudden she comes on our trip.

P S-C: What did you say to your dad?

Doug: Nothing. I went into my room and stayed by myself—he knows what's wrong.

P S-C: Are you sure?

Doug: Yes.

P S-C: It must feel like you lost him twice—first when he left your mom and then when he got a girlfriend.

Doug: (*Starts crying.*) How can he do this to my mom? She's all alone, and I can't help her with everything. I thought he might come back and live with us.

P S-C: I wish I could make it all happen the way you want. It makes me feel pretty helpless. You know you aren't alone in all of this, don't you?

Doug: I know I have my mom and that you will help me. But I don't want to see him anymore.

P S-C: Right now you are pretty mad—that's OK. I think maybe you need some time to think. When are you supposed to go with your dad again?

Doug: The end of this month. I'm not going.

P S-C: Well, that's your decision. Why not wait a while to see how things go. Did your mom talk to your dad?

Doug: Yes. She said I hurt his feelings—too bad—he hurt me. See how he likes it.

P S-C: Well, can you just see how things go the next couple of weeks?

Doug: I'm not going with him.

P S-C: I'm not saying you need to—just that you wait and see how you feel. I'd like to talk about this a little bit more next week. You know, I think I understand the picture of the mountain you drew last week a little bit more. Can you tell me about it now?

Doug: Well, I felt like my dad had let me down and that he wasn't going to be helping me anymore.

P S-C: So the mountain was how you felt—like life was dangerous and at any time you could have a life change. You have to be watchful and really careful. Having your dad fall off the mountain—what did that mean?

Doug: I was mad—I thought he might as well be dead—he wouldn't help me anymore.

P S-C: You were all by yourself. That is scary. How do you feel now?

Doug: Better. But I still think about what will happen.

During the following week, Doug spoke to his father on the telephone. He was still angry but his mother also told him that she wouldn't want to live with his father anymore even if he didn't have a girlfriend. Doug decided to go for the weekend and asked his father for some time alone with him without the girlfriend.

Doug continued to make progress in our weekly sessions and became more adept at identifying his feelings and talking with his mom and dad about what he was thinking. He reluctantly let go of his fantasy of his parents reuniting. He couldn't accept his father's girlfriend but they established a sort of truce to share his father's attention. Doug's father set aside individual time during his visits when no one else was allowed to go with him. After approximately three months, we began discussing ending our sessions. The following excerpt concerns this issue.

P S-C: It sounds like things are going pretty well for you.

Doug: Yes—my mom and I are going to the cabin this summer. She said I could bring a friend.

P S-C: That sounds like fun. We only have a couple weeks of school left. I'm wondering how you will feel about not coming here anymore.

Doug: Sad. I like talking with you.

P S-C: Do you remember how you felt when I first met you?

Doug: I was mad and sad all together.

P S-C: How do you feel now?

Doug: Sometimes like I used to, but now I can talk to my mom and she helps me think about what's happened.

P S-C: You have really worked hard to feel better. I see you as doing what you need to make things better. I don't see you looking as sad anymore. I think we should start talking about ending our work in the next few weeks. It's a good time because summer vacation is coming up.

Doug: Does that mean I can't see you anymore?

P S-C: No, I'll be here if you need me. It means that I think you are ready to try things without seeing me every week. I would like to take the next three weeks to talk about ending our meetings.

Doug: I thought we'd stop when school was out?

P S-C: Well, we will go almost to the end of school. I think we should take our time saying good-bye.

Case 2

Sherry

Sherry was referred for therapy because of concerns about her refusal to comply with her mother's direction. She was 15 when she first began treatment. Sherry had a history of school difficulty since first grade. She was currently in slower paced high school classes and was volunteering in a local day care facility. Sherry also had difficulty keeping friends and was described by her teachers as "quiet and sad." She was eager for help and willingly began treatment.

Sherry: I was really happy you agreed to see me. Things have really been hard for me this year. I'm having trouble in school and at home.

P S-C: It sounds like there's problems in all areas of your life. Is anything going right for you?

Sherry: I have a new boyfriend.

P S-C: Tell me a little about him.

Sherry: Well, he's really tall and has a car. His name is Billy and he's in some of my classes. He's really smart and good-looking.

P S-C: What's he like when he's around you?

Sherry: He takes me places and we do a lot of things together.

P S-C: Is he nice to you?

Sherry: Pretty nice—I don't have many friends you know.

P S-C: Why is that do you think?

Sherry: I don't know—they are mean to me.

P S-C: In what way?

Sherry: They call me names and make fun of me. Sometimes they pretend they like me and ask me to do things. Then when I do, they laugh and then they won't talk to me.

P S-C: That sounds pretty hurtful.

Sherry: It is. I don't know why I do what they say—I keep hoping they will like me. Boys like me but not girls. I think they are jealous of me.

P S-C: Have you ever had a girlfriend?

Sherry: I have friends but they never seem to last very long. They always seem to make friends with someone else and then they don't have enough time for me.

P S-C: Tell me more about that.

Sherry: Well, I'll have a friend and then they will want another girl to come with us too. I can just tell the new person doesn't like me. They should want to just be with me. So then we aren't friends anymore.

P S-C: It sounds like it's been hard for you to have one friend who will only be your friend.

Sherry: No one really knows how I feel. For some reason they always leave me.

P S-C: I don't really know very much about your background. Can you tell me about your parents?

Sherry: There's not much to tell. My dad left just after I was born. I haven't even seen him since I was five. He just left my mother with me and my older sister. My mom had to work to support us and I never had as nice clothes as the other girls in school. My sister was ten when he left so she remembers him. She has always done well in school and is now in college. She has lots of friends and has never had many problems. Her name is Carol.

P S-C: How do you and Carol get along?

Sherry: Pretty good. She makes me mad when she starts bossing me around just like my mother. I don't need to be told what's wrong with me all the time.

P S-C: Who does that?

Sherry: My mom and sister. They always say how much of a problem I am and that I'm no good at anything.

P S-C: Is that what they say?

Sherry: Sometimes. Most of the time they just say, what is wrong with me. It seems like I can never do anything right.

P S-C: That must be hard for you.

Sherry: It is. I don't think anyone really loves me. They always want me to change into something else.

P S-C: So you are never good enough for your mother, or sister, or the girls at school.

Sherry: That's right. That's how I feel. Never good enough. Why can't they just like me without changing me?

P S-C: Well, why don't you tell me what you like about yourself?

Sherry: I think I am a nice person. I don't hurt anyone's feelings. I'm pretty good at making things.

P S-C: Is there anything about you that you would like to change?

Sherry: I'd like to know why people don't like me.

P S-C: What else?

Sherry: I wish I was smarter. I don't think I can do many things very well. Everything is harder for me than for other kids.

P S-C: What would you like to find out in therapy?

Sherry: I'd like to find out why people don't like me as much as I think they should.

P S-C: And what would you like to find out about yourself?

Sherry: I guess, how I can be happy?

P S-C: Do you think we can meet for an hour every week?

Sherry: Sure.

Sherry continued in treatment for the next two months. She began to see how her behavior could affect other people. She also began to realize that part of her difficulty was that she reacted to any type of threat with rejection before her fear of rejection could come true. The following session revolved around a rejection she had just experienced with her boyfriend.

Sherry: It has been really hard for me. I refused to have sex with my boyfriend, and he said he wouldn't see me anymore.

P S-C: What will you do about it?

Sherry: I almost changed my mind and slept with him. But then I remembered what we talked about—that I needed to feel good about what I do—not what other people think of me. I thought I'd wait until we had some time to talk.

P S-C: I'm proud of you. That was a very hard thing to do. How do you feel about it now?

Sherry: Better, I guess. I still wish I had a boyfriend. Now I have nobody to do things with.

P S-C: So you are alone again.

Sherry: Yes.

P S-C: Is it as scary as you thought it would be?

Sherry: No. I guess now that it's happened, I'm OK. I just wish I had someone I could count on.

P S-C: You know Sherry—sometime you will need to realize that it's important to count on yourself. It's interesting you don't see your mom or sister as being someone you can call on if you needed to.

Sherry: They always think I could be better.

P S-C: Is there anything they like about you?

Sherry: Well . . . I guess they have to like me because they are my mother and sister.

P S-C: Is that the only reason?

Sherry: I'm not sure.

P S-C: Do you feel you could ask them?

Sherry: I'm afraid of what they might say.

P S-C: What are you afraid of?

Sherry: I guess that they won't be able to think of anything they like.

P S-C: Are you willing to take that risk?

Sherry: Do you think it's important?

P S-C: Yes. I think it may give you some information you don't have, and I think you may be surprised by what you find out.

Sherry: OK.

P S-C: I look forward to hearing about it next week. Our time is almost up.

Sherry came to the next session with a smile. She was excited about her conversations with her mother and sister and about meeting a new friend.

Sherry: I had a really good week.

P S-C: Tell me about it.

Sherry: Well, I talked to my mom and sister. I asked them what they liked about me. They were really surprised I didn't know it. My mom said she liked my art skills and that I could make her laugh with my jokes. My sister said she liked how I could make things out of junk and that I liked to do the same things she did so we had fun together.

P S-C: Tell me what you thought they might say before you asked them.

Sherry: I was afraid they would say there was nothing they liked about me.

P S-C: That would be sad to hear.

Sherry: I always think other people don't like me.

P S-C: I wonder who it is that doesn't like you.

Sherry: I don't know. Other girls in school.

P S-C: Sometimes people who don't feel good about themselves will believe that other people don't like them.

Sherry: Do you think I don't like myself?

P S-C: I think it's a possibility—what do you think?

Sherry: I think when I first started coming here, I didn't like myself very much because I couldn't see that I could do anything right. Could that cause me to fail at everything?

P S-C: Certainly when you don't feel much confidence in yourself you go into situations believing you might fail or others might not like you.

Sherry: I still feel like that most of the time.

P S-C: That's some of the things we need to work on. You know our work here in this room is just the beginning of the process that you need to work on when you aren't here. Our time is almost over. I think you have made good progress so far.

Sherry called and canceled the next session. She came the following week and was very quiet in the beginning of the session.

Sherry: I couldn't come last week. Did you get my message?

P S-C: Yes. I missed seeing you last week. What happened?

Sherry: I had to go to a meeting at school I had forgotten about. Were you upset?

P S-C: Did you think I would be mad?

Sherry: Yes. I was afraid to come today.

P S-C: Tell me what you thought might happen.

Sherry: I thought you'd be mad and tell me that I wasn't doing very well.

P S-C: It's interesting that you felt that after our last session where I told you I was proud of you.

Sherry: Did you?

P S-C: Yes. Sometimes when people are not sure of themselves, they will worry that they can't keep up the good work and that they will fail.

Sherry: I feel that way all the time. Sometimes I feel like I am faking it even when I do well and that eventually you will find out how bad I am.

P S-C: When you have those kind of fears, what do you say to yourself about them?

Sherry: I don't know. I can't remember.

P S-C: I want you to think about it the next time it happens and write down what you have said to yourself.

Sherry: OK. I'll try it.

P S-C: You haven't said much lately about how it is going with your mother.

Sherry: It's OK most of the time. I still think she's going to criticize me all the time. But now at least I don't start a fight with her when I think I have done something wrong.

P S-C: When did you change that?

Sherry: After you asked me to talk to her about what she liked about me. I guess I thought she didn't really like me. I knew she loved me because I'm her daughter, but I didn't think she liked me much.

P S-C: And now?

Sherry: I think it's better. It's still hard for us, but I think it's better.

P S-C: What is it like for you to admit that you are doing something better?

Sherry: It's different.

P S-C: One of things I'd like you to try to do is to give yourself compliments when you deserve them. Do you think you can do this?

Sherry: I can try.

Sherry continued in treatment for the next several weeks. I continued to work on her ability to see positive interactions as well as her ability to effect change by her attitude. We continued to discuss her tendency to see people as threats to her security. She made progress in her sense of herself and her ability to begin seeing situations from more than her own point of view. Sherry appeared to be at a developmental emotional stage that was pretty narcissistically based. She continued to experience significant difficulty with any type of perceived criticism, real or not. The following excerpt is from one of the sessions toward the end of our meetings. Sherry had begun a friendship with another girl and had weathered several crises where her friend included others in their activities.

P S-C: How do you think it has been going for you?

Sherry: I feel much better than I used to. I still have times when I feel everything is going wrong and no one likes me.

P S-C: What do you do when that happens?

Sherry: I tell myself to wait and see if there really is a problem. I know now that sometimes I expect the worst to happen rather than the best.

P S-C: What do you think about the other person now?

Sherry: Well, I am trying to think about how they might feel. It's hard to realize that they do things because of how they feel, not just to make me feel better. I do that now with my friend, Sally. Right away I always think she's doing something to hurt me but now I try to think about what has happened and how she thinks about it. Like the other night . . . I just wanted to go to the movies alone with her but she invited another friend. At first I was really angry and didn't want to go. I finally asked her why she invited someone else, and she was surprised that I was hurt. She said she just thought the other person would like to go and it would be fun. It was a surprise that it had nothing to do with me.

P S-C: Did you think at first that it was because she didn't have enough fun with just you?

Sherry: That's right. And it had nothing to do with that.

P S-C: You never would have known that unless you had asked. Do you feel what this change in approach has done to modify your expectation about their reaction?

Sherry: I think I wouldn't have even talked about it with her and would have been mad and then found some excuse to end the friendship.

P S-C: It's pretty hard to keep friends if you do that often enough. What about the other girls in the class at school? Are they still laughing at you?

Sherry: I don't see it as much.

P S-C: I wonder if they were laughing at you?

Sherry: It felt like it to me.

P S-C: Could it relate to your insecurity about people liking you?

Sherry: Maybe. It doesn't happen so much anymore so maybe they have stopped laughing.

P S-C: Or maybe you don't feel it now because you feel better about yourself.

Sherry: I have been telling myself to try to think of reasons why they might be doing something other than just that they don't like me.

P S-C: That was a huge burden for you to carry all these years. I wonder why you had it?

Sherry: I don't know. I just know I always felt like I wasn't good enough.

P S-C: Do you think it has anything to do with your father leaving before you were born?

Sherry: I don't know. I hadn't really thought about that—maybe. Do you think so?

P S-C: Sometimes when kids are young, they feel they have more power than they do. It's possible you instinctively felt that he left your mother because you weren't good enough to stay around for.

Sherry: I always wondered if he left because he was disappointed that I wasn't a boy.

P S-C: So in some sense you felt not good enough for your dad.

Sherry: I also thought Mom blamed me for his leaving.

P S-C: Did she?

Sherry: I don't think so. I think it was me, and I would fight with her so that she paid some attention to me.

P S-C: Even if it was negative.

Sherry: I guess.

P S-C: You've been doing a lot of thinking about all of this. Do you feel strong enough to talk with your mother about it?

Sherry: I'll be scared—what do you think she'll say?

P S-C: What's more important—what are you afraid she'll say?

Sherry: That she really was disappointed in having me rather than my father.

P S-C: It's possible she'll say that—but what is more likely?

Sherry: Probably that she loves me.

P S-C: Why would she say that?

Sherry: I guess because she stayed with me and she always took care of me.

P S-C: I think it's important for you to put some of the fears you have been carrying for a long time to rest.

Sherry: OK. Could you be with me when I talk with mom?

P S-C: I can if you want me to, and if it's OK with your mother.

The following session took place two weeks later with Sherry and her mother.

P S-C: Sherry wanted you to come to our session to talk about when Sherry's father left.

Mom: OK. What would you like to know?

Sherry: Why did Dad leave when I was born?

Mom: We were having lots of trouble in our marriage—lots of fighting and problems. It started before you were born.

Sherry: Was he disappointed that I wasn't a boy?

Mom: What makes you think that?

Sherry: I thought maybe he left because I was a girl.

Mom: He left because we weren't getting along and because I asked him to leave.

Sherry: So he didn't leave because he didn't like me?

Mom: Why would you think that?

Sherry: I thought it was my fault. I thought maybe you were mad that you had me and not him.

Mom: Where did you get that idea?

Sherry: I don't know—I guess because he didn't leave when my sister was born. I was afraid you held it against me all this time.

Mom: Oh Sherry—I never said that or felt it. I was relieved when he left but also scared because we were all alone. It was hard for me and there weren't many single mothers in our town.

P S-C: Sherry has felt that she is to blame for a lot of things and this has caused her problems in how she feels about herself. Sherry, how did these fears affect how you reacted to your mother?

Sherry: I think I fought with you to see if you would still love me. I guess if I was bad enough and you stayed with me, then you loved me.

Mom: It has been better the last couple of months. We aren't fighting as much and I think you consider my feelings more. I wish we could have talked about this before.

Sherry: I was afraid to ask you.

Mom: Do you think we can talk about things now? I love you—you're my daughter.

Sherry continued in treatment for four more months. She is currently in vocational school and looking forward to a career in interior design. Sherry continues to have some difficulty holding onto relationships, particularly with men. She now sees another therapist in her new community and is making progress in this area too.

10

Group Therapy

Group therapy provides an alternative method of treatment to individual treatment that is appropriate for certain types of problems. Some topics for group intervention include children of divorce, development of social skills, anger management, and homework completion.

Setting Up Group Therapy

Group therapy methods give the clinician a number of advantages. First, more children can be seen within the same time period. Rather than using the 30-minute period to work with one child, you can see four or five children, thus reducing the cost for services as well as allowing some children service that otherwise may have been denied. Second, peers can provide assistance, modeling, and support in the development of some skills. Third, peers can provide support outside of the therapy session. Fellow group members can provide reinforcement of behaviors during hours beyond the session. Finally, a group provides a feeling to the child that he or she is not the only person experiencing that type of problem. Children and adolescents with similar concerns can reduce the feelings of isolation that often occur.

    Group therapy also has some disadvantages which need to be evaluated carefully when deciding whether such therapy is appropriate for a particular client. Groups require the child to be willing to talk about problems in front of more than one person. Confidentiality is more difficult to enforce and children may have difficulty keeping the conversations within the group itself. Also, for clinicians not within a school setting, it can be very difficult to coordinate schedules in order to set up a group.

Group therapy can be very successful when correctly managed. The choice of clients for participation in the group, the structuring of the group sessions, the purpose for the group, and the management of the group all influence the success of this form of treatment. Each of these areas is discussed in the following sections.

Choice of Clients

Not all children can benefit from participation in a group setting. Some children who are very quiet and withdrawn may have considerable difficulty talking about their concerns or providing support for other group members. Conversely, other children are so out of control that they could continually disrupt the group, thus preventing treatment from taking place. Still other children are unable to tolerate the expression of strong feelings by a peer, and others are unable to share the "spotlight" with another child.

A child with difficulty in any of the above areas is most likely not a good candidate for group therapy. To determine which children are appropriate for your group, you should interview each candidate individually. During this interview it is helpful to answer a number of questions.

- Does the child want to be in the group?
- Why does the child want to be in the group?
- What does the child expect to get out of the group?
- Can the child defer his or her own needs when appropriate?

Your observations of the child within the classroom setting as well as input from the teacher and parents can assist you in determining whether a child can profit from a group intervention. For some children, it may not be an appropriate time for an intervention to take place. You will need to explain carefully that although they will not be participating in the current group, you will consider them for a later group.

Selecting the Group

You are now at the point of selecting your group participants. You want to select children who can work together and yet complement each other. It can be very difficult to work with a group of children who are all withdrawn. Similarly, a group of children who all act out will be problematic. I find the best balance is to select children who are on a continuum of behavior not too removed from one another. The group should have children who run from a moderate range of the behaviors targeted for the group to a more extreme range. For example, when establishing a group dealing with divorce, it works best to select children who are adapting somewhat to the divorce as well as children who are experiencing some difficulties that are more extreme.

One group I worked with had difficulties making friends. Of the five boys attending the group, two had one friend each, one had no friends, and two were able to make friends but unable to hold onto their friendships. This group was more balanced and allowed the children who could make friends to share their ideas with the child who could not make friends. The two children who were able to keep at least one friend were able to assist the children who could not maintain relationships. When you work with a balanced group, you can utilize the experience of the group members to provide a backdrop for discussions.

Exclusionary Criteria
If a child is not appropriate for a group when you are initially setting it up, you may wish to reevaluate the child after a period of time. Sometimes when a child participates in individual treatment for a while, he or she will be more ready to discuss feelings in a group. If the child is motivated to be in a group setting rather than in individual treatment, it may be important to select a group that will provide the child with support and allow the child to participate. You should clarify well in advance what behaviors will be expected and which will result in losing group privileges. For other children, it is important to strike an agreement about the behavior that may be preventing their group participation. For example, if a child constantly talks out and monopolizes the conversation, then the child will need to agree to allow others to speak. If the child disrupts the group, then the child needs to learn self-control before participating in a group. Such goals can be arrived at with the child and a contract which sets out the type of behavior to be improved and can be established with a time frame for such improvement.

Certain children are not appropriate for a group setting. These include children with severe aggressive behaviors, autistic children, children with severe speech and language skill deficits, children with thought disorders, and very withdrawn children. Groups may be painful for these children or their behavior may be such that they are too difficult to control when more than one child is present.

Group Contracts
After you select the children for a group, develop a contract with them about their participation. They need to agree to attend the sessions and participate fully. While this contract can be in oral or written form, I find it most helpful to put it into written form and provide each child with a copy of the contract at the first session, when everyone signs it.

Obtaining Permission
It is important to secure permission before beginning your group. Such permission needs to be obtained from the parents of the children as well as from the child. Your request for permission from the parents requires you

to discuss the duration of the group, probable topics of discussion, and issues of confidentiality.

Scheduling

One of the more difficult aspects of working with groups is arriving at a time when all members can attend. This aspect is particularly difficult for private clinicians and often forestalls the use of group therapy in private practice. In the schools, scheduling needs to take into consideration the school day, individual teacher needs, and schedule conflicts. It is possible to schedule your group during part of a lunch period. At schools where the children walk to school, groups can be scheduled before or after the school day. At other schools, you can schedule groups during the period generally labeled as health. I have also scheduled groups during the study period time. It is important to avoid the main academic periods as much as possible as well as subjects the children enjoy (i.e., gym, art). As with everything else, the good clinician needs to be very flexible and able to switch meetings so as not to conflict with special programs, music rehearsals, and other occasions that occur.

Structuring the Group

As the group begins, it is important for you to establish its duration. Some groups may meet as few as six times while others may meet for a year. Each group's duration is dependent on its purpose as well as the goals the group establishes for itself.

Goals

One of the ways to have a group fail is to not provide structure in order to develop and meet group goals. Each group needs to develop its own goals. These goals should contribute to the overall reason for the group's existence as well as facilitate individual participation during the sessions. While you should establish the topic for each session, the group should, with your help, set up its own goals. For example, one group I worked with on completing homework decided an appropriate goal was for each of them to develop a homework worksheet that their teacher agreed to check at the end of the day. Another group, working on making friends, established a goal to help each other on the playground if they saw a group member walking alone. These goals help establish cohesiveness both within the session and on the outside of the therapy room.

Rules

I generally establish two initial rules. One of these rules is that no one may talk about what is said within the group outside of the group. Group therapy can pose confidentiality difficulties since there are times when group members will share information with a nongroup member. If this occurs, it is important to process such concerns during the next group session. You should review the need for confidentiality and facilitate how the group will deal with such indiscretions. Some groups have expelled the member while others have decided not to take any action and to offer the member another chance. I find it most useful to discuss these issues with the group at large after I have talked with the offending member to ascertain what has been happening. It is important for you as the group leader to determine whether children and adolescents who breach confidentiality need to drop out and pursue individual help rather than continue in the group.

The first session should clearly discuss the issue of confidentiality and the need for this rule. It is also important to talk about safety in the group as well as respecting the rights of members. Rules can help with outward behaviors but still not provide the safety that is needed for clients to discuss painful concerns. In groups safety comes with time as members begin to trust one another. The group facilitator can assist in this process by encouraging members to talk and allowing time for group members to feel comfortable with one another. Structure sessions to talk about issues such as the time when the member was most happy or most embarrassed, what the member wants out of life, and so on. In topical groups it is somewhat easier to help bridge the gap as the earlier sessions are structured and members share a common experience (i.e., learning disabilities, divorce, and so on).

The second major rule is that nothing and nobody can be hurt during the sessions. From this point on I facilitate the establishment of rules. It is usually helpful to write the rules on a large piece of paper that can be hung up for each session. These rules generally consist of standards for conduct and need to include the following:

- One person speaks at a time.
- There is no name-calling.
- Everyone in the group is important.
- We all help one another work out problems.
- What we talk about stays only in the group.

Topics
It is helpful to structure each of the sessions around a topic. Not only does this help organize the session, it also provides accountability for staying on topic during the session. Select the topics before the group begins and present them during the first session. Group members can then have input as appropriate, and topics can be added, combined, or deleted. For some types of groups, commercial products are available for the sessions. The ASSET program for social skills training (Hazel et al., 1981), ACCEPTS and ACCESS

(Walker et al., 1983), and *Developmental therapy in the classroom* (Wood et al., 1986) are just a few of the commercial programs currently available. These programs are fine for a beginning clinician and for groups whose goals concern social skill development. The more experienced therapist may wish to supplement these materials or tailor-make programs for each group. Topics for various types of groups are discussed later in this chapter.

Limit Setting

As with any other enterprise, it is important to establish limits as well as consequences for behaviors that interfere with group functioning. These limits need to stem directly from the rules the group has established. Limits for the group should also be well-defined before problems can arise. In the case of misbehavior, you will be well-advised to enforce the limits in the beginning sessions in order to set the tone for later meetings.

Behaviors that will result in expulsion from the group need to be well-defined. Behaviors—such as belligerence which blocks the group process, name-calling that reflects refusing to respect the other members of the group, or divulging group discussions outside of the group—are sufficiently serious that expulsion from the group should be considered. Hopefully your screening procedure has eliminated this type of client from consideration prior to the group's beginning session. If you have a group member with this type of difficulty, allowing her or him to remain in the group can prevent the group from functioning.

If the decision is to expel a member, then it is very important that you spend a session discussing how the group feels about such an action as well as providing support to the group for their decision. The group member who is expelled should also be offered individual sessions to deal with his or her feelings about what has transpired.

For more minor infractions, the group can determine appropriate consequences. For many groups, bringing the difficulty to the child/adolescent's attention has generally been sufficient to correct the problem. For others, you may need to take a more active position in assisting the child to change his or her behavior through active reinforcement of appropriate behavior.

Social Competence as a Group Therapy Issue

One of the best predictors for good adult adjustment is the development of adequate social skills. Various types of competing behaviors can interfere with social functioning. Problems with anger management, difficulty knowing which appropriate behaviors to select to fit a particular situation, and inappropriate social behaviors can impact negatively on a child's relationships as well as his or her overall adjustment.

Social skills include the ability to join and maintain conversation appropriately, inhibit impulses that could interfere with socialization, and share in the attention of the social group. Many children learn these skills from their environment while others require direct teaching to master social exchanges. Still other children have the requisite skills but are unable to put these skills into practice because of competing and/or interfering behaviors. For example, a child who is unable to wait his or her turn or who monopolizes the conversation will often be rejected by peers. Similarly, a shy or withdrawn child, who may have the requisite skills to interact appropriately with peers, may not practice these skills because of lack of opportunity. Treatment for each of these children will vary depending on the competing difficulty.

Social Skills

Social skills are an important part of a child's or adolescent's development. Children who do not know how or are unable to play and interact with others will have a very difficult time in school. One of the most common complaints parents will bring to your attention is their child's difficulty making and/or keeping friends. Some children can make new friends easily but find it is very difficult to keep them. Others have problems even approaching other children to make contact. Still other children seem to have a sign pasted on their back that says "victim." Each of these types experiences real pain as they are continually reminded they are not accepted.

One boy the author worked with began treatment individually. He was seven years old and had been rejected by his second-grade classmates. The boy was the older of two children and had had parental attention and reinforcement for everything he did. He was seen by his parents as so special that during his first six years of life he had felt he could do no wrong. His life was peopled only with adults who found his precociousness cute. The first difficulties he experienced were in kindergarten, where he attempted to direct social activities and demanded that the others play using only his rules. These problems escalated in first grade and came to a head at the beginning of second. His parents had numerous friends and could not understand what had gone wrong for their son. By the time he was referred for assistance by the school psychologist, he was angry and reluctant to talk about any of his problems.

The initial sessions were held with the boy to discuss his views of the difficulty he was having making friends. The following excerpt is from one of the first sessions.

P S-C: Do you know why I asked to see you?

Boy: Yes. My mother said it was because the other kids are mean to me.

P S-C: Is that why you think you are here?

Boy: Sure. They pick on me all the time. I hate school.

P S-C: Can you tell me about how they pick on you?

Boy: They call me names and make fun of me.

P S-C: Why do you think that happens?

Boy: *(shrugs)*

P S-C: Tell me what happens after they call you a name.

Boy: Well, I usually get mad and then hit them. It's their fault, you know.

P S-C: So what happens before they call you the name?

Boy: Sometimes they just call me the name before anything happens at all. I am walking in the hall and they call me nerd or stupid.

P S-C: And then what happens?

Boy: I get mad and yell at them and sometimes I hit them.

P S-C: Does everyone do that?

Boy: Some of the boys just ignore me. That almost hurts as much. One time I had made a friend and things were going real well. Then all of a sudden he didn't want to play with me anymore.

P S-C: Can you help me to understand what happened? Tell me about one of these children.

Boy: Well, Tommy said I could be his friend. He came over to my house and we played with my toy trains. It was lots of fun and I thought we were best friends.

P S-C: And then what happened?

Boy: Well, we were in school and I wanted to play 4 square and he wanted to be with the kids playing soccer. They won't let me play—they say I always boss them around. He played with them and left me all alone.

P S-C: So you were all by yourself.

Boy: MmMm. I wouldn't play with him the next time he asked. He liked them better than me.

P S-C: So because he chose not to play with you one time, you then felt he wasn't your friend?

Boy: Yes.

P S-C: One of the things we will work on in the group I talked to you about is how to keep friends as well as thinking about how the other child feels. Does that sound like something you might like to be in?

Boy: Well . . . Maybe—

P S-C: Why don't we try a few meetings and see how things go? Would that be OK?

Boy: OK.

This child was unable to see any part that his behavior played in his difficulty keeping friends. Through structuring a group that role-plays the above scenario with other players and then discussing the session, this child can be assisted by his peers in learning new ways of reacting to disappointment.

Make-Up of the Group
Each group you work with on social skills will differ depending on the individual players' make-up. I find it useful to include children with varying levels of ability in the group. It can be very difficult to have a group of children who all have the same difficulty. In this case there is no one to provide peer modeling for new and emerging behaviors. To mix the group members—those who have the skill but don't use it with those who have not developed the skill—assists the group facilitator in role-playing situations. The following section discusses ways the group can utilize the strengths of individual members for learning and practicing new behaviors.

Practicing Behaviors
One of the assets of group treatment is that it allows group members to practice new behaviors with one another. In groups where a child is learning a new behavior, it is easier to practice this new behavior in front of other children/adolescents who have accepted the client and with whom the client feels confident enough to try something new. This ability to practice with peers is particularly important when developing new social behaviors.

For one group of sixth graders who were developing skills in making friends, it was particularly important for the members to try out new methods of interacting. It was exceptionally painful for one very shy girl to try out new skills. One of the other members helped her by not only coaching her within the group setting but also by agreeing to help her outside the group by staying near her as she tried to talk with one other girl, an assignment agreed on by the group members. In other instances the members would decide to take other parts and act out how to deal with peer rejection or name-calling. Through this type of structured practice, the group provided support as well as alternative behaviors appropriate for various situations.

Peers can not only assist their group members in practicing new behaviors, but they can also assist in helping members select behaviors from their existing repertoire. Some children may already possess the needed skills but be unable to utilize them in an appropriate and/or timely manner. The group can be used to role-play situations when various behaviors are appropriate. In this manner, all group members can practice behaviors for different situations you set up.

Some children may be able to participate in the role-play in the safe environment of the group. Eventually it is important for you to facilitate transfer of this learning to situations outside of the group session. One way to accomplish this task is to help group members provide support outside of the treatment room. Through active coaching and support during the day by both group members and interested teachers, children can learn to apply the skills.

You can take an active role in the transfer of these skills by setting up situations that have proved to be problematic for group work for the child. Identification of these situations can be accomplished through observations gathered from playground supervisors and teachers. Group discussions then can proceed about what was tried unsuccessfully in the everyday situation and what could have been done to correct the difficulty.

Some of the topics which are appropriate for social skill training include the following:

- Meeting other kids
- How to say hello
- How to enter a group
- How to find kids you can play with
- Things to say in a conversation
- How to wait for your turn to talk
- How to show other children that you understand what they have said
- Listening skills
- Sharing/Taking turns
- Leaving a game
- Feelings

Problem-Solving Groups

Another type of group process which can be utilized with children and adolescents is that of teaching problem-solving skills. Problem-solving skills include the ability to assess a situation and then select alternative behaviors appropriate to the situation, the ability to evaluate one's own behavior and its effect on others, and the ability to evaluate others' behavior and adapt to these effects.

For many children these skills do not come automatically and need to be taught. Like social skill development, problem-solving skills can be more easily taught within a group setting, which allows for role-playing as well as support both within and outside of the group setting. It is important for you to break down into manageable units the problem-solving difficulties each group presents. I find it helpful during the initial sessions of the group to have each child begin a diary of experiences for the week. This diary can contain situations that occur, how the child managed the situation, and what happened before and after the situation.

These situations can then be shared within the group session and charted as to problem and solution the child/adolescent used. Then the group can discuss alternative methods that could have been selected, how they see the client, and how others may have reacted to the client's action. The group may discuss how the client feels about trying new solutions when a similar situation arises.

These diaries can serve as a basis for evaluation of the child's problems and as a foundation for later sessions. It is important to build time into each session for each client to evaluate his or her own performance during the week. To assist with helping the client to evaluate her or his behavior realistically, you should gather independent information on the client's functioning from teachers and parents. I find it helpful (and time-saving) to ask for teacher and parent observations through the use of a short note they return to me. Areas of disagreement between the client and other observers of his or her behaviors can then be discussed during the group session.

Topics which can be discussed within the sessions may include:

- What is a problem; whose problem it is; why the member should change
- Decision making
- How to choose other behaviors
- When what feels natural is the wrong thing to do
- Looking at what happens before and after the problem
- Evaluating one's own behavior
- Understanding another child's behavior
- How the member's actions may affect another person

Discussions of these areas can lead to additional topics which you can tailor-make for the individual group. The most important group dynamic is assisting the members to understand the impact of one member's behavior on other children.

Anger Management Groups

Children and adolescents who experience difficulty managing their anger also tend to have difficulty with social relationships and problem-solving situations. Anger management groups therefore contain elements of both the social skill and problem-solving group paradigms. In addition, these groups require additional discussions about feelings as well as ways of helping members explore their flash points. The use of charts and diaries can prove invaluable in sorting out these problematic areas. They can also assist the client in looking at antecedents and consequences of his or her behavior, thus helping to develop strategies for managing these areas of conflict.

The use of a group setting to acquire management skills for handling intense feelings is helpful for several reasons. First, the client is provided an opportunity to see other children or adolescents at her or his age level struggle with similar problems. This opportunity allows the client to see that he or she is not alone in this area of difficulty. Second, the client can benefit from the experiences of his or her peers in handling problem areas. The group can discuss what has worked for some of them in some situations and what has not worked. Finally, the opportunity is present for role-playing different situations and practicing various behaviors.

Groups whose purpose is to discuss intense feelings need to spend additional time examining what certain emotions mean and what it is like to experience such reactions. It may be difficult for children and adolescents who have difficulty managing their feelings to distinguish anger from sadness or guilt. These clients may only allow themselves to feel anger. It may not be acceptable to them to feel sadness or to experience guilt (Teyber, 1990).

Situations which should bring out feelings of sadness are therefore converted into anger because the client finds the sadness or guilt so uncomfortable that he or she changes it into something more manageable. The client may also subconsciously feel that anger provides a more powerful method for coping with his or her feelings. Thus, it is important to spend sufficient time to analyze the client's underlying feelings, with an eye toward what those feelings may represent for the client.

Children and adolescents who experience difficulty managing their anger often are hard put to talk about any other feelings they may have. By reconstructing activities and situations that provoke sadness you can provide instruction as to how to handle such feelings without the child fleeing into anger or hostile action. The use of videotaped sections from movies can assist in illustrating natural reactions to environmental stimuli. It also allows you to construct situations that can serve as the basis for discussions about how the hero/heroine feels and the resulting actions from such feelings.

Many clients who experience difficulties with anger management do not appear to be able to consider other alternatives before they act. An essential part of groups working on anger management is the need to develop a menu of substitute behaviors to use when anger begins to be felt. Some clients are not aware of their feelings until they erupt; they may also be unaware of situations that are likely to provoke their anger. It is important to help the group members develop an awareness of the triggers for their angry behavior. When these situations arise, they can then be prepared to use an alternative behavior. It is particularly important to assist them in learning how to *act*, not just react, to the environment. Sometimes the best action is one that avoids the problem in the beginning.

In order to use such instruction, the client also needs to be able to read her or his reactions before they get out of control. It is helpful to discuss with the group such topics as what it is like to be angry, when a person knows if he or she is angry, and what the first signs of anger may be. Then the group can develop actions to take when these first indications appear.

Group topics may include the following areas:

- What feelings are
- What goes on in your body when you are angry, sad, lonely, and so on
- Tuning into your body
- Anger/sadness/guilt
- Alternatives
- Relaxation techniques
- Avoidance techniques

Groups for children who have difficulty managing intense emotions need to have built-in consequences for clients who act out on their feelings. These consequences can be decided either within the group setting or individually. Following an infraction it is important to discuss how the client felt and which alternative actions may have changed the result.

Divorce Groups

Groups for children of divorce are often helpful in assisting the child to cope with the results of parental actions. Divorce groups are generally time limited and rarely extend beyond a six- to eight-week period. In divorce, children and adolescents are often helpless in controlling their lives and they may feel that things are spinning out of control. Discussing such feelings among other children/adolescents who have experienced similar situations can help the client feel that he or she can effect some changes in his or her life and exert some control over what happens to him or her.

A group may well include children at various stages in the divorce process. It is helpful for the children to hear how other children have coped with a divorce, how others feel about it, and to express what their own feelings are. These groups may also serve the purpose of having the children provide support for each other beyond the time of the group sessions.

There are common topics and experiences for children of divorce. These topics can serve as guide for the sessions. Some suggestions include

- Why do parents divorce?
- What will happen to me?
- Where will I live?
- What feelings are normal?
- Why do I feel so bad? sad? happy?
- Does dad/mom still love me?
- Can I be divorced?
- What will happen on holidays?

You probably can think of other appropriate topics. Your group may also be able to think of different topics which are particularly relevant for them. These topics can be inserted into the group curriculum and utilized for treatment. Groups for children of divorce need to include work with parents to help them cope with their child's problems. You may wish to conduct parent groups to assist them with understanding their child's struggles with divorce.

Conclusions

Group treatment can be a useful way of assisting children deal with difficulties in their lives. It is an economical method that can provide services for children experiencing similar difficulties. Some children will benefit from group work while others may not be emotionally ready for a group experience. You should provide sufficient time for screening candidates for services and consult with both parents and teachers as to a child's needs.

You need to establish well-thought out goals for treatment within the group session. Groups that are not organized and goal-oriented usually accomplish little more than keeping children out of some of their classes. Group goals need to be evaluated both during the sessions and immediately afterward. It is also important to conduct a follow-up evaluation to assess the success of the treatment, including obtaining information from teachers, parents, and the clients themselves. Such a follow-up assists in evaluating the effectiveness of your treatment as well as informing you about needed changes.

Group work not only allows you to work with more children, it can provide the opportunity to learn and utilize additional therapy skills. Group therapy provides another tool for your arsenal that can be used to help children and adolescents. It allows you to be more of a facilitator than a leader and can help to diffuse the responsibility for change among the various members. With the appropriate children and with well-thought out goals, this treatment modality is an important alternative for the busy clinician.

11

Therapy with
Special Populations

Children with disabilities have much in common with children without disabilities in their need for therapeutic intervention. Although many of the previously discussed treatment techniques are appropriate for them, these children also bring to therapy special needs that can impinge on treatment. For example, a child who has a medical disorder may need assistance coming to terms with his or her feelings as to how this disorder makes him or her feel different as well as with any other emotional difficulties being experienced. Similarly, a child with a diagnosed learning or neuropsychological disability shares adjustment difficulties with the typically developing child while dealing with his or her disability in learning. Because many clinicians will have children with various disabilities referred to them for therapy, it is important to discuss the special needs these children and their parents bring to treatment.

This chapter discusses treatment strategies that may be helpful with special needs children. Children with learning disabilities, attention deficit disorders, and closed head injury are frequently referred for therapy to assist them in dealing with their specific disorder as well as their problems with self-esteem. Children with medical disorders can also require assistance in their coping ability and are candidates for a therapeutic intervention. All of these groups may feel that they are different from their peers in important ways. Such feelings of difference can contribute to questions of self-worth and efficacy. Since these children frequently present with emotional difficulties, it is important for the school and private clinician to evaluate how the disorder contributes to development. A discussion of the specific therapy needs of children with pervasive developmental disorder or severe speech and language disability, children who are members of ethnic groups who do not approve of counseling, and children with thought disorders is not within the scope of this book.

Learning Disabilities and Attention Deficit Disorders

Children with learning disabilities and attention deficit hyperactivity disorder (ADHD) experience the common emotional and behavioral adjustment problems associated with development as well as having additional concerns relating to their disability. You need to be sensitive to the areas of concerns these children bring to the treatment session and the stress that may be experienced by the family. Particular attention needs to be paid to the child's adjustment to special education classes as well as her or his participation in mainstreamed classes. These children/adolescents may experience difficulty with feelings of low self-worth because of problems in school with academics and behavior. Other children without these disorders do not need to make such an adjustment.

Learning Disabilities

Children with learning disabilities are a heterogeneous population. A *learning disability* is defined as a discrepancy between aptitude and areas of achievement ranging from reading and written language to mathematics. This discrepancy is generally assumed to be due to a central nervous system disorder which manifests in a difficulty in processing visual or auditory information (Wyngaarden, 1987). Some children with learning disabilities have a family history of learning problems while others do not. Moreover, children with learning disabilities often have other types of developmental problems. Approximately 35 to 50 percent of children with learning disabilities may also have ADHD (Semrud-Clikeman, Biederman, et al., 1992). Treatment is more problematic when working with children with comorbid disabilities and needs to be adjusted to take in both areas of concern.

No psychological profile fits all children with a learning deficit. They vary widely in their ability to cope and compensate with the difficulties they find in learning. Early research with children with learning disabilities suggests that they experience more peer difficulties, emotional disturbance, and later adult adjustment problems (Bryan, 1974). Later research has found that while many children with learning disabilities do experience these problems, many others do not (Semrud-Clikeman & Hynd, 1990).

The children who do not experience significant emotional and behavioral disabilities may well be those who have an area of success in their lives. They may be successful in their ability to relate to other children because their peers see them as possessing qualities that are more similar to them than dissimilar. Children with learning disabilities who are adept at sports or games have fewer emotional and behavior difficulties than those who are clumsy, unable to play cooperatively, and do not understand other children's feelings. These latter children tend to be ostracized or isolated by their peers, which results in emotional difficulties.

Children with learning disabilities who have difficulty expressing themselves because of language disorders are often unable to enter into conversation at the same level as their peers. One of the hallmarks of emotional development is the ability to relate to peers through conversation, both in beginning a conversation and maintaining it. If these children experience difficulty expressing their thoughts, understanding the speaker's point of view, and/or taking conversational turns, it is hard for them to relate to their peers.

Some children with learning disabilities may also experience difficulty interpreting facial expression, gestures, and idiomatic speech (Semrud-Clikeman & Hynd, 1991a). It may be very problematic for these children to relate appropriately to the ambiguous social situations often experienced in everyday life. They may not understand social information the same way their same-aged peers do. Normal children generally do not understand why these learning disabled children cannot relate to them. They are therefore often pushed away by peers because they do not fit into the continuum of normal behavior and reactions.

An example of the above type of learning disabled child is a girl I worked with from the age of 3 to 10. At age three she had significant language difficulties, particularly in expression and understanding. Her reactions to other children ranged from indifference to overreaction. During her early school years, she learned how to read single words but experienced significant difficulty with reading comprehension. Particular difficulty was noted in mathematics and spatial knowledge. She was referred for therapy in third grade when her peers began teasing her unmercifully because of her immature and often inappropriate reactions to them. She was also being emotionally abused by her older sister, who saw her as an embarrassment. The girl had little understanding about why her peers related to her in such a manner and frequently was confused by their reactions. The following excerpt is from a session where Sheila had been the target of teasing in her classroom.

Sheila: They were calling me names.

P S-C: What kind of names?

Sheila: Dummy. Dumb like a turkey.

P S-C: Tell me what happened before they called you names.

Sheila: I was sitting at my desk coloring. It was a picture of a turkey. I took it up to my teacher to show her and they started making fun of me. They said I was dumb like the dumb turkey I drew.

P S-C: What did your teacher do then?

Sheila: She told them to stop. But on the playground they started calling me a turkey again, saying I was stupid.

P S-C: What did you do then?

Sheila: I was crying and went and told the teacher. She said to stand with her.

P S-C: Sheila, why do you think they were calling you that name?

Sheila: Because I am stupid. I can't do the math like they do—my teacher gives me some things I can do—like coloring and they call me a baby.

P S-C: What do you want to do?

Sheila: I just want to have a friend. And for them to stop calling me names.

P S-C: Would it be OK with you if I talked with your classroom about how difficult it is for you to learn some things? Maybe that way they can understand why you are coloring instead of doing math.

Sheila: Do I have to be there?

P S-C: No. I think it might be better if you were with Mrs. Jones during that time. I'd like to call your mom and make sure it's OK with her too.

Sheila: When will you do it?

P S-C: Probably Friday. I need to talk to your teacher first about what is happening.

Sheila: OK.

P S-C: After I talk with the class, I will meet with you.

Sheila's mother gave permission and a conversation with the teacher indicated that the class was causing Sheila difficulty. It seemed to the teacher that there were about four children who were particularly cruel to Sheila. A time was set up for me to meet with the class. The discussion described what a learning disability was, explained that you aren't "dumb" if you have a learning disability, and pointed out that Sheila didn't understand why they were picking on her. The class discussion also talked about ways the children in the class could help Sheila, and children volunteered to help her learn some of the games. They also shared complaints about some of

Sheila's behavior. The behaviors included her tendency to bother the class when they were trying to do their work, her not respecting their things by touching them and taking them without permission, and Sheila's tendency to monopolize conversations. All of these areas were targets for treatment. It should be noted here that children without learning disabilities may have difficulties similar to Sheila's. What may differ is the problem Sheila had in recognizing and interpreting social situations compared to other children her age. She experienced significant difficulties interpreting facial expressions, voice inflection, and gestures. These areas of social interaction are called *prosody*. When a child has significant problems in prosody, the world can be a very confusing and terrifying place. He or she may be unable to anticipate social exchanges correctly or misinterpret behaviors (Semrud-Clikeman & Hynd, 1990, 1991a).

Sheila frequently misunderstood the actions and statements of her peers. An example of one such misinterpretation of a figure of speech happened one day when it was raining hard. Sheila came running into my office yelling that cats and dogs were dying outside. I asked her, as calmly as I could, "What do you mean?" She replied that her teacher had said that it "was raining cats and dogs." Sheila interpreted the statement to mean that cats and dogs were falling out of the sky and dying from such a long fall.

Some children with learning disabilities may have difficulty understanding cause-and-effect relationships. Such reasoning is necessary for successful social interaction. In the give and take of social exchanges it is important to be able to anticipate the consequences for certain statements and actions on the part of the listener. If the child cannot accurately predict what his or her behavior may occasion in another child, then that child may not link his or her behavior to the peer's resulting behavior. If such links are not forged, then the child is unable to learn from past experience.

For children like Sheila, this inability to learn from past experience often translates into significant adjustment problems. Interventions for these types of learning problems include work with role-playing similar to what has been described in earlier chapters. This role-playing needs to be adapted to the individual child's needs and ability. For Sheila it was important to take situations from her everyday life and role-play them the way the situation took place as well as to practice alternative behaviors.

A videotape is also helpful to use in developing skills and in teaching the child how to analyze the results of his or her behavior. Sheila was regularly videotaped interacting with peers on the playground. These tapes were then viewed and discussed with Sheila and role-plays were developed to practice new skills. One of the problems inherent in this process was that Sheila was able to learn particular skills for particular situations. It can be very difficult, however, to provide the child with all possible alternative behaviors for various situations that can arise. For children with severe social learning disabilities this limitation makes treatment difficult. Fortunately, most children are able to apply and generalize what they learn to new situations.

Group Treatment
Many children and adolescents with learning problems do not understand what these difficulties include. Many children with a diagnosis of learning disability describe themselves as "different" or "dumb." They may also feel that they are alone in these feelings. It can be very helpful for these children to have time-limited group sessions to discuss what their learning disability means to them and to others. The groups can discuss topics such as

- What is a learning disability?
- How did I get it?
- Will I grow out of it?
- What can I do to make it better?
- College and the learning disabled student
- Peer problems
- Family problems

The use of group therapy can help children and adolescents deal with their feelings about their disorder. A group can also provide support against feelings of isolation and "differentness." The universal feeling of wanting to be like everyone else can put additional stress on developmental tasks contained in preadolescence and adolescence. Periodic meetings to discuss such feelings and to develop coping strategies for these children are helpful.

Attention Deficit Disorders

Attention deficit disorders (ADD) may include difficulties in controling one's activity level, problems in behavioral inhibition, and disorders in planning and organization. As a heterogeneous disorder, attention deficits are thought to affect 3 to 5 percent of the school population (Barkley, 1990). Similar to children with learning disabilities, children with ADD may range from having serious emotional and behavioral disturbance to fairly normal behavior.

Attention disorder is one of the major clinical and public health problems in the United States. As such, this disorder is of concern both clinically and educationally because of financial cost, family stress, school and educational disruption, and its tendency to be associated with criminality and drug abuse regardless of whether medication is utilized (Mannuzza et al., 1989). The disorder has been found to persist into adulthood and has been linked to psychopathology in later life (Gittelman et al., 1985; Weiss et al., 1979).

Subtypes
The emerging behavioral/cognitive profile indicates that children with attentional problems may involve subtypes. One subtype, generally called attention deficit disorder without hyperactivity (ADD/noH) consists of those children who experience difficulty with attention and organizational skills. Another subtype is that of attention deficit disorder with hyperactivity (ADD/H). These children experience problems with attention as well as overactivity. A final subtype is that of the child with attention deficit with hyperactivity and aggressive tendencies—children who show attentional problems, overactivity, and conduct disorder (Frick & Lahey, 1991).

Not only are there differences in activity levels among these subtypes, there are also differences in behavior. Children with ADD/noH may have more of a problem with the information-processing component of attention, speed of cognitive processing, and mental preoccupation. They are exquisitely sensitive to environmental interference. In contrast, children with ADD/H may possess more of a deficit in sustained attention and the disinhibition component of attention. They are unable to inhibit their motoric behavior, which in turn negatively correlates with maintaining attention to task.

Children with ADD/H evidence problems with behavioral organization and disinhibition, whereas the children with ADD/noH demonstrate a slow cognitive tempo and inwardly directed attention problems. Thus, a different cognitive and attentional pattern is suggested for the child with ADD/H and the child with ADD/noH.

Behavioral Inhibition
The clinician working with children with ADD needs to be sensitive to their particular problem in behavioral inhibition. Inhibition difficulties are particularly important for the understanding of attention disorders. An inability to delay a response long enough to evaluate various alternative behaviors makes it difficult to learn new behaviors as well as to develop compensatory skills. Children with attention disorders often have a problem delaying their responses to environmental stimuli. They have also been found not to respond readily to environmental feedback as to their behavior (Douglas, 1983). This inability to utilize feedback may be grounded in difficulty in inhibiting their responses long enough to profit from feedback. These difficulties may well impact on the therapy session. You need to be aware of problems in inhibition and attention and plan accordingly by utilizing point systems for appropriate behaviors, shortening sessions, providing breaks in longer sessions, and rewarding proper behavior.

When tasks are complicated, the demands for planning, organizing, and executive regulation of behavior are increased. Children with ADD display fewer attentional or behavior problems in novel or unfamiliar settings or when tasks are unusually different, colorful, or highly stimulating (Barkley,

1990). Symptoms of ADD are noticeable when the demands of the environment or the task exceed the child's capacity to sustain attention, regulate activity, and/or restrain impulses. Examples of this poor regulation and inhibition of behavior include responding quickly to situations without understanding what is required, failure to consider consequences, difficulty waiting one's turn, and seeking immediate gratification or rewards that require less work to achieve rather than working toward a long-term goal and larger reward. Thus, poor inhibitory regulation of behavior may appear as an attention deficit but is explained more clearly as a dysfunction of behavioral inhibition.

In addition to attention difficulties, recent studies have supported a hypothesis of a generalized self-regulatory deficit that affects information processing, inhibition of responses, arousal/alertness, planning, executive functions, metacognition, and self-monitoring ability that spans the various sensory modalities (Douglas, 1988). An inability to inhibit excess behavior and stimulation impacts negatively on the child's ability to learn in the classroom, not only in terms of negative classroom behavior but also in terms of impacting on attention resources. Because attention is not directed, the child cannot focus appropriately and thus takes in irrelevant as well as relevant details. An interaction between inattention and disinhibition thus impacts negatively on information processing and on school achievement and social adjustment.

These deficits may also depend on the situation the child faces. For children with ADD, attentional problems become more evident in situations requiring sustained attention on a repeated task (Milich et al., 1982) or in structured situations (Porrino et al., 1983). Moreover, on tasks that are novel or when behavioral consequences are immediate, children with ADD show great ability to contain attentional problems (Douglas, 1983). Some researchers suggest that the primary difference in ADD children may not be in attention but in the way the child's behavior is regulated by consequences (Barkley, 1990; Frick & Lahey, 1991).

Issues in Treatment
When you are working with children and adolescents with ADDs, it is important to remember that they may react differently to consequences and to feedback about their behavior than would be expected. For many of the adults who teach and work with these children, their misbehavior may "feel" willful in nature rather than being a result of the attention disorder. It is important to realize that these children are exquisitely sensitive to their environment and react accordingly.

Children with attention problems often do not understand why people and events relate to them in certain ways. They can be very frustrating clients. Even with the best of intentions, ADD children frequently cannot modify their behavior without intensive assistance from teachers and parents. Moreover, children with overactivity and attention problems often feel they cannot control their reactions, let alone their body. Imagine not being able to sit still no matter how much you want to. Imagine also adults telling you that you are not trying hard enough even when *you* know you are doing *everything* you possibly can.

Concurrent Disorders in Mood

One child I worked with, who had an ADD diagnosis, reflected to me that he felt he never did anything right. Although he was highly motivated to control his behavior, he would have times when he felt very sad about his progress. He felt his life was difficult and he couldn't see any end in sight for the problems. He was 10 years old when he felt that his life would never improve.

It is not uncommon for children with attention problems to present with mood disorders as well (Biederman, 1990). Concurrent mood disorders may complicate treatment and certainly affect it. When you are working with ADD children and other disorders, it is important to deal with all aspect of the problem. You should not mistake depression overlaid on attention problems as the only area of difficulty.

A 16-year-old girl was referred to the author for assessment of possible depression. She was described by her teachers as "lazy, unmotivated" and her parents were thoroughly frustrated with her. She came to the session reluctantly and was very quiet and withdrawn. She answered questions with a yes or no and did not expand her answers unless pressed to do so. Difficulties were apparent in sustained attention and in her ability to screen out extraneous noises. Structured interviews and measures of attention indicated that problems lay both in feelings of sadness and significant attention deficits. The intervention recommended included medication along with cognitive-behavioral therapy. Consultation with her parents and teachers was also recommended to assist with changing their attitudes toward her behavior. She responded well to the medication and began to work on self-monitoring of her behavior.

Group Treatment

Children with ADD can benefit greatly from groups that provide support and guidance as well as a forum for the development of new behaviors. Group treatment similar to that discussed in Chapter 10 for problem-solving and social skills training is appropriate for work with ADD children. If, as Douglas (1988) believes, part of the difficulty lies in self-regulation, it is important to assist these children in evaluating their behavior and planning alternative methods of adjusting to environmental demands.

It is likely that the most effective treatment may differ between subtypes of ADD (Hynd et al., 1991). Generally, children with ADD/noH show difficulty with academic achievement, work completion, nonverbal reasoning, and social skills. They do not often act out and are not disruptive in class; more often, these children are described as lethargic. Therefore, the most efficacious behavioral treatment for children with ADD/noH would include social skills training and academic interventions. Inservice training for teachers of children with ADD/noH should include sensitivity to these types of children and point out the need to encourage them to attempt tasks. Teachers will need to be versed in helping these children stay on task and decrease daydreaming. Behavioral charts of work completed, academic tasks given one at a time, directions given only a few steps at a time, positive reinforcers in the form of preferred activities provided for work completion, and assignment notebooks to provide organization are strategies to assist with attention to task and work completion. Each of these areas lends itself to group support and treatment.

In contrast to children with ADD/noH, children with ADD/H show difficulty with behavior management, activity level, work completion during independent work times, social rejection, and oppositional behaviors. Treatment for these children would revolve around behavioral interventions, problem-solving skill development, and often anger management—all appropriate for group intervention. Teachers will need to be trained in providing these children with frequent and specific feedback. Moreover, the use of behavioral contracting for work completion and reinforcement of appropriate behavior coupled with consequences for off-task behavior (i.e., out of seat, talking out in class) is applied in the classroom and reinforced in the group setting.

Training in problem-solving skills (Braswell & Bloomquist, 1991; Kendall & Braswell, 1985) involves teaching the child to recognize how he or she approaches problem situations. The child is then taught to engage in a step-by-step approach for solving the problem. Activities are then provided to give practice in these skills with modeling by the therapist and support from the group. The most important problem-solving skills to incorporate into the group treatment for children with ADD/H are the ability to perceive that a problem exists, to generate different solutions to a problem, to be aware of the steps needed to achieve the solution, to understand the result of acting in a particular way or choosing a solution, and to understand how events relate to each other over time and in different situations.

Working with Parents

One time while presenting a workshop for parents of children with learning and attention difficulties, I was brought down to reality by a parent who raised his hand and said that many professionals have difficulty remembering that the parents of these children may also have learning and attention-based difficulties. When you work with parents of children who have developmental problems, it is important for you not only to recognize the child's problems but also entertain the possibility that the parents may have similar difficulties.

A mother of a child who had severe language and learning problems was invited to a meeting to discuss his educational needs. She came to the meeting smelling of alcohol and we eventually learned she had significant reading problems and that it was frightening for her to enter school. She needed to have several drinks to fortify herself against her own memories of school experiences as well as the fear of being expected to read lengthy and wordy forms and to listen to extensive reports to learn about her child's problems.

Both of these examples illustrate that clinicians working with the parents of children with educational needs have a particular need to be sensitive to the possibility for similar difficulties for the parent. There are support groups for parents of children with educational needs (see Appendix B). Frequently, it is also helpful to have parent groups within the school setting provide these parents with information about school requirements as well as to form alliances to assist with parenting difficulties. Although a full discussion of these types of groups is beyond the scope of this book, topics useful for group discussions include the following:

For Elementary Children

- What a learning disability/attention deficit disorder is
  - Etiology, developmental course, treatment
  - Heritability, involvement of professionals, Public Law 94-142
- Praise, time-outs, and natural consequences
- Peer relationships
- Teacher conferencing
- Section 504 of the Americans with Disabilities Act
- Transitions to middle school

For Middle and High School Children

- What a learning disability/attention deficit disorder is
  - Etiology, developmental course, treatment
  - Heritability, involvement of professionals, P.L. 94-142, Section 504
- Praise, time-outs, and natural consequences
- Peer relationships
- Teacher conferencing
- Sexual development
- Drugs and alcohol
- Vocational and college preparation

Many of the groups may begin with one session a week for six to eight weeks, with follow-up sessions on a monthly basis. It can be helpful to begin the sessions with a discussion of problems that occurred during the previous week and then proceed to the topic at hand. I have also found it helpful to have the group decide on any additional topics they may wish to add to the agenda.

These groups can help to support the parents as well as assist the clinician in working with children with developmental disorders. Moreover, they can help parents become more comfortable with the school and the clinician. Too often parents can feel overwhelmed by the myriad of regulations and professionals they face when asking the school for assistance for their child. A group where the clinician becomes an ally and smooths the way for the parents can pay dividends for the child's school experience.

Neuropsychologically Based Disorders

Neuropsychologically based disorders are disorders that are disturbances in behavior due to brain damage, resulting from such causes as head injury, stroke, and head trauma. Although not all clinicians are expected to possess in-depth knowledge of neuropsychologically based disorders, it is important for an informed and ethical clinician to gather sufficient information if he or she begins to work with a child with this type of problem. Children with this type of disorder may need assistance in dealing with the aftermath of their injury as well as their feelings around the loss of their previous skills. In addition, parents of these children need to come to terms with their feelings of loss, anger, and/or fear for their child's future. These dynamics make it very important for the clinician to be aware of the interactions of various systems in a child's life.

Figure 11–1 illustrates how the systems interact. The child is the pivotal point where different systems come into play. Medical, school, and home systems come together in working with the child. Each of these groups participates in the child's life and has important expertise to provide for the child's recuperation. For a child who has experienced a trauma, it is very important for these systems to be coordinated. You can play an integral role in this process and assist the various systems in communicating the needs of the child.

Similar adjustment problems may be present for children who experience a stroke, a head injury, or head trauma. Important variables to consider when evaluating a child for treatment include the pre-injury functioning levels, age at injury, extent of the injury, and the coping skills of the family. Family variables interact with the child's ability to cope with the disorder.

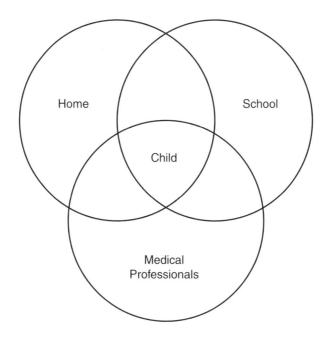

FIGURE 11–1 Interaction of Home, School, and Medical Professionals who Serve Children with Special Needs

Even when you are working individually with the child, it is important to be cognizant of the effect these variables can have on the child's eventual adjustment.

Family Variables

During this time a marriage may encounter significant stress which in turn can impact on the child's recovery. For example, a child I worked with contracted meningitis at 18 months of age. Prior to this time, he had developed normally and was considered to be within developmental expectations for his age. On release from the hospital he had lost the use of his right arm, his speech was significantly affected, and he had lost his ability to walk. He received speech and language, occupational, and physical therapy from two years of age until age six. At first grade he was referred for evaluation because of difficulty learning to read. An acquired learning disability was identified, and he began receiving assistance in reading, written language, and mathematics. Emotionally he had made a good adjustment and was well-liked by his peers. His disposition was generally happy and he had developed ways to play softball, volleyball, and other sports even though he had not regained use of his right hand.

One of the key components for his good recovery was the support he received from his parents. I began working with his parents directly following his release from the hospital. They required assistance in dealing with the grief associated with the loss of their "perfect" child as well as the normal feelings of "why us?" They also needed to come to terms with their fear of the future for their child. At the time that I began to work with his parents, they did not know the extent of the possible cognitive delays he might experience. Their greatest fear was of significant mental retardation. As he recovered, it became clearer that major problems in speech and language existed but that he showed excellent receptive language skills and good auditory comprehension. These parents were able to cope with the difficulties their child experienced and worked as a unit to help in his recovery. The stress on their marriage was significant, and without their ability to deal with such stress, there may have been severe marital problems or even divorce.

They developed the attitude that their child would accomplish as much as he could. They encouraged him to try things and to compensate for his difficulties. For example, his father worked with him to develop a method to play softball. He learned to catch a ball with his left hand by trapping the ball with his body. The feeling they communicated to him was that whatever he could try was fine with them, whether he failed or succeeded.

It is not uncommon for difficulties to surface in marriages when additional stresses, such as significant medical problems, are applied. You need to be aware of this tendency and provide needed assistance as required. Several couples that I worked with were unable to cope with these stresses and were divorced. In these families, however, often problems were present before the medical problems occurred. The medical problems and the associated stress can throw a marriage into overload and negatively impact on the shaky foundation.

Particular difficulties occur when the marriage partners are unable to come to terms with the guilt they may experience and any resulting blame one partner puts on the other. An example of this type of problem was presented by a case referred to me at an outpatient clinic. A third-grade girl had recently experienced her first grand mal seizure when her parents requested counseling for her. She was described as having significant problems with her peers and resisted taking her seizure medication. A parental conference indicated her parents were feeling considerable stress about the seizures, fear for the girl's future, and a fear of what else the child would have difficulty with since she already attended a class for children with severe behavioral disorders. Her parents were generally angry and this anger seemed to be directed at each other. Her mother appeared to be depressed and her father was working long hours and frequently was away from home on business trips.

Difficulty continued for this family, with her father becoming less and less involved in the child's life and treatment. Eventually the mother was able to share that the father had had a seizure disorder since childhood. This disorder was a family secret and was seen as shameful by both parents. When the child also experienced a major seizure, the father was unable to cope with his feelings of guilt. He believed the child had inherited his disorder and that the child's problems were "his fault." His method of coping with these feelings was to avoid both the feelings and his child. Unfortunately, he continued to be very resistant to any discussions about his feelings and eventually removed himself from the child and the marriage.

The child continued to experience difficulty coping with her problems and resisted any discussion about them. When the father left the home, the mother became more willing to help with treatment. A conference with the mother and girl began the healing process. The "family secret" was discussed and the girl's feelings of being a "freak" were finally revealed as well as her anger at her father. The girl and the mother, with their realization that her father could not face the problems, accepted that whatever healing was to occur was up to them.

Head Injuries

Closed head injuries are one of the most commonly experienced injuries for children under the age of 10 (Bengali, 1992). Head injuries can leave subtle effects, ranging from increased irritability to lethargy. Some children with closed head injuries may not show any effects after the injury while others may show changes in behavior ranging from subtle to overt. The most difficult scenario is when the behavior changes are subtle and occur in a dysfunctional family setting. It can very problematic to decipher the effects of both situations.

In addition to the severity the head injury has on adjustment, the age at which the child suffers such head injuries is important. Age interacts both in terms of brain development and outcome following trauma. There is a direct parallel between the length of any coma the child may experience and his or her later intelligence. More severe cognitive deficits are generally seen when the child is younger than eight years of age after recovery than for children over 10 years of age (Brink et al., 1970; Woo-Sam et al., 1970).

Similarly, children injured in their first year of life tend to have severe global deficits (Woods, 1980). In contrast, children injured after one year of age show more lateralized effects specific to the site of injury. Moreover, brain damage appears to have its greatest effect on new learning (Hebb,

1942). Children injured at a very early age have less accumulated knowledge and experience. They may therefore be greatly affected in their attempts at new learning.

Deficits may not be identified until several years after the injury, when brain development brings damaged areas into focus. For example, the frontal areas of the brain serve to orchestrate the ability to observe and evaluate one's own behavior (executive functions). These areas of the brain do not develop functionally until around 12 years of age. While damage to this area is frequently seen in head injuries, the effect of such injury in terms of cognitive flexibility and independent thinking will not show up until development of these areas occurs. Thus, development as well as age, site of injury, and severity are important variables to keep in mind when developing treatment plans. An excellent resource for school personnel is *Head Injury in Children and Adolescents* by Vivian Bengali (1992).

Treatment Variables
Teachers and parents are frequently unprepared by medical personnel to deal with the resulting emotional problems often seen with children with head injuries (Carney & Gerring, 1990). When you work with children and adults with any head injury, you should not only incorporate treatment which addresses the social and emotional difficulties experienced by the client but also evaluate the need for rehabilitation (for the adolescent or adult) or training (for the child who has never developed the skill to be rehabilitated) as part of the intervention.

Children who suffer brain injuries have been found to be acutely aware of their lost skills (McCabe and Green, 1987). The child's emotional development may be forestalled and/or derailed by the injury with resulting problems in their sense of self. Motivation and attention problems may significantly interfere with the acquisition of new learning. The child may continue ineffective behavior in a situation because of the perseveration tendencies frequently accompanying head injury. Teachers and parents should be prepared for these "behaviors" as usual accompaniments to head injury and not willful or psychopathological actions. The attainment of such developmental milestones as achieving a driver's license, getting a job, and dating may be delayed for the adolescent with a head injury. The frustration which can arise by having to delay or lose such experiences can impede the child/adolescent's development. Parents and teachers need to be aware that the child/adolescent will need to mourn over these losses and may become moody, angry, and/or depressed as he or she observes peers making life transitions.

Children often experience diffuse damage from head injuries, resulting in more global cognitive, behavioral, and emotional deficits (Pirozzolo & Papanicolaou, 1986). Deficits in emotional and behavioral control can impact on the developing child's ability to establish emotional boundaries between themselves and others, recognize others' feelings and motivations, develop empathy, control impulse, and develop self-awareness—all of which are developmental tasks (Lehr, 1990). For older children self-awareness problems are a particular concern. The use of videotapes, mirrors, and role-plays helps in the development of self-awareness. Children with impulse-control difficulties not only experience more negative interactions with their environments, but they also are at higher risk for psychopathology (Breen & Barkley, 1984).

These children also show poorer social skill development. Social skills often need to be directly taught. Role-plays and the use of puppets and videotapes may assist in the child's ability to recognize and label emotions. Assistance in the generation of alternatives also needs to be part of the social training. The sole use of social skills training programs is frequently not successful with these children since additional work may be needed in basic skills as well as applications. Because children with head injuries frequently have difficulties with memory and attention, skills need to be reviewed, reinforced, and practiced in many situations in order for them to profit from these interventions.

A developmental perspective is required for treatment of children. Treatment needs to be structured so that it changes with the child's age. As mentioned in the preceding section, the age at injury impacts on the treatment of the child. Moreover, skills which emerge at later ages may consequently be affected by earlier damage. Thus, assessment following injury may not determine a later deficit. Executive functions which begin developing after age 10 may not show damage when assessed at a younger age. The clinician who works with younger children and their families will therefore need to provide information to the families about such skills that develop later and assist them in coping with the resulting difficulties.

Parents of children with a head injury must also come to terms with the loss of the child they had before the injury. It is necessary for parents to acknowledge their loss before interventions with the child can be successful. The family needs to reconnect with their injured member after an injury (Martin, 1988). The person they had known may not be the same person following the injury.

The case of an eight-year-old girl with a severe head injury referred to the author for assessment provides an example of family, school, and medical interventions working at odds with each other. She had fallen off a jungle gym and hit her head on the cement. The injury was severe and she needed surgery to relieve the pressure on the left side of the temporal region of her brain. She was in a coma for six hours following surgery and was released from the hospital into her parents' care after two weeks. There were no significant neurological signs of the injury noted during her follow-up visit to the neurologist one month later.

Her mother contacted the neurologist six months later because of concerns about the girl's behavior. She noticed her daughter "blanking out" during conversations. She also felt her daughter showed more irritability and mood volatility. The girl's performance in school was reported to be satisfactory, but her teacher expressed concern about the girl's change of affect since the injury. The teacher reported that the girl was withdrawn and seemed not to be interested in playing with other children.

An interview with the girl's parents and teachers indicated a child, prior to the injury, who had age-appropriate social skills and was well-behaved. Following the injury the child showed more volatility, less ability to tolerate disruptions in routine, and more dependent behaviors. No neurological or psychological measurement tests indicated deterioration of cognitive or motor skills. An interview with the child's neurologist indicated that he felt the child was showing "emotional disturbance" not related to the injury.

Therapy with the girl's parents revealed severe parental stress and guilt over the injury and some overcompensation due to these feelings. Her mother in particular was consumed with guilt because the girl had been injured while in a baby-sitter's care when the mother was at work. The mother had feelings that the girl would not have been hurt if she had been there to take care of her. This belief translated into the mother's developing need to protect the child and in her frequently demanding assistance from the neurologist. He reacted by backing off from the client and assigning these problems to the mother's "hysteria." As she demanded, he moved away and finally referred the child and mother for therapy. The interaction between the parent and the child continued to be fairly negative prior to the beginning of therapy.

The "softer" signs of problems in adjustment, which appeared to be emotional in nature for this girl, were consistent with behavioral changes often seen with traumatic brain injury (Bengali, 1992). It was important to work initially with the mother and father around their concerns about the child's development. The strain of the injury on her parents was coupled with the inability to relate to the medical establishment. The parents' stress in turn was communicated nonverbally to the child, increasing her feelings of vulnerability which were heightened following the accident. Treatment proceeded by assisting the parents and teachers in training the child in methods of soothing herself, developing self-talk when she felt the need for support, and using training to help with both expected and unexpected environmental transitions. It was also recommended that the girl be monitored to evaluate her progress both emotionally and cognitively as she developed.

For clients with head injuries and other traumatic experiences, it is thus important to deal with the emotional aftermath from an approach melding the various arenas of the child's life. Moreover, therapy with clients with neuropsychological disorders needs to address the frequently seen disorders of attention, memory, and inability to evaluate one's own behavior. Most families with head-injured members have been found to be moderately to significantly impacted by that member's disorder (Livingston & McCabe, 1990). Emotional stress following injury has been found to be more closely related to emotional and behavioral factors rather than to cognitive deficits.

School Involvement

It is particularly important to involve teachers in the treatment plans for these children. Frequently schools are not informed about changes in behavior and emotion that may occur following a head injury. Behaviors, which may look like anxiety, low frustration tolerance, depression, or poor motivation, may be more related to moderate head injury than to *personality* variables. Without preparation and assistance, clients with head injuries and other trauma may experience additional unnecessary adjustment problems in school. It may be necessary to help the child cope with changes in their pace of school learning; the person in the best position to do this is the teacher.

The school can provide educational assistance as well as assisting with the transition from hospital to classroom. It is important to plan for the child's reentrance into the school through modifications such as half-day attendance, preferential seating in the classroom, and assistance as needed in basic academic subjects. The teacher's understanding of head injury and how she or he prepares the classroom are instrumental in smoothing the child's reentrance. It is important for the other children to understand that the child may have different behavior than she or he had before the injury and to ask for their patience in the transition. By being proactive in helping the teacher and classroom prepare for the child's reentry, you can forestall as many problems as possible.

Medical Problems

Children with medical problems bring their own set of difficulties to therapy, aside from the usual developmental and emotional problems. Although acute medical problems are stressful, if they resolve over a short period of time, they generally have few long-term effects. In contrast, children who experience chronic medical conditions run a higher risk of developing accompanying emotional problems (Siegel et al., 1991).

Chronic medical conditions include diabetes, heart condition, cancer, asthma, allergies, and bowel disorders. Each of these can make a child feel very different from his or her peers as well as requiring the child to make adjustments in his or her daily life. Diabetic and food allergic children must carefully monitor their diet, and some foods are forbidden. This difference becomes particularly evident when the child participates in activities which include these forbidden foods. A birthday party can pose difficulty for a child with diabetes or allergies. Trips to fast-food restaurants can be very problematic and require the adolescent to make choices to go with his or her peers or do what is medically recommended.

Children may deal with such problems in various ways. Some may choose to ignore their disorder, making choices that are unhealthy for them. Others may abide by medical recommendations but become angry and resistant to direction. Still others may withdraw from social interactions so that they do not need to make difficult choices. Each of these compensations carries its own consequences.

The child/adolescent who ignores his or her condition must face medical consequences. One of the more difficult situations is the diabetic child who decides to eat what his or her peers are eating despite the resulting rise in blood sugar. Parents and teachers can try reasoning and cajoling to little avail until the child decides the consequences are not worth what happens to his or her body after indulging.

One 12-year-old child I saw briefly for treatment presented with this type of problem. He was allergic to any product made of wheat. Most sweets and breads have some wheat in them. When invited to a party, he was reluctant to refuse the birthday cake for fear of being seen different or "weird." Treatment revolved around discussing his feelings of being different and his anger about having this disorder. It turned out that he was attempting to deal with his disorder by pretending the doctors were wrong. Each time he would eat the wheat products he would have difficulty breathing and would wheeze for several hours. His mother's usual routine was to admonish him severely and then provide him with additional attention and care. His physician reported that the child would not have long-term effects from the wheat ingestion but just the nasal congestion and wheezing. A discussion with the mother with the child present went something like the following.

Mother: I get so upset when he eats something that makes him sick. I imagine him going to the hospital and getting very sick.

P S-C: So, when he eats the wheat, you become worried that he could die. What does the doctor say about that?

Mother: That he won't die—but I still think about it—you know, like some people are allergic to bee stings and have only 30 minutes to live if stung.

P S-C: So, even though the doctor says that Charles will be uncomfortable at worst, you envision more drastic results.

Mother: It sounds silly when you put it that way. I guess I have always worried about him and now that he's twelve, he is with his friends and I don't know what he is doing.

P S-C: So I wonder if you are worried about the loss of control you have on his diet now.

Mother: It's possible. I'm not sure what he eats when he's not home.

P S-C: I wonder if some of these difficulties are because he is moving toward being away from home more and is growing up. It may be that he needs to try some of these behaviors to see how far he can go by himself.

Mother: I have always made those decisions for him.

P S-C: What do you think might happen if you were able to let him make some of his own decisions about what he eats?

Mother: He'd probably eat what he shouldn't.

P S-C: And then what?

Mother: Well, he'd come home and be unable to breathe.

P S-C: Totally unable to breathe?

Mother: Well, no. He'd have problems.

P S-C: So, who would be the most uncomfortable?

Mother: Mmm. Well, both of us.

P S-C: Tell me about that.

Mother: I'd feel like he let me down and he'd have trouble breathing.

P S-C: So you'd feel like you had lost control. Can you tolerate that feeling for a few times to see what happens?

Mother: I don't know. I have had to watch out for him for so many years now, it's hard to stop.

P S-C: It is hard to stop. You have done a great job taking care of his needs. But now he needs to try to make some of the decisions himself. It's hard to let go, but it really seems that he's telling you with his behavior that he needs to make some decisions in his life and that you need to let him face the consequences for those decisions, within reason. Would you be willing to try not to react when he comes home from a party or from hanging around with his friends and it is obvious that he has eaten something he should not have?

Mother: What should I do instead?

P S-C: What would you like to do that would take you out of the room?

Mother: Well, I could go and work on my painting—that might help. It will be hard for me not to say something.

P S-C: I know it will be hard and you may have times when you can't stop yourself. But, I think it would be helpful for you to try.

A few weeks later the mother reported that she had tried to ignore her son. One time he had actually pursued her, talking about his problems breathing. She was able to hold on to her resolution and ask him why he was having problems. When he told her he had been to a fast-food place and eaten fries and a hamburger, she said that he knew what would happen and now must deal with how he felt. She kept busy doing something else at the time.

Children also may attempt to deal with their medical difficulties through withdrawal from their peers. In this case, they will refuse to place themselves in situations where they may encounter restricted foods or activities. These children are more difficult to work with; the clinician and parent will need to encourage them to work with these situations. The medical condition of some children may provoke abuse from peers. In these cases it is important to work with the child, the peer situation, and the home setting.

One child of 14 whom I saw had an irritable bowel. He did well until he experienced stress, and then he would have three or four soiling incidents. His peers began teasing him, which made the incidents increase even more. Understandably, he decided to stay home and be home-schooled. His parents were supportive of his decision but concerned about his lack of peer involvement. The following discussion took place during a therapy session.

P S-C: Your parents have told me that you have decided to stay home and have a tutor come to present your school work.

John: Yes. I just can't go to school right now—I never know when I'll have my problem.

P S-C: That uncertainty of when you will have a soiling incident must be hard.

John: It can happen at any time and then all the kids in my class start making fun of me because I smell.

P S-C: Tell me what happens after a soiling incident occurs.

John: I usually go to the office and get cleaned up. I just want to go home and not go back to class. That's why I'm staying home now. They just make noises when they see me and hold their noses.

P S-C: I can imagine how hard that must be.

John: Well, I'm not going to see them anymore.

P S-C: You know, that sounds pretty lonely to me.

John: It is, but the other way is worse.

P S-C: It sounds like neither is what you want.

John: No, I want to be like all the other kids. They don't know what it's like.

P S-C: I wonder what it would be like to tell them how you feel.

John: It won't happen—I'm not going to see them again.

P S-C: Well, I still wonder what it would be like—can you imagine it for me?

John: Well, maybe they would understand that I can't help it.

P S-C: And then what?

John: Maybe they wouldn't make fun of me.

P S-C: Then you could go to school?

John: Yes—and be like them.

P S-C: Well, is there any way you can think of that could help them learn about your problem?

John: I'm not going to tell them—they wouldn't listen anyway.

P S-C: Are you giving up?

John: Why not?

P S-C: That would probably be the easiest thing to do. But would it be what you need to be happy?

John: It's the only way.

P S-C: I wonder what would happen if someone talked to groups of your classmates about your problem.

John: Who would do that for me?

P S-C: Well, I could or maybe one of your teachers could help. What do you think?

John: Then everyone would know my problem.

P S-C: They know something's wrong now—and what they think is worse than the truth—don't you think?

John: That I do it on purpose?

P S-C: Yes. You know, even if we do this, some kids will still make fun of you—I wonder if we can talk about what you can do about that next week?

John: Mmm.

P S-C: I'd also like you to think about our talking to your classmates. So I'll see you next Wednesday?

John: OK.

The hardest thing is to get the child to try again with your support. You also need to obtain the parents' and teacher's support and assistance in drawing the child out of his or her self-imposed exile. As with any preadolescent or adolescent, John desperately wanted to be like everyone else. His medical problem continually reminded him of his differentness.

Involving Parents

With any child/adolescent it is important to include the parents in the treatment. This practice is particularly important for children with medical problems because these parents have had to deal with their child's special needs many times, often from birth. All parents want their children to be "normal" but parents of children with special medical needs are reminded daily of their child's uniqueness. Some parents are able to weather these extra demands with little additional effort while others may seek to distance themselves from their child's problems by avoiding dealing with them or looking for solutions by "doctor-shopping." Still other parents become very protective of their child and seek to shield him or her from any difficulty he or she may encounter. Each of these coping styles brings its own attendant problems which can negatively impact on therapy that is seeking to assist the child face the challenge of the medical problems. For treatment to be successful, these coping styles must be incorporated into the therapy and some resolution to the conflicts needs to be provided.

Conclusions

Children who present with special needs frequently require assistance in coping with their difficulties. They bring to treatment the same types of emotional difficulties as children and adolescents in general. Treatment is complicated by the concurrent difficulties they may experience in controlling their bodies, understanding their environment, and/or dealing with a medical disability.

Parents, teachers, and peers may relate differently to such children because of their special needs. Social relationships can be fraught with problems, and these children can become the brunt of teasing and ostracism. Just as it is important for therapy for any child to involve parents and teachers, it is doubly so for the child with special needs. It is also particularly important to work with the child's peers as their acceptance (or even in some cases just tolerance) can mean the difference between helping the child develop coping skills and withdrawing from all interaction.

Consultation is a very important part of working with special needs children. By working with parents and teachers, using a voluntary and problem-centered approach, you can deal with all aspects of the child's life. Envisioning the child as the intersection of school, home, and medical institutions can provide more assurance that her or his treatment will be successful. The final chapter in this book discusses the use of consultation as a means of working with all of the parts of a child's life.

12

Consultation

Children and adolescents have far less of a say in the control of their lives than do the adults around them. Treatment with children and adolescents, therefore, must of necessity involve the other important players in their lives. In therapy with children and adolescents the astute clinician will find it profitable to maintain a consultative relationship with the client's teachers, parents, and, as necessary, a physician. You see the child one hour a week while the teacher and parents see the child most of the other 167 hours. Consultation with teachers and parents can assist in extending the treatment into those additional hours. Moreover, information from such consultations can allow for adjustments to be made so therapy will address emerging issues in the life of the child or adolescent which may not be apparent within the therapy room.

Consultation has been defined as a voluntary relationship between two parties that is focused on a problem of a third party and where the players are equal in their areas of knowledge and expertise (Meyers et al., 1979). The use of a problem-centered approach allows you to enlarge the therapeutic area. If the purpose of psychotherapy is to assist the client in developing coping ability (Koocher, 1983), it becomes important to evaluate the client's performance in areas beyond the therapy room in order to facilitate the development and application of these coping skills. To accomplish this end you will need to consult with the major players in the child's life. Moreover, once individual treatment ends, consultation can help assist the continuance of gains made in therapy. This chapter discusses the use of consultation with parents, teachers, and physicians to facilitate therapy. Issues in consultation, consultative techniques, and ethical issues are discussed.

How Consultation Differs from Therapy

Consultation differs from therapy in that consultation works on the problems of a *third* party rather than the problems of either player present in the room. There may be points when the issues facing one of the participants require individual therapy. Such areas are not the purview of consultation, and the consultee should be referred for therapy outside of the consultation process.

When the consultee evidences a need for therapeutic intervention, it is important for the consultant gently to suggest the possibility of treatment. If such a suggestion is rejected, then it is important for the consultant to work diligently to redirect discussions to the problems of the child or adolescent—not of the consultee. Words such as "I'm sure that was difficult for you, but let's talk about how Johnny is doing at home (or in class)" or "We really need to focus on how we can work together to help Johnny" should help redirect the discussion.

Lack of Professional Objectivity

The lines can blur between therapy and consultation when the consultee presents with issues that blur his or her ability to be objective about the problem of the child/adolescent (Meyers et al., 1979). In this situation, the consultee has a lack of professional objectivity. Such difficulty may stem from simple identification with the child to personality problems. Consultees with severe personality problems, which are negatively influencing their relationship to the child/adolescent, should be referred for outside treatment. Consultees who identify with the child/adolescent because of similar attributes (e.g., sex, color, background experience) or who transfer feelings from past experience with a similar child to this child/adolescent will require the consultant to *unlink* these similarities.

A lack of professional objectivity between a consultee and the child/adolescent is frequently present when the consultee is highly emotionally charged about the child's/adolescent's problems. The consultee may show unusual fascination with the details of the case and relate personal or somewhat tangential information in the problem description. The consultee may also show anxiety during case discussions. To help the consultee and consultant move beyond this roadblock, gentle confrontation can be used. In addition, the consultant may use theme interference reduction (Caplan, 1970). This technique allows the consultant to unlink the inevitable outcome the consultee has linked to this child because of previous experience with a similar child or in their own life.

For example, a teacher approached me about a kindergarten boy I was working with in treatment. She was experiencing significant problems controlling the boy's behavior in her classroom and was convinced that the boy was heading for problems in life.

P S-C: You wanted to talk with me about how Bobby is doing. What can you tell me about his behavior?

Ms S: He is just out of control. We have to do something soon or he will end up in real trouble.

P S-C: I appreciate your concern about Bobby. Can you describe what it is that he's doing in your class?

Ms S: He's always out of his desk. If I tell him to sit down, he does for a few minutes and then he's up again. The other day he shot another child in the face with his pencil.

P S-C: That sounds pretty serious—can you tell me how it happened?

Ms S: Well, I was in the corner of my room talking with my aide. When I turned around, some of the kids came to me and said that Bobby had shot Timmy in the face with his pencil—he could have punctured his eyeball. I tell you he can be dangerous—he didn't even think about what he was doing.

P S-C: It sounds like the incident really scared you. What did Bobby say about the incident?

Ms S: Well, he of course said he didn't do it on purpose—he was just kind of aiming his pencil like a sword or something and it slipped. It doesn't really matter what he said—he could have really hurt the other boy.

P S-C: But that didn't happen. I wonder how it felt to you to have this happen when you were right there?

Ms S: Well, I can't keep my eye on him all the time—I do have 20 other children.

P S-C: I can appreciate how challenging Bobby can be. I wonder why he seems to get you so upset?

Ms S: I just worry about him. He can go either way at this age and I'm afraid he'll wind up as a delinquent. I've seen other kids with his behavior who have gone on to break the law and be bad kids. (*Theme: Boys who act this way become delinquents.*)

P S-C: So your real fear for Bobby is that if we don't do something major now, he will end up like those other boys.

Ms S: Yes. He's like my stepson. He started off having little problems like this and then he eventually got into drugs and is now in juvenile detention. We have to do something to stop Bobby from having this happen to him. *(Theme: Boys who, like my stepson, are hard to manage and don't consider the consequences of their behavior, will be troublesome and uncontrollable in adolescence. When faced with hard-to-manage young males, I become incompetent—just as I was unable to handle my stepson's difficulty.)*

P S-C: I can see how much you care about Bobby. *(Gently here)* He's not your stepson though or any of the other boys you were talking about. Is there any difference you see between them? *(Beginning unlinking of the theme).*

Ms S: Not really.

P S-C: Well, I wonder if the other boys you worked with were as well-liked by their peers.

Ms S: That's true. Bobby still has lots of friends.

P S-C: Mm. That's interesting—I wonder why?

Ms S: Well . . . They don't seem to think he means to do what he has done.

P S-C: So his misbehavior is not malicious?

Ms S: Now that I come to think of it, no. They generally are accidents. But, if he keeps it up, he will be without friends and he could hurt someone.

P S-C: I can see what you mean—it's hard to worry about him hurting someone but since he's not thinking before he acts, what can we do to facilitate his safety and the safety of others in the classroom? He has been diagnosed with attention deficit hyperactivity disorder and children with that type of disorder often act impulsively without thinking about the consequences. *(Unlinking: He's not your stepson.)*

Ms S: Well, he doesn't seem to do as much of that when either my aide or myself are near him.

P S-C: You know—you are an excellent teacher and I have observed you working well with many children with more severe behaviors than Bobby is showing. You were able to help Tommy last year when you gave him a strict schedule and both of you charted his progress in not fighting.

Ms S: Yes, he really turned around.

P S-C: I wonder if there's something like that you could do with Bobby. *(Beginning to take the focus off of Bobby's uncontrollability to what can be done about it—also providing unlinking from the other theme involved here, namely, that of the teacher's feelings of helplessness and incompetence.)*

In the preceding example the teacher needed assistance in unlinking what she considered an inevitable outcome for this child. She based this outcome on her unsuccessful experience in working with her own stepson. Basically this teacher had excellent skills of management. If problems had also been present in her behavioral management skills, such skills would need to be taught by the consultant to help the teacher manage the child. Some information was provided as to the area of attention deficit hyperactivity disorder and its relation to problems with impulse control. Thus the consultee may reveal a lack of skill, knowledge, self-esteem, and/or professional objectivity, attributes which need to be addressed during the consultation (Gutkin & Ajchenbaum, 1984; Gutkin, 1981).

Expertise

Consultation differs from therapy in another important way. Therapy generally assumes that one of the participants is an expert and the other is in need of treatment. In contrast, consultation assumes that both participants possess expertise which they bring to the consultation (Meyers et al., 1979). Such an assumption levels the playing field—both members contribute information and expertise about the child or adolescent. Many consultees will see the clinician as possessing all the expertise. In a true consultative relationship it is important for you to invite the consultee to utilize his or her knowledge to assist in resolving some of the issues surrounding the child/adolescent involved in therapy.

Not only does this stance empower the consultee, it also shares the responsibility for the outcome. If the ownership for solving difficulties the child or adolescent is experiencing lies solely with the therapeutic relationship, successful treatment becomes more elusive than if all caretakers are involved in treatment. There are points in their lives over which children and adolescents, particularly, have limited control. Involving the adults, who do possess this control, in the treatment can assist the child/adolescent to successfully adapt their behavior and coping skills.

Prevention Based

A final major difference between therapy and consultation is the fact that therapy is often remedial. It is meant to resolve a problem which currently exists. In contrast, consultation is prevention based and is meant to provide information that can be utilized the next time the consultee encounters a similar problem. While it is true that the solutions, which are generated at the time of the consultation, are directed toward remediating the current problem, it is also accurate to say that the solutions are generated to help the consultee develop additional skills, insight, and knowledge about similar problems.

Stages of Consultation

It is important to discuss the reason for meeting with the teacher or parents about the identified child/adolescent. I find it helpful to introduce the meeting as a problem-solving time to assist the child. I also find it most efficacious to select an area of concern to work on during the consultation meeting. In this manner, the resolving of a problem necessitates that the consultee will be involved in the solution. When a teacher perceives he or she has control of the situation, he or she is more likely to see that something can be done to assist the child (Medway, 1979). Moreover, when teachers are taught skills and assist in coping with children's behavior, referral rates for special education placements have been found to be lower (Ritter, 1978).

Inviting Consultee Participation

The initial interviews will be devoted to gathering information about the area of concern. It is frequently most helpful to allow the teacher or parents to discuss their areas of concern. Although it can be difficult, it is important for the consultant to provide pertinent questions throughout the interview without jumping to quick suggestions or solutions for problematic behavior. Giving the consultee an open invitation to speak about his or her concerns, reflecting the consultee's feelings accurately, and providing empathy and genuineness to the interview will provide the impetus for a full disclosure of problem areas. Gathering information without a set agenda allows the consultee to freely disclose all areas of concern.

Problem Specification

This stage begins the process of selecting specific areas of behavior for attention. Behavioral parameters—how often the behavior occurs, how long it lasts, its intensity—allow for beginning to understand the extent and scope of the areas of concern. Similarly, additional information about the behavior needs to be gathered—how the teacher or the parent responds, how the child's peers respond, what incompatible behaviors the child also performs (when working, he or she can't talk)—and the response given to the child when he or she is exhibiting the behavior.

At this point the consultant needs to determine what areas of intervention the consultee is willing to pursue. For example, a mother asked for a meeting with the therapist to assist her with the child's behavior. The mother was adept at discussing areas of concern about her 10-year-old child. She could readily delineate how often the difficulty was present (several times a day), how severe the behavior was (he would escalate misbehavior until the mother intervened), and what incompatible behavior was present (when she spent time with him or was near him, he did not engage in the difficult behavior). She was also able to discuss how often she reinforced appropriate behavior (infrequently) and what methods she used for discipline of inappropriate behavior (yelled at him). However, when the problem specification process began, this mother began using techniques I call "yesbutting." She would say, "Well, I could do that, but it won't work because I have three other children" or "He would like to do that but I don't have time."

In this case it became evident that, although the mother had the best of intentions, she did not have the energy to put any intervention into effect. She was in a basic conflict since she was unable to state this inability up front because of her need to appear as a worthy parent to the consultant while at the same time feeling overwhelmed by the demands of being a single parent. Once the consultant was able to specify this as part of the problem, it became evident that the case required supportive treatment for the mother along with intervention for the child. Consultation would not be enough support for this parent because she needed to come to terms with her own issues before being able to provide the parenting necessary for her child. At this point in the consultation, therefore, the consultant helped the parent to see that what she needed was more than could be provided in the interview.

Another case provides an example of an appropriate use of consultation with a parent. In this case the 16-year-old boy was seeing me for treatment. He expressed concern about how his mother dealt with her anger. An appointment was made with the mother without the boy being present but with his permission. The mother indicated concerns about the challenges the boy was making to her authority. She was disturbed by his frequent arguing with her over directions and the lack of respect she felt he was showing her. The behaviors had been present since about the time of the parents' divorce but had escalated in recent months. His mother was able to detail the areas of conflict, ways she had attempted to solve the problem, and methods that had worked for her in the past. She was able to discuss various alternatives to work with the areas of concern and agreed to return to other consultations in the next few weeks.

Therefore, consultation is one method the therapist can use to assist teachers and parents to work with the therapeutic client in other areas of his or her life. It is not the same as therapy and should not be considered as such. When therapy is required for the parent or teacher, it is appropriate to broach such intervention. It is not best practice for the consultant employed by the school district to provide therapy to a teacher. To do so would constitute a dual relationship (colleague and client), which is unethical under the Code of Ethics of both the National Association of School Psychologists and the American Psychological Association.

It is rarely advisable to enter into a therapeutic arrangement with a parent of a child/adolescent you are working with in addition to your work with the child. Difficulties with confidentiality between yourself, the child/adolescent, and the parent; problems with rapport and trust from the client's point of view; and the high probability of overlapping needs make it wise to avoid such a practice. This is not to say that it is not appropriate to meet with parents around the progress of the child/adolescent and areas of concern. Consultation meets this need most appropriately.

Consultation Evaluation

As consultation begins to end it is important to evaluate the effectiveness of the process. While there are always important areas for improvement, it is equally meaningful to ascertain what went right about the consultation. Around the end of the consultation you need to ask the consultee what he or she felt was gained through the process as well as what more he or she may have wished to attain. It is important to listen to the evaluation with as open a mind as possible. I find it helpful to develop a relaxation response before the feedback begins and to listen closely to what the consultee is saying—not to develop a response until the consultee has finished. While the consultee is speaking, I try to determine what the feeling under the words is. To be able to do this, I find it helpful to summarize what the consultee has said in order to clarify the meaning. Moreover, it is useful for you to realize how you are feeling about what is being communicated. This is not a time to defend your actions—only to evaluate what the consultee is sharing with you. As you listen to the feedback, it is important to note what helpful material might be used for future consultations.

Providing feedback to the consultee can be difficult and in some cases needs a light touch. Some beginning consultees seem to feel that if they keep saying what they believe is the crux of the problem, the consultee will finally "get it." What happens more often is that the consultee goes away from the session feeling totally misunderstood with little motivation to come to the next meeting. It is important to provide feedback to the consultee. *Feedback* is any type of information that informs the consultee about the effects of her or his behavior on the problem at hand. When giving feedback, you need to determine the usefulness or potential influence your communication will have on your *relationship* with the consultee (Conoley, 1991).

Secondly, it is important to describe your observations in a nonevaluative manner and to provide a description of how the behavior affected you. For example, when a parent talks about hitting her child as a method of discipline, you need to communicate concerns about child abuse as well as to discuss other methods of changing behavior. After talking a bit about how hitting can escalate into physical damage, I find it helpful to discuss whether hitting will change the behavior on a long-term basis. It is appropriate to share your concern about the child abuse issue but not appropriate to have the parent leave your session feeling he or she can no longer share his or her actions with you.

For some types of feedback it is best to phrase the area of concern as a hypothesis. For example, "I wonder if your yelling at him provides him with attention and that's why he doesn't seem to end his behavior." In this case it is up to the consultee to determine whether he or she will seek more information about the areas of concern or adopt some changes in his or her own behavior. Your feedback should include aspects of behavior that *can* be changed. One of the failures I have found in consultation is when the consultant focuses on behaviors that the consultee is unable or unwilling to change. The single-parent mother described above was unable or unwilling to change her method of interacting with her son. The consultant continued to try to convince the consultee to change her behavior, but it quickly became apparent that the mother was not going to modify her behavior no matter how hard he worked to convince her to change.

Finally, it is important for you to check the understanding of the consultee about the message provided. I repeatedly find it interesting to hear information attributed to me that I cannot remember stating. When I query the person telling the story, I find the understanding of what I said was very faulty. You can avoid this pitfall by having the consultee summarize his or her understanding of what has been said.

Ending

It is just as important to provide an ending for the consultation process as it is in therapy. This ending should be active and explicit. You should remember that there is a relationship forged which requires an active method of saying good-bye, for example, by statements such as "When we began to meet, we agreed to talk about this problem. I think it is time for us to stop talking about this problem because . . ." It is important to provide a summary of the progress (or nonprogress) seen as well as pitfalls both of you discovered along the way and the methods used to resolve such areas of difficulty. It was appropriate to state to the mother who was unwilling or unable to work on her son's difficulty that "I think we need to stop talking about these areas of concern for now. You seem overwhelmed by just trying to do what you need to do to live, and I feel to ask you to anything more will overload you to the breaking point. I'd be glad to speak to your new therapist with your permission."

For most consultees the ending of the consultation is easily accomplished. It is appropriate to tell the consultee to contact you if difficulties reemerge that need additional sessions. For other consultees the ending of the sessions can be more problematic. Issues of dependency or feelings of helplessness may reemerge when termination is broached. In this case it is important to provide support for the individual but also to gently remind him or her that the consultation contract was for a limited period of time and the problems which were previously present have now been resolved. You may need to ease out of the relationship by spreading the sessions out by scheduling longer and longer periods of time between each one.

Consultation with Physicians

For children and adolescents with some disorders it may be necessary to involve the pediatrician in the therapy because of medication and medical concerns. Seizure disorders, asthma/allergies, neurological problems, attention deficit hyperactivity disorder, among others, usually require medication as well as medical follow-up. Because many of these children and adolescents may also require therapy at some point, it is important for the clinician to be prepared to make contacts with medical personnel. Prior to this occurrence I find it helpful to make myself known to area pediatricians through offering to come and speak at a meeting or in their office at their convenience. Clinicians who are based in the schools or in clinics need to be proactive in introducing themselves to area medical personnel. I found that sending a letter which introduced myself to the pediatricians who were most frequently listed on children's health cards served to assist in later contacts about a particular child.

For some cases it is important to keep the physician updated as to the client's progress. The first step, of course, is to secure parental permission to speak with the physician. Once permission has been granted, I find it most appropriate to call the physician's nurse to determine a good time to talk with the doctor and then arrange to call at that time. In this way the physician has time to have the chart brought to him or her and to review his or her notes.

You should keep your consultation with the physician brief and to the point. Planning what you need to ask in advance of the phone call is important. If a physician feels you are just calling to chat, cooperation at later times will be problematic. By outlining areas of concern as well as possible ideas of underlying problems, you can utilize the time with the physician in the most efficient manner. Behavior needs to be objectively described but scores on standardized testing should be kept to a minimum; you can always offer to send the report if the physician wishes to read it.

For most clinicians it is helpful to know which medications, if any, the child is on in order to inquire about side effects. One child I worked with, both through consultation and individual treatment, had a serious seizure disorder. She was on multiple anti-seizure medications and showed signs of extreme lethargy and apathy. Her ability to learn was declining rapidly and great concern was expressed by her teachers that something was drastically wrong. During consultation the neurologist was provided with the areas of behavioral concern as well as the observations of classroom and resource room teachers. This data provided the neurologist with information indicating that he needed to reevaluate the medication the child was on. He ultimately hospitalized her in order to take her off all medications and monitor her reaction to different medication regimens. The data provided to him were descriptions of behavior, behavioral counts of time she seemed to "space out," and the frequency of possible seizure activity as evidenced by staring periods.

As more children with medical issues are mainstreamed in school, it becomes more and more important to involve the physician in the child's life. Most physicians are very willing to work with clinicians as long as their time is appropriately utilized. If it is appropriate, you may wish to consider providing information about the special education programs available through the school system. I also supply information about our Child Find system for referring children with learning and behavioral problems and the kindergarten screening program in place in most school districts. Pediatricians are in a perfect position to refer children for evaluation at early ages and to assist parents understand the needs of their child from a medical standpoint.

Conclusions

In conclusion, consultation is a technique that allows the clinician to utilize the expertise of people involved in the life of the child or adolescent. These people are in a position to expand the work begun in the therapy room. A basic tenet of consultation is that the process is voluntary, problem-centered, and involves a third party. It is not therapy, teaching, or supervision, although aspects of each of these disciplines may be present in various parts of the collaborative process. Consultation involves the establishment of a contract between the consultant and consultee. Such a contract involves discussions of confidentiality, responsibilities and roles of each participant as well as a time frame for the consultation. The contract can be reviewed and modified as needed throughout the process.

Consultation consists of stages that involve problem identification and specification, development of an intervention plan, and finally evaluation and termination. Although the consultation process may encompass some needs of the consultee, each of these stages focuses primarily on the needs of the child/adolescent and specific areas of difficulty.

As an adjunct to therapy, consultation can provide additional support for the child/adolescent. Consultation may also be utilized as a support for the termination process as the client is moved out of therapy. Monitoring of progress following termination and providing support within her or his environment to ease the transition are other important uses for consultation.

Skills in consultation build on the therapy skills of empathic listening, clarification, summarizing, and reflecting. Knowing how to be a therapist, however, does not necessarily prepare you to do consultation. You need to be able to move out of the therapeutic stance into one of a "resource collaborator" to provide assistance and support to the consultee (Conoley, 1991). In this model, the influence is bidirectional—that is, the consultee and consultant influence each other. What is shared by the consultee informs the consultant about how the child/adolescent performs, which in turn may inform and modify the therapeutic application. In this way treatment truly becomes circular, with each player in the situation contributing his or her unique perception and information to the case at hand.

A team approach allows for a fuller understanding of the child or adolescent as well as an ecologically valid approach involving all parts of his or her life. Consultation allows for such a team approach to be utilized in the most efficient manner. It also communicates to the parents, teacher, and/or physician their equal role and shared responsibility for working with the child or adolescent.

References

Achenbach, T. (1990). Conceptualizations of developmental psychopathology. In M. Lewis & S. Miller (Eds.), *Handbook of developmental psychopathology* (pp. 3–13). New York: Plenum Press.

Achenbach, T., & Edelbrock, C. S. (1983). *Manual for the Child Behavior Checklist and revised child behavior profile.* Burlington, VT: Department of Psychiatry, University of Vermont.

Ainsworth, M. (1979). Infant–mother attachment. *American Psychologist, 34,* 932–937.

American Psychiatric Association. (1994). *Diagnostic and Statistical Manual* (4th edition). Washington, DC: Author.

American Psychiatric Association. (1987). *Diagnostic and Statistical Manual* (3rd edition-revised). Washington, DC: Author.

American Psychiatric Association. (1980). *Diagnostic and Statistical Manual* (3rd edition). Washington, DC: Author.

American Psychiatric Association. (1968). *Diagnostic and Statistical Manual* (2nd edition). Washington, DC: Author.

American Psychiatric Association. (1950). *Diagnostic and Statistical Manual.* Washington, DC: Author.

Axline, V. (1947). *Play therapy.* Boston: Houghton Mifflin.

Barkley, R. A. (1990). *Attention deficit hyperactivity disorder: A handbook for diagnosis and treatment.* New York: Guilford Press.

Barona, A., & Garcia, E. E. (1990). *Children at risk: Poverty, minority status, and other issues in educational equity.* Washington, DC: National Association of School Psychologists.

Bengali, V. (1992). *Head injury in children and adolescents* (2nd ed.). Brandon, VT: Clinical Psychology Publishing Company.

Berlin, I. N. (1986). The use of competitive games in play therapy. In C. E. Schaefer & S. E. Reid (Eds.) *Game play: Therapeutic use of childhood games* (pp. 197–214). New York: John Wiley & Sons.

Bettlheim, B. (1972). *Play and education. School Review, 81*, 1–13.

Biederman, J. B. (1991). The diagnosis and treatment of adolescent anxiety disorders. *Journal of Clinical Psychiatry, 51(5, supplement)*, 20–26.

Biederman, J. B., Newcorn, J., & Sprich, S. (1990). Comorbidity of attention deficit hyperactivity disorder with conduct, depressive, anxiety, and other disorders. *American Journal of Psychiatry, 148*, 564–577.

Biederman, J. B., & Steingard, R. (1989). Attention deficit hyperactivity disorder in adolescents. *Psychiatric Annals, 19*, 587–596.

Braswell, L., & Bloomquist, M. (1991). *Cognitive-behavioral therapy with ADHD children: Child, family, and school interventions.* New York: Guilford Press.

Breen, M. J., & Barkley, R. A. (1984). Psychological adjustment in learning disabled, hyperactive, and hyperactive/learning disabled children as measured by the Personality Inventory for children. *Journal of Clinical Child Psychology, 13*, 232–236.

Bretherton, I., & Waters, E. (1985). Growing points of attachment theory and research. *Monographs for the Society for Research in Child Development*, Serial No. 209, *50*, 1, 2.

Brink, J., Garrett, A., Hale, W., Woo-Sam, J., & Nickel, V. (1970). Recovery of motor and intellectual function in children sustaining severe head injuries. *Developmental Medicine and Child Neurology, 12*, 565–571.

Brooks, L., & McKinley, W. (1983). Personality and behavioral change after severe blunt head injury—A relative's view. *Journal of Neurology, Neurosurgery, and Psychiatry, 46*, 336–344.

Brophy, J. E., & Good, T. L. (1970). Teacher's communication of differential expectations for children's classroom performance. *Journal of Educational Psychology, 61*, 365–374.

Bryan, T. H. (1974). Peer popularity of learning disabled children. *Journal of Learning Disabilities, 7*, 621–625.

Buss, A. H., & Plomin, R. (1984). Temperament: Early developing personality traits. Hillsdale, NJ: Lawrence Erlbaum Assoc.

Caplan, G. (1993). The organization of preventive psychiatry programs. *Community Mental Health Journal, 29*, 367–395.

Caplan, G. (1970). *The theory and practice of mental health consultation.* New York: Basic Books.

Carney, J., & Gerring, J. (1990). Return to school following severe closed head injury: A critical phase in pediatric rehabilitation. *Pediatrician, 17*, 222–229.

Cassem, N. H. (1991). *Massachusetts General Hospital handbook of general hospital psychiatry.* St. Louis: Mosby Year Book.

Conoley, Jane C. (1991). *School Consultation.* New York: Pergamon.

Douglas, V. I. (1988). Cognitive deficits in children with attention deficit disorder with hyperactivity. In L. M. Bloomindale & J. Sergeant (Eds.)., *Attention deficit disorder: Criteria, cognition, intervention.* A book supplement of the *Journal of Child Psychology and Psychiatry* (No. 5). New York: Plenum Press.

Douglas, V. I. (1983). Attention and cognitive problems. In M. Rutter (Ed.), *Developmental neuropsychiatry* (pp. 280–329). New York: Guilford Press.

Erikson, E. (1950). *Childhood and society.* New York: Norton.

Fine, M. J., & Carlson, C. (1992). *Family–school intervention.* Boston: Allyn and Bacon.

Frick, P. J., & Lahey, B. B. (1991). Nature and characteristics of attention deficit hyperactivity disorder. *School Psychology Review, 20,* 163–173.

Gibbs, J. T. (1989). *Children of color: Psychological interventions with minority youth.* San Francisco: Jossey-Bass.

Gittelman, R., Manuzza, S., Shenker, R., & Bonagura, N. (1985). Hyperactive boys almost grown up. *Archives of General Psychiatry, 42,* 937–947.

GoPaul-McNichol, S. A. (Ed.). (1992). Mini-series: Understanding and meeting the psychological and educational needs of African-American and Spanish-speaking students. *School Psychology Review, 21.*

Greene, B. A. (1992). Racial socialization as a tool in psychotherapy with African American children. In L. A. Vargas & J. D. Koss-Chioino (Eds.), *Working with culture* (pp. 63–84). San Francisco: Jossey-Bass.

Gresham, F. M., & Elliott, S. N. (1989). Social skills assessment technology for LD students. *Learning Disability Quarterly, 12,* 141–152.

Gutkin, T. B. (1981). Relative frequency of consultee lack of knowledge, skills, confidence, and objectivity in school settings. *Journal of School Psychology, 19,* 57–61.

Gutkin, T. B., & Ajchenbaum, M. (1984). Teachers' perceptions of control and preferences for consultative services. *Professional Psychology: Research and Practice, 15,* 565–570.

Harter, S. (1986). Processes underlying the construction, maintenance, and enhancement of the self-concept in children. In J. Suls & A. Greenwald (Eds.), *Psychological perspectives on the self* (vol 3, pp. 10–33). Hillsdale, NJ: Erlbaum.

Hazel, J. S., Schumaker, J. B., Sherman, J. A., & Sheldon-Wildgen, J. (1981). *ASSET: A social skills program for adolescents.* Champaign, IL: Research Press.

Hebb, D. O. (1942). The effect of early and late brain injury on test scores, and the nature of normal adult intelligence. *Proceedings of the American Philosophical Society, 85,* 275–292.

Hodges, K., McKnew, D., Burback, D. J., & Roebuck, L. (1987). Diagnostic concordance between the Child Assessment Schedule (CAS) and the K-SADS in an outpatient sample using lay interviewers. *Journal of the American Academy of Child and Adolescent Psychiatry, 26,* 654–661.

Holmes, D. S., & Urie, R. G. (1975). Effects of preparing children for psychotherapy. *Journal of Consulting and Clinical Psychology, 43,* 311–318.

Hynd, G. W., Lorys, A. R., Semrud-Clikeman, M., Nieves, N., Huettner, M., & Lahey, B. B. (1991). Attention deficit disorder without hyperactivity: A distinct behavioral and neurocognitive syndrome. *Journal of Child Neurology, 6,* Supplement, S37–S43.

Jacob, S., & Hartshorne, T. (1991). Ethics and law for school psychologists. Brandon, VT: Clinical Psychology Publishing Co., Inc.

Kagan, J. (1984). *The nature of the child.* New York: Basic Books.

Kazdin, A. E. (1988). Childhood depression. In E. J. Mash & L. G. Terdal (Eds.), *Behavioral assessment in childhood disorders* (2nd ed., pp. 157–195). New York: Guilford Press.

Kendall, P. C., & Braswell, L. (1985). *Cognitive-behavioral therapy for impulsive children.* New York: Guilford Press.

Kister, M. C., & Patterson, C. J. (1980). Children's conceptions of the causes of illness: Understanding of contagion and use of immanent justice. *Child Development, 51,* 839–846.

Kohut, H. (1971). *The analysis of self.* New York: International Universities Press.

Koocher, G. P. (1983). Competence to consent: Psychotherapy. In G. B. Melton, G. P. Koocher, & M. J. Saks (Eds.), *Children's competence to consent* (pp. 111–127). New York: Plenum.

Koocher, G. P., & Keith-Spiegel, P. C. (1990). *Children, ethics, and the law.* Lincoln, NE: University of Nebraska Press.

Lehr, E. (1990). A developmental perspective. In E. Lehr (Ed.), *Psychological management of traumatic brain injuries in children and adolescents* (pp. 41–98). Rockville, MD: Aspen Publishers.

Livingston, M. G., & McCabe, R. J. (1990). Psychosocial consequences of head injury in children and adolescents. *Pediatrician, 17,* 255–261.

Mahler, M. S., Pine, F., & Bergman, A. (1975). *The psychological birth of the human infant.* New York: Basic Books.

Mannuzza, S., Gittelman-Klein, R., Horowitz-Konig, P., & Giampino, T. L. (1989). Hyperactive boys almost grown up, IV: Criminality and its relationship to psychiatric status. *Archives of General Psychiatry, 46,* 1073–1079.

Martin, R. P. (1988). *Assessment of personality and behavior problems.* New York: Guilford Press.

Mash, E. J., & Terdal, L. G. (1988). *Behavioral assessment in childhood disorders.* New York: Guilford Press.

Masten, A. S., Garmezy, N., Tellegen, A., & Pellegrini, D. S. (1988). Competence and stress in school children: The moderating effects of individual and family qualities. *Journal of Child Psychology & Psychiatry & Allied Disciplines, 29,* 745–764.

McCabe, R. J. R., & Green, D. (1987). Rehabilitating severely head-injured adolescents: Three case reports. *Journal of Child Psychiatry and Psychology, 28,* 111–126.

Medway, F. J. (1979). How effective is school consultation? A review of recent research. *Journal of School Psychology, 17,* 275–282.

Meyers, J., Parson, R. D., & Martin, R. (1979). *Mental health consultation in the schools.* San Francisco: Jossey-Bass.

Milich, R., Loney, J., & Landau, S. (1982). The independent dimensions of hyperactivity and aggression: A validation with playroom observation data. *Journal of Abnormal Psychology, 91,* 183–198.

Neighbors, H. W. (1985). Seeking professional help for personal problems: Black Americans' use of health and mental health services. *Community Mental Health Journal, 21,* 156–166.

O'Connor, K. J. (1991). *The play therapy primer: An integration of theories and techniques.* New York: John Wiley & Sons.

Orvaschel, H. (1985). Psychiatric interviews suitable for use in research with children and adolescents. *Psychopharmocology Bulletin, 21,* 737–745.

Pirozzolo, F. J., & Papanicolaou, A. C. (1986). Plasticity and recovery of function in the central nervous system. In J. E. Obzrut & G. W. Hynd (Eds.), *Child neuropsychology: theory and research* (Vol. 1, pp. 141–154). San Diego: Academic Press.

Porrino, L. J., Rapoport, J. L., Behar, D., Sceery, W., Ismond, D. R., & Bunney, W. E. (1983). A naturalistic assessment of the motor activity of hyperactive boys. *Archives of General Psychiatry, 40,* 681–687.

Quay, H. C., Routh, D. K., & Shapiro, S. K. (1987). Psychopathology of childhood: From description to validation. *Annual Review of Psychology, 38,* 491–532.

Ramirez, M., & Castenada, A. (1974). *Cultural democracy, biocognitive development and education.* Orlando, FL: Academic Press.

Reich, W., & Welner, Z. (1989). *Diagnostic Interview for Children and Adolescents— Revised.* St. Louis: Washington University, Division of Child Psychiatry.

Reynolds, C. R., & Kamphaus, R. W. (1992). *Behavior assessment system for children.* Circle Pines, MN: American Guidance Service.

Ritter, D. R. (1978). Effects of school consultation program upon referral patterns of teachers. *Psychology in the Schools, 15,* 239–242.

Rogers, C. R. (1961). *On becoming a person.* Boston: Houghton Mifflin.

Rothbart, M. K. (1986). Longitudinal home observation of infant temperament. *Developmental Psychology, 22,* 356–365.

Rutter, M. (1987). The role of cognition in child development and disorder. *British Journal of Medical Psychology, 60,* 1–16.

Sampson, E. E. (1988). The debate on individualism: Indigenous psychologies of the individual and their role in personal and societal functioning. *American Psychologist, 43,* 15–22.

Scarr, S. (1984). Personality and experience: Individual encounters with the world. In J. Aranoff, I. A. Rabin, & R. A. Zucker (Eds.), *The emergence of personality* (pp. 49–78). New York: Springer.

Schaefer, C. E., & Reid, S. E. (1986). *Game play: Therapeutic use of childhood games.* New York: John Wiley & Sons.

Selman, R. L. (1980). *The growth of interpersonal understanding: Developmental and clinical analyses.* New York: Academic Press.

Semrud-Clikeman, M., Biederman, J., Sprich-Buchminster, S., Lehman, B., Faraone, S. V., & Norman, D. (1992). Comorbidity between ADDH and learning disability: A review and report in a clinically referred sample. *Journal of the American Academy of Child and Adolescent Psychiatry, 31,* 439–448.

Semrud-Clikeman, M., & Hynd, G. W. (1991a). Specific nonverbal and social-skills deficits in children with learning disabilities. In J. E. Obzrut & G. W. Hynd (Eds.), *Neuropsychological foundations of learning disabilities: A handbook of issues, methods, and practice* (pp. 603–630). San Diego: Academic Press.

Semrud-Clikeman, M., & Hynd, G. W. (1991b). Review of issues and measures in childhood depression. *School Psychology International, 12,* 275–298.

Semrud-Clikeman, M., & Hynd, G. W. (1990). Right hemispheric dysfunction in nonverbal learning disabilities: Social, academic, and adaptive functioning in adults and children. *Psychological Bulletin, 107,* 196–209.

Serok, S., & Blum, A. (1982). Rule violating behavior of delinquent and nondelinquent youth in games. *Adolescence, 17,* 457–464.

Siegel, L. J., Smith, K. E., & Wood, T. A. (1991). Children medically at risk. In T. R. Kratochwill & R. J. Morris (Eds.), *The practice of child therapy* (pp. 328–366). New York: Pergamon Press.

Sroufe, L. A. (1979). The coherence of individual development. *American Psychologist, 34,* 834–841.

Sutton-Smith, B., & Roberts, J. M. (1971). The cross-cultural and psychological study of games. *International Review of Sport Sociology, 6,* 79–87.

Teyber, E. (1990). *Interpersonal process in therapy* (2nd ed.). Pacific Grove, CA: Brooks/Cole Publishing Co.

Todd, C. M., & Perlmutter, M. (1980). Reality recalled by preschool children. In M. Perlmutter (Ed.), *New directions in child development: Vol. 10. Children's memory* (pp. 69–85). San Francisco: Jossey-Bass.

Vargas, L. A., & Koss-Chiono, J. D. (1992). *Working with culture: Psychotherapeutic interventions with ethnic minority children and adolescents.* San Francisco: Jossey-Bass.

Walker, H. M., McConnell, S. R., Holmes, D., Todis, B., Walker, J., & Golden, H. (1983). *The Walker social skills curriculum: The ACCEPTS program.* Austin, TX: Pro-Ed.

Weiss, G., Hechtman, L., Perlman, T., Hopkins, J., & Wener, A. (1979). Hyperactives as young adults: A controlled prospective ten-year follow-up of 75 children. *Archives of General Psychiatry, 36,* 675–681.

Winnecott, D. W. (1971). *Playing and reality.* London: Penguin Books.

Witt, J. C., Cavell, T. A., Heffer, R. W., Carey, M. P., & Martens, B. K. (1988). Child self-report: Interviewing techniques and rating scales. In E. S. Shapiro & R. R. Kratochwill (Eds.), *Behavioral assessment in schools: Conceptual foundations and practical applications* (pp. 384–454). New York: Guilford Press.

Wood, H., & Wood, D. (1983). Questioning the pre-school child. *Educational Review, 35,* 149–162.

Wood, M., Combs, C., Gunn, A., & Weller, D. (1986). *Developmental therapy in the classroom* (2nd ed.). Austin, TX: Pro-Ed.

Woods, B. T. (1980). The restricted effects of right-hemisphere lesions after age one: Wechsler test data. *Neuropsychologia, 18,* 65–70.

Woo-Sam, J., Zimmerman, I. L., Brink, J. A., Uyehara, K., & Miller, A. R. (1970). Socioeconomic status and post-traumatic intelligence in children with severe head injuries. *Psychological Reports, 27,* 147–153.

Wyngaarden, J. B. (1987). *Learning disabilities: A report to the U.S. Congress.* Washington, DC: Interagency Committee on Learning Disabilities.

Zakich, R. (1975). *The ungame.* Anaheim, CA: The Ungame Company.

Appendix A

Parent Interview Format

Name of Child _____ Sex _____

Birthdate _____ Age _____ Grade _____

Address _____ Phone _____

Father's name _____ Age _____ Occupation _____

Mother's name _____ Age _____ Occupation _____

Child lives with (   ) both parents; (   ) father; (   ) mother.

Parents (   ) live together; (   ) are divorced; (   ) separated

Father's education _____ Mother's education _____

Siblings:

Name	Age	Grade	Areas of Difficulty

Any one else living in the home? (Grandparents, aunts, uncles, etc.)

Are there any family pets? If so, what is the child's relationship to the pet?

Where do you live? (   ) single-family home; (   ) apartment; (   ) other
How many moves has this child made?

What language(s) are spoken at home? Is the child fluent in those languages?

Who referred you to me?

Why are you seeking help?

What other interventions have been attempted with your child?

What has been successful with your child? What has not worked with your child?

Developmental History
(I am now going to ask you questions about your pregnancy with this child.)
Please tell me about your pregnancy with this child? (how long was the pregnancy? any unusual occurrences during pregnancy? how long was labor? what did the child weigh at birth?)

At what age did the child sit alone?   take his/her first steps?

walk alone?   speak his/her first words?

speak in sentences?

Can others understand his speech?

How many directions can he/she follow?

When was he/she toilet trained?

Which hand does he/she prefer?

How would you describe your child's temperament?

Who in you or your spouse's family does your child remind you of?

What does your child like to play? What doesn't he/she like to play?

What type of discipline do you use with your child? How frequently do you need to discipline him/her? How does she/he react to your discipline? How effective do you feel your discipline is? Who disciplines the child the most?

Medical History
(Now I will ask you some questions about your child's medical history.)
How is your child's general health?

When was his/her last medical examination? Name of physician and the phone number.

Has your child had any illnesses? injuries? surgeries? head injuries? Has he/she been hospitalized?

When were your child's eyes last examined? What were the results of this exam?

When were your child's ears last examined? What were the results?

Has your child had ear infections? When and how many?

Does your family have a history of any type of medical problems (high blood pressure, diabetes, autoimmune, etc.), psychological disorder, or learning disability (ADHD, etc.)?

School History
(Now I would like to ask you about your child's school history.)
What was his/her first school experience? Did she/he attend preschool and/or day care? How often? What was his/her reaction to going to school?

Has he/she repeated any grades? If so, why? Was retention ever suggested?

Has your child ever been psychologically tested? What were the results? Where can a report be obtained?

Has your child ever had counseling? What was his/her reaction? How did you feel about it?

How would you describe your child's social ability? Does he/she have friends? Can he/she make friends easily? Does he/she keep these friends?

Would you describe your child as a leader or a follower?

What hobbies does your child have?

What organizations does your child belong to (Girl Scouts, Boy Scouts)?

What does your child like to do when he/she is alone? Can he/she entertain himself/herself?

Can your child take care of her/his personal needs?

What chores does he/she have around the house? What responsibilities does he/she have? How well does he/she perform these?

Appendix B

Resources for Parents and Teachers

Computer Software

You may order a catalog for educational software entitled "Special Times: Special Education Software for Grades K–8" from:

Cambridge Development Laboratory Inc.
214 Third Avenue
Department NUMEROBIN
Waltham, MA 02154
1-800-637-0047
(617) 890-4640 in Massachusetts

Another resource for word-processing software is:

Scholastic Inc.
2931 East McCarty Street
Jefferson City, MO 65102
1-800-541-5513

Organizations

Learning Disabilities Association (LDA)
4156 Library Road
Pittsburgh, PA 15234
(412) 341-1515

Orton Dyslexia Society
724 York Road
Baltimore, MD 21204
(301) 296-0232

Council for Exceptional Children (CEC)
1920 Association Drive
Reston, VA 22091
(703) 620-3660

Children with Attention Deficit Disorder (CHADD)
300 NW 70th Avenue, Suite 102
Plantation, FL 33317
(305) 792-8100

Author Index

Subject Index

nontraditional families, 16–17
psychiatric history of, 62
referrals from, 16
right to refuse services, 16
step-, 17
support groups for, 197–198
wishes vs. child's needs, 84
Patterson, C. J., 36
Peers
relationships with, 13
support by, 173, 182
Performance deficits, 84–86
Perseveration, 202
Physicians, consultations with, 222–223
Play, 113–134
board games in, 121–125
cheating in, 123–125
defined, 113–114
and development, 113–114
dollhouses in, 117–119
figure drawing, 131–134
as ice breaker, 114
incomplete pictures, 130
incomplete stories, 129–130
interpretation in, 118, 131, 134
puppets in, 116–117
and role-playing, 119–121
scribble games, 125–127
scribble stories, 127–129
selecting session activities, 119
as self-expression, 114–121
word games, 125–130
Positive regard, 102–103
Practicums, 3, 140
Problem-solving skills, 196
and group therapy, 182–183
topics for, 183
Process, in therapy, 103–111
and conflict, 105–111
and defenses, 104–105
and emotional understanding, 103–104

Prognosis, in case formulation, 64
Prosody, 189, 191
definition of, 191
Puppets, 116–117 (*see also* Play)

Q
Questioning, formats for, 49–51

R
Reactivity, 11
Recess, 122
Reenactment of issues, 109–111
Referrals
determining need for, 4–6
for evaluation, 223
in schools, 15
and scope of problem, 6
for special education, 6, 15, 218
Reflection, 76–77 (*see also* Listerning)
Relationships
ability to utilize, 10, 25–26, 44
to caretakers, 11, 13, 93–94
case study in, 163–172
to peers, 13
therapeutic, 8–9, 73–89
Role-playing, 119–121, 184
and confrontation, 120
as practice, 120
Routine, importance of, 75

S
Sadness, and anger, 184
Schedule for Affective Disorders and Schizophrenia for School-Age Children, 27
School Psychology Review, 32
Schools (*see also* Institutional expectations)
-based assessment, 60